THE GREENING OF SAINT LUCIA

THE GREENING OF SAINT LUCIA

ECONOMIC DEVELOPMENT
AND ENVIRONMENTAL CHANGE
IN THE EASTERN CARIBBEAN

BRADLEY B. WALTERS

THE UNIVERSITY OF THE WEST INDIES PRESS
Jamaica • Barbados • Trinidad and Tobago

The University of the West Indies Press
7A Gibraltar Hall Road, Mona
Kingston 7, Jamaica
www.uwipress.com
© 2019 by Bradley B. Walters
All rights reserved. Published 2019

A catalogue record of this book is available from the
National Library of Jamaica.

ISBN: 978-976-640-705-6 (paper)
       978-976-640-706-3 (Kindle)
       978-976-640-707-0 (ePub)

Book and cover design by Robert Harris
Set in Minion Pro 10.5/14.5 x 27

Printed in the United States of America

CONTENTS

FIGURES

TABLES

PREFACE

I had the good fortune to first travel to Saint Lucia in 1990 to work as an intern with the Caribbean Natural Resources Institute, a non-governmental organization then based in the southern town of Vieux Fort. The focus of the institute's work then was mostly coastal resources management (Walters and Renard 1992), but it was apparent that the country's most urgent environmental problems at that time were unfolding in the rural countryside. Saint Lucian farmers were pushing ever deeper into the island's rugged, mountainous interior, cutting and clearing forests to plant bananas and ground provisions like yams, sweet potatoes and dasheen. Illegal farming was rampant within the public forest reserves. Soil erosion and agrochemical pollution of waterways was widespread. Conservationists expressed increasing alarm about threats to the island's wild animal and plant species, including the iconic, endemic Saint Lucian parrot (*Amazona versicolor*), which was endangered because of habitat loss and hunting (Christian et al. 1996). I departed the island in 1991 feeling much apprehension about the country's environmental future.

After a fifteen-year absence, I returned in 2006 and was astonished by how much Saint Lucia's countryside had changed. On the one hand, residential housing and tourism infrastructure had expanded dramatically, replacing huge tracts of valley-bottom farmland and coastal scrub forest. The quiet country abode where I had resided outside of Vieux Fort was unrecognizable, the mixed farm–dry forest landscape transformed into an expanse of residential subdivisions and commercial developments. Seeing all this was unsettling yet not surprising, because one comes to expect these kinds of changes with the forward march of development (Potter 1993, 1995).

What did genuinely surprise, however, were changes in the country's rural interior, where large tracts of hillside farmland were abandoned and returning to forest. There was still some concern in 2006 about deforestation, soil erosion and agrochemical contamination, but these were problems cited mostly as localized cases. There was no longer the sense of nationwide urgency about these things that had predominated in the 1980s and early 1990s. By 2006, illegal incursions into the island's network of protected forest reserves had become rare occurrences. The once-endangered Saint Lucia parrot was now thriving, its population having grown about fivefold since the early 1990s and its range now expanded well beyond previously isolated interior forests.

In fact, despite growing development pressures in the lowlands and near the coast, Saint Lucia's wider rural landscape has more land under forest today than at any time in at least seventy-five years, perhaps much longer. This change is profoundly significant in light of the many ongoing efforts to achieve sustainable development on small-island states like Saint Lucia. More generally, this seemingly good news story runs contrary to most conventional narratives about the worsening state of the environment in the Caribbean and elsewhere. It begs various questions of interest to citizens, activists and policymakers who strive to reconcile continued economic development and environmental conservation, among these: How did this remarkable change come about? What role did government, the private sector and other actors play in this? What are the links between this environmental change and wider changes in the Saint Lucian economy, politics and society? Is there more to this story than meets the eye? These and related questions will be explored in this book.

ACKNOWLEDGEMENTS

I am grateful for the support of the Government of Saint Lucia and, in particular, members of the Forestry Division, including Michael Bobb, Adams Toussaint, Michael Andrew, Rebecca Rock, Methodeus Fouscher and Anais Vernai. I am also extremely grateful to Melvin Smith, Marshall Symons, Lisa Hansen, Jennifer Sargent, Nigel Selig, Frances Ross and Shannon White for assistance with fieldwork. Lisa Hansen's diligent work on plant identification and Roger Graveson's generous sharing of his knowledge and data base of Saint Lucia plants were invaluable. Special thanks also to Yves Renard, Kai Wulf, Gregor Williams, Chistina Tardif, David Barker, Peter Jackson, Chris Alcindor, Michael Oatham, Amy Deacon, Donnie Mackinnon, Charles Cartwright and Mariana Baptista. Finally, I would like to thank Pete Vayda, Tom Rudel, Jolien Harmsen, Kevin Flesher and anonymous reviewers for editorial suggestions on earlier drafts of this book or chapters therein. This research was supported by grants from the Social Sciences and Humanities Research Council of Canada and Marjorie Young Bell Faculty Fund of Mount Allison University.

This book includes material that has already been published, albeit in revised form. Specifically, chapter 1 and the conclusion draw in part from B.B. Walters, 2017, "Explaining Rural Land Use Change and Reforestation: A Causal-Historical Approach" (*Land Use Policy* 67:608–24); chapter 3 draws from B.B. Walters and L. Hansen, 2013, "Farmed Landscapes, Trees and Forest Conservation in St Lucia, West Indies" (*Environmental Conservation* 40 [3]: 211–21); chapter 5 draws from B.B. Walters, 2012b, "Do Property Rights Matter for Conservation? Family Land, Forests and Trees in St Lucia, West Indies" (*Human Ecology* 40:863–78); chapter 6 draws from B.B. Walters, 2016a, "Migration, Land Use and Forest Change in St Lucia, West Indies" (*Land Use Policy* 51:290–300); and chapter 7 draws from B.B. Walters, 2016b, "Saint Lucia's Tourism Landscapes: Economic Development and Environmental Change in the West Indies" (*Caribbean Geography* 21:5–23).

ABBREVIATIONS

ACE	abductive causal eventism
ACP	African, Caribbean and Pacific Group of States
GATT	General Agreement on Tariffs and Trade
LCS	land change science
SES	socioecological systems
SLBGA	Saint Lucia Banana Growers Association
UFC	United Fruit Company
WINCROP	Windward Island Banana Growers Crop Insurance
WTO	World Trade Organization

INTRODUCTION

THE NATURAL HERITAGE AND BEAUTY OF THE ISLAND CARIBBEAN has long been celebrated, yet the environment and environmental change have remained background concerns in most Caribbean scholarship. This book is different. It is an interdisciplinary study of the changing relationships between people and the environment. Specifically, it examines how people in Saint Lucia, West Indies, have used the land and changed its forests. It asks why the island's forests were for so long degraded, and why in recent decades they have seemingly recovered. It is, in short, a story about environmental change and the wider social and economic developments that brought this change about.

In many respects, the story presented here about Saint Lucia's "greening" is an optimistic one. It suggests that environmental conservation and economic development may co-occur under the right circumstances, or at least that *some forms* of environmental conservation may co-occur with *some forms* of economic development. That the two phenomena might be causally related is an especially intriguing prospect, given the conventional wisdom about environmental protection being a constraint to, and typically undermined by, economic development. If the state of Saint Lucia's forests contravene such wisdom, it is important to understand why.

AGRICULTURE, DEVELOPMENT AND FOREST CHANGE

Economic development and agricultural expansion throughout history have typically proceeded in tandem and at the expense of forests (Williams 2003). The island Caribbean's biologically rich and diverse forests were among the first in the Americas to be extensively cleared for agriculture, as Europeans colonized and established plantations throughout the region to grow cotton, sugar cane, coffee and cocoa beans, fruits, and spices for export back to their homelands (Watts 1987; Kimber 1988; Harmsen et al. 2014). Over four centuries, all but the most remote, impenetrable lands were cleared of forests to make way for agriculture of one kind or another.

The conversion of tropical forest to agricultural landscapes has been central to the historical development of the region, but Caribbean island environments are especially vulnerable to damage, given their rugged geography and the highly restricted habitat distributions that result from steep topographic and climate gradients and island insularity (Lugo et al. 1981; Kueffer and Kinney 2017). Many plant and animal species are endemic to one or a few islands and so are at heightened risk of extinction from deforestation. Likewise, removal of forest cover from island watersheds increases the risk of flooding, soil erosion and landslides during rainfall events and leads to reduced stream flows during dry periods (Bruijnzeel 1991; Bonell and Bruijnzeel 2004; Pattanayak 2004; Trancoso et al. 2010). These are especially pressing concerns for Caribbean countries as they become more dependent on fresh water-demanding industries like tourism and face increasing risk of damaging weather events associated with climate change (Courchamp et al. 2014; Walters 2016b; Moore et al. 2017).

The findings presented in this book are important for these as well as other reasons. Conventional narratives about the environment in the Caribbean have long emphasized its worsening conditions. There is still much truth to this sentiment, especially considering the degraded state of coastal environments throughout the region. But findings presented here reveal a very different picture about the current state of Saint Lucia's upland environment. In short, the conditions of Saint Lucia's upland environment have improved dramatically in recent decades because of widespread reforestation of the landscape (Walters and Hansen, 2013). Why has this happened?

At the most general level, Saint Lucia has transitioned over the past half-century from an agricultural to a predominantly post-agricultural economy or post-agrarian society. Caribbean scholars have for years documented aspects of this transition, including accelerated urbanization, outmigration, growth of the tourism and services sector industries, and restructuring of labour markets (Peach 1967; Lowenthal 1972; Hope 1986a, 1986b; Momsen 1986; Conway 1993; Potter 1993, 1995; Byron and Condon 2008). But few scholars have considered the consequences of these changes for Caribbean island environments.

In contrast, a growing body of research from tropical regions outside the Caribbean has documented what appear to be similar trends of widespread reforestation on lands that had been previously deforested for agriculture (Brown and Lugo 1990; Corlett 1995; Finegan 1996; Guariguata and Ostertag 2001; de Jong et al. 2001; Chazdon 2003; Aide et al. 2013). The term "forest transition" was first coined by the geographer Alexander Mather to describe such historical reversals in forest cover change where these have manifested at regional or national levels (1992). Initial research on the topic focused on historical studies of forest change in Europe and North America, where it was found that many countries displayed a shift from net forest loss to forest gain as they industrialized and urbanized (Mather and Needle 1998; Agnoletti and Anderson 2000). Attention has since shifted to include studies of land use and forest change in the global south, where evidence suggests such transitions may also be underway in some developing countries (Rudel et al. 2005; Aide et al. 2013; Keenan et al. 2015).

The idea of a "forest transition" originated as a historical generalization about how forest cover often changes – from net loss to net gain – as economies and societies develop. Theoretical explanations to account for this tend to take one of two general forms (Rudel 1998; Rudel et al. 2005). The first of these – referred to as the "forest scarcity thesis" – is microeconomic in character and argues that forest transitions reflect a relative shift over time in the value placed on forests and forest products/services. As forests are depleted over time, their value grows, and this eventually incentivizes widespread action to protect and restore them. Barbier et al. (2017) adopted this kind of microeconomic approach but framed it more explicitly in terms of the relative value of alternative land uses (i.e., land used for agriculture vs forest, etc.).

The second, "economic development thesis" emphasizes broader structural and technological changes as central to explaining forest transitions. In short, as societies industrialize and urbanize, rural people – especially younger adults – are drawn from the countryside to live and work in urban areas, sapping the rural farm sector of the labour needed to sustain it. Farms are downsized and farmlands are abandoned as a result. These trends are reinforced by the mechanization of agriculture and food production which redirects investment to the most productive farmlands only and drives down food prices so that marginal producers can no longer compete.

I will not attempt at this point to evaluate the merits of these respective theories, although both claim evidential support from the literature (Rudel et al. 2005). Arguably, the two are not mutually exclusive but rather differ in their points of explanatory emphasis. For example, both forest scarcity and economic development theses anticipate that reforestation be concentrated on more marginal farmlands. Theoretical interpretations are also complicated by the fact that most scholars have applied the forest transition concept using a fairly broad brush and, by doing so, typically overlook socio-economic, geo-graphic and ecological variations within the areas bounded by their analyses (Robbins and Fraser 2003; Perz 2007).

In this study, these shortcomings were largely overcome by integrating information on national trends with findings based on detailed, field-based investigations. As well, the analytical approach used here, abductive causal eventism (ACE), and described in the following chapter explains reforesta-tion in particular places in Saint Lucia by constructing event-causal histories specific to those places, not by appealing to theory or models of forest change more generally. In this regard, the most relevant ideas from the forest transi-tion literature are those about events – specifically events that have been shown elsewhere to contribute to forest transitions. Such events include farm produc-tivity declines, farm input cost increases, farm commodity price declines, rural outmigrations, enacted policies that redirect incentives away from agricultural development and towards promotion of forest conservation and tree planting, and so on (Mather and Needle 1998; Rudel et al. 2000; Foster and Rosenzweig 2003; Robbins and Fraser 2003; Rudel et al. 2005; Aide et al. 2013).

In fact, recent scholarship on Caribbean forests suggests that Saint Lucia may not be alone among island states in the region in its experiencing a forest transition (Helmer et al. 2008; Alvarez-Berrios et al. 2013; Timms et al. 2013; Keenan et al. 2015; van Andel et al. 2016; Newman et al. 2018). For example, a forest transition in Puerto Rico has been well documented and its causes thor-oughly studied (Rudel et al. 2000; Grau et al. 2003; Pares-Ramos et al. 2008). But Puerto Rico aside, research on other Caribbean islands has focused on national-level assessments of land use change only or, in the case of Jamaica, on intensive study of just one district. As such, little is still known about the specific character and causes of forest transitions within the island Caribbean (Walters 2017). A central aim of this book is therefore to enlarge our understanding of the causes and consequences of forest transitions by in-depth examination of the Saint Lucian experience.

EXPLAINING RURAL LAND USE AND FOREST CHANGE

Saint Lucia's rural landscapes are now heavily forested, but not all forests are alike, and sometimes a forest is not exactly what it seems. For example, forests that have been planted or regrown naturally on former agricultural land are likely to differ in composition and structure from the original, primary forests that once existed there, although they may still be rich in native species and can quickly re-establish a complex vegetation structure that helps conserve soil and water (Corlett 1995; Grau et al. 2003; Chazdon 2003; Junqueira et al. 2010). Even some types of agriculture, including home gardens and agroforestry (growing of tree crops), each of which are widely practised in the Caribbean, can generate economic benefits while also harbouring diverse plant and animal species and contributing to soil conservation and watershed protection (Denevan and Padoch 1987; Brierley 1992; Perfecto et al. 1996; Naughton-Teves 2002; Schroth et al. 2004; Sambuichi and Haridasan 2007; Bhagwat et al. 2008; Norris 2008; Jose 2009; da Silva Moco et al. 2009; Asase and Tetteh 2010).

Given such considerations, research on Saint Lucia's forests must first obtain a clear picture of the environmental changes that have actually occurred in the landscape. What are Saint Lucia's forests like and how have they changed in recent decades? Where in the landscape are forests actually returning? Are some lands more prone to reforestation than others? What is the ecological structure and species composition of these recovering forests? Are these recovering forests predominantly "natural" in their species composition or has deliberate tree planting played a part? To answer these questions, two representative watersheds were selected and studied intensively, using a combination of field-based and remote-sensing techniques (chapter 1).

As the ecological character of the forests and watershed landscapes became clearer, research then sought to explain key patterns and changes observed. For example, in what ways is the expansion of forest causally linked to changes in land use, and is this in turn causally linked to wider environmental, economic and political factors? To guide the analysis, I employed an analytical approach whereby explanations of environmental change are sought by constructing causal histories of those changes. ACE is described in chapter 1. Because ACE methodology is novel for studies of land use change, another central aim of this book is to provide an empirical illustration of its application.

Explaining reforestation and land use change in Saint Lucia proved a complex task. As will be shown in chapters 3 and 5, local factors like topography and land tenure could account for particular patterns of reforestation in the landscape. But robust explanations of reforestation in general could not be established without stepping back and understanding the influence of larger socio-economic and political causes. Specifically, Saint Lucian agriculture has long been shaped by international political and market forces, and recent changes are no exception to this. In fact, one of the more interesting findings revealed by the study of Saint Lucia's agricultural history (detailed in chapters 2 and 4) is that the recent bout of reforestation is not unprecedented. Periods of agricultural expansion and contraction (with associated deforestation and reforestation) have recurred at different times in the island's history. This raises an intriguing question: Is the recent forest transition going to last, or might we eventually see a return to widespread deforestation on the island?

To contemplate this question, one needs to appreciate that Saint Lucia's recent agricultural troubles reflect more than declining export markets. Farms are downsizing and often abandoned outright because rural people – especially the young – view farming as among the least attractive opportunities for making a living, so many are choosing to leave farming or are avoiding it altogether. Outmigration has long been pursued by Saint Lucians as a means to diversify livelihood options, and it has arguably been an underappreciated cause of reduced farming and reforestation in the past (Walters 2016a). As we shall see in chapters 6 and 7, Saint Lucian society has modernized and its economy diversified, so opportunities to remain on the island and work have also grown considerably in recent decades. Tourism and construction, in particular, have become the preferred industries of work by otherwise would-be farmers. Development in these areas is driven by more than just foreign, multinational investment in the tourism sector. Significant employment has been created and sustained by a long-lasting boom in residential house construction financed by remittance income and waves of elderly Saint Lucian migrants returning home from years living and working abroad. The effects of this "boomerang urbanization" – where rural outmigrants to urban centres elsewhere later return and contribute to urbanization back home – are visible in the form of sprawling residential subdivisions around towns across the island.

Finally, tourism in Saint Lucia has grown gradually since the 1960s, but expansion of the sector accelerated in the 1990s as a result of deliberate and sustained policy support (Walters 2016b). Tourism infrastructure and its impacts are concentrated near the coast. Chapter 7 will show how an emphasis on eco- and heritage tourism plus growing political support for water supply protection has contributed to upland forest conservation and reforestation on both public and private lands. While tourism's demand for fresh fruits, vegetables and flowers has stimulated growth in some agricultural sectors, these effects are simultaneously offset by employment generation in tourism, which draws people away from farming and so contributes further to upland reforestation.

OUTLINE OF THE BOOK

The first two chapters of this book establish some historical and theoretical context for the study. Specifically, chapter 1 provides an overview of Saint Lucia, specific study areas and methods. It then compares and contrasts different approaches that have been used by scientists to study human-environment interactions and describes a novel research methodology – ACE – that was applied here to study land use and forest change in Saint Lucia. Chapter 2 then provides an overview of Saint Lucia's agricultural history up to the collapse of the sugar industry in the 1950s.

Empirical findings from watershed vegetation and land use surveys are presented in chapter 3. These reveal widespread decline in agriculture and expansion of trees and forests across the rural landscape of both study watersheds. The four following chapters seek to explain these changes. Specifically, chapter 4 examines the history of the Saint Lucia banana industry and its dominant, but now waning influence on the rural economy and landscape. Chapter 5 considers the role that land tenure has played shaping patterns of land use, tree planting and forest conservation. The influence of human migration and shifting labour markets is then explored in chapter 6. Finally, tourism's increasingly dominant place in the Saint Lucian economy and its consequences for rural environmental change are examined in chapter 7. The book concludes with some reflections on study findings and their wider relevance to concerns about economic development and environmental change in the small-island Caribbean and beyond.

A NOTE TO READERS

The material presented in this book is based on an interdisciplinary research project that draws from environmental science, social science and historical sources of information. Its analytical strength derives from the integration of these diverse sources, but it is inevitable that certain material may be of less interest to some readers than to others. For example, the analysis of environmental variables, presented mostly in chapter 3, includes tabular summaries of numerical data and statistics. Environmental scientists will likely view this material as critical to interpretation of the overall story. However, readers lacking a technical-scientific background may struggle to make sense of some details presented. Recognizing this, I have sought to present information and arguments throughout this book in a clear, readable manner, while also not depriving those readers who might be especially interested in key technical or theoretical details. Those less interested in such details should feel free to skim or skip these sections. Key points will be highlighted so readers will not lose the main threads of the story by doing so. As well, I provide brief summaries at the end of each chapter that highlight especially important findings.

CHAPTER 1

EXPLAINING LAND USE CHANGE AND REFORESTATION IN SAINT LUCIA

ONE OF THE CENTRAL AIMS OF THIS BOOK is to demonstrate the application of a novel research methodology, abductive causal eventism, which uses causal-historical analysis to understand interactions between people and the environment. However, this is not in a conventional sense a book on Caribbean history, because the research draws heavily on various natural and social scientific methods as well as historical information to build its causal history. The material presented in this book should therefore be of interest to historians, social scientists and environmental scientists alike.

In this chapter, I detail the research methods and methodology used in the study. The chapter is organized in two main parts. The first part provides general contextual information about Saint Lucia and the field study sites and then details the specific methods used in this study. Readers will be well served by reading the background section on Saint Lucia and the description and rationale for the selection of study watersheds. Otherwise, the descriptions of the particular methods can be skimmed or skipped with little cost to understanding the findings presented in subsequent chapters.

The second part of the chapter makes the case for using the ACE approach to study land use change and reforestation. This discussion is the most theoretically complex of the entire book and provides the analytical framework upon which the different components of the study hang together, so to speak. That said, the larger story presented in this book will not be significantly compromised by skimming these sections.

RESEARCH CONTEXT AND STUDY AREAS

Saint Lucia is a small (616 km²), English- and French Creole-speaking nation in the Windward Islands of the Eastern Caribbean (figure 1.1). It has a wet tropical climate, with highest precipitation from July to November and the driest conditions typically from January to April. The island is characterized by mostly rugged, mountainous topography and steep relief, with about two dozen significant watersheds draining eastward and westward from a central range of mountains. Interior lands are mostly steep-sloped and inaccessible by vehicle. Terrain nearer the coast is typically less steep, and large expanses of flat, valley-bottom land can be found within several of the larger watersheds (Roseau, Cul de Sac, Mabouya, Soufrière) and on the north (between Castries and Gros Islet) and south (around Vieux Fort) ends of the island. Soils are of relatively recent volcanic origin and generally fertile, which, combined with favourable temperatures and rainfall, means that the land is generally well suited for growing a variety of crops (Stark et al. 1966; GOSL 1991a).

Landscapes of Saint Lucia have been modified by settlement and agriculture for centuries, a history described in detail in following chapters. Briefly, since the mid-1700s the economy has been founded on export-oriented agriculture (cotton, sugar, etc.), with most exportable produce being grown on estates concentrated on the flat bottomlands and lower slopes of the island's valleys. Smallholder farming on adjacent hillsides, ridgetops and remoter lands of the interior was initially focused on subsistence, but it surged following emancipation and diversified, eventually displacing the estate farming sector in significance as bananas replaced sugar as the predominant export crop following World War II (Romalis 1975). From the late 1950s until the late 1990s, bananas were the dominant agriculture crop in Saint Lucia and had pervasive effects on the island's economy, landscape and environment. As bananas grew in significance, so did other sectors of the wider Saint Lucian economy, most notably tourism but also small-scale manufacturing, construction, real estate and administrative services (Walters 2016a, 2016b). Even before the crash of bananas in the mid-1990s, major changes were already underway that were reshaping the economy and redefining Saint Lucia as a predominantly post-agricultural society.

Mamiku and Soufrière Watersheds

These changes have unfolded island wide, but a compelling analysis of the causal dynamics requires attention to on-the-ground details of farm-level decision making, changing land use practices and ecological change. To do this, the watershed was used as the basic unit of field study because it enabled sampling of a wide variation in topography and the full range of forest habitats – from coastal mangrove and dry scrub to wet mountain rain forest – and situated these within a wider landscape of changing land use. Saint Lucia is bisected, north to south, by a steep, central range of mountains. Watersheds that drain eastward and westward have long constrained the settlement and agricultural development of Saint Lucia's rugged, mountainous terrain. Most rural roads ascend from the coast inland along valley bottoms, roughly parallel to river courses; but few upland roads cross between watersheds. Watersheds are also increasingly used as the basis for land use and conservation planning in Saint Lucia.

I selected for primary study sites one watershed that drains eastward (Mamiku = 790 ha) and one that drains westward (Soufrière = 1570 ha) (figure 1.1). Both are midsize watersheds, but each spans a wide range in elevation and topographic variation. Their selection from opposite sides of the island was intended to capture some of the country's variation in geography and agricultural history. Topography on the east coast is typically less rugged than on the west coast, but conditions are drier and windier. Farming has thrived best on the east coast during periods of robust demand for less water-demanding crops like cotton, sugar, coconuts and livestock. These same conditions also made Mamiku and surrounding areas favourable for intensive banana cultivation, which by the 1970s dominated farming in the watershed.

By contrast, the west coast, including Soufrière, is geologically younger, so the terrain is especially rugged and soils more fertile. Local climatic conditions are also particularly amenable to diverse agricultural production. Lying in the western shadow of the tallest mountains in Saint Lucia, Soufrière receives the highest rainfall on the island and is significantly protected from easterly prevailing winds that often damage crops during storms. These factors, com-bined with the locating of the first centre of French colonial administration in Soufrière, established this area as an early epicentre of plantation agriculture on the island (Breen 1844; Harmsen et al. 2014). The rugged, but otherwise favourable environmental conditions also encouraged widespread planting of tree crops like cocoa, coffee, coconut and lime.

Soufrière's rugged terrain and relative geographic isolation from the rest of the island have, nonetheless, posed special challenges for development. Through most of its history, Soufrière was only accessible by sea or inland foot/mule paths. This posed little problem during the days of sailing ships, but lack of good road

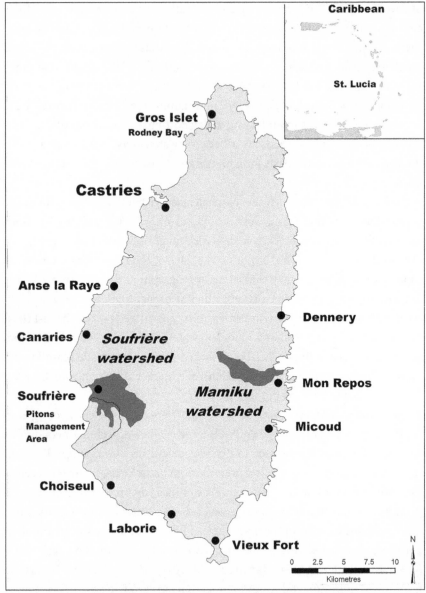

Figure 1.1. Map of Saint Lucia, including study watersheds

access disadvantaged Soufrière with the advent of steamships and the locating of centralized shipping terminals in the north and south of the island (Gregor Williams, personal communication; Harmsen et al. 2014). These challenges were especially pronounced with bananas because they cannot tolerate extended travel over rugged terrain without bruising. Unlike in Mamiku, farmers in Soufrière were thus often reluctant to convert existing tree crops wholesale to banana production. Banana cultivation became important in Soufrière but never dominated to the extent it did on the east side of the island.

Vegetation Surveys

Vegetation surveys of the two watersheds were completed between February and April 2006. To assess vegetation characteristics quantitatively, a quadrat-census plot (10 m × 10 m) method was used (Walters and Hansen 2013). To sample widely and minimize site selection bias, a systematic, stratified sampling protocol was employed by using predetermined Geographic Positioning System grid coordinates to identify specific sampling sites. Plots were thus located in a large grid across each watershed, with individual plots 500 metres apart north to south and 1000 metres apart east to west (figures 1.2 and 1.3). Specific plot site coordinates were preprogrammed into a GPS, which was then used to guide researchers to sampling locations. Using this approach, a total of fifty-six plots were sampled, thirty-four in Soufrière and twenty-two in Mamiku (numbers

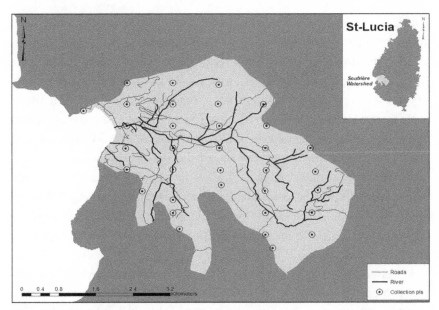

Figure 1.2. Map of Soufrière watershed, showing thirty-four sampling points for vegetation plots

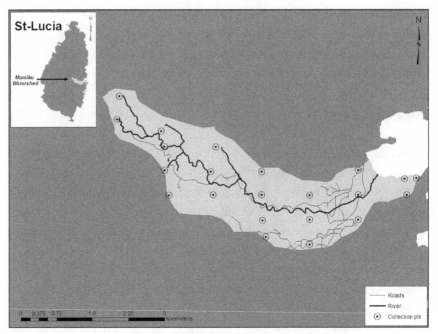

Figure 1.3. Map of Mamiku watershed, showing twenty-two sampling points for vegetation plots

reflective of differences in watershed size). Severe terrain compelled small deviations from the grid-designated locations in a few cases.

The plot sampling protocol captured a wide variety of habitat and land use types, including coastal mangrove forest, coastal dry scrub forest, mixed wet-dry tropical forest, wet tropical forest, agroforest, annual crop agriculture, pasture land, residential property, a grassy schoolyard and the rock caldera and grassy emission plume field of a semi-active volcano. At each field plot site, altitude, slope and aspect were recorded and other characteristics noted, including evidence of human or natural disturbance. Information about land tenure, landholding size and land use history of each site was sought through interviews with local farmers and by consulting official land registry maps. The distance from the site to the nearest drivable road was later estimated, using air photos and maps.

Within each of the 56 vegetation plots, every tree greater than 2.9 centimetres diameter at breast height was numbered, mapped and measured, for a total of 1,699 trees. Tree species were identified on site by local guides in either the local Creole patois dialect or Latin nomenclature. Appropriate samples of leaves, flowers or fruit were collected where possible, along with photographs. Post-identification was assisted by Graveson (2005), and verifications were later made at the Saint Lucia Herbarium following collections and Howard (1974). Trees were classified as being planted or natural, where planted referred to trees which were known to be traditionally cultivated by Saint Lucians and natural referred to trees which were not. Some commonly cultivated trees (e.g., guava, mahogany) have become naturalized in Saint Lucia in that there are individuals established and growing through natural reproduction alone. Nonetheless, through the course of the fieldwork there was rarely any doubt about the origins of specific trees that were measured. The distinction made between natural and planted is thus justified.

Tree canopy height for each sample plot was derived by taking the mean height of the largest (by diameter at breast height) individual trees (n = 4) within each of the plots' four sub-quadrats, where individual tree heights were measured using a clinometer. Canopy structure was classified by walking through the centre, along the length of the horizontal and vertical axis of each plot, stopping every metre and observing the canopy vertically above. Canopy structure was thus derived from twenty measures that were summed up and converted to plot percentages. Canopy structure was classified as either "gap" (fully open), "expanded gap" (under tree foliage but proximate to a gap) or "closed canopy" (completely covered by tree foliage) following Walters (2005).

Quantitative data were analysed statistically using SPSS. Vegetation plot measures were log transformed for statistical analysis when they did not meet the test for homogeneity of variances (Zar 1984).

Air Photo Assessments

Near-comprehensive, aerial-photo coverage for both watersheds (1966, 1977, 1992 and 2004) plus recent Land Remote-Sensing Satellite (GoogleEarth) imagery (2009/13), were combined with field observations from 2006 and 2015 to assess trends in five general land status categories over time: "developed" (built infrastructure, etc.), "annual agriculture" (short-lived crops like bananas or vegetables, as well as animal pasture), "agroforest" (tree crops), "secondary forest" (young, post-agricultural forest) and "mature forest" (long-established forest). To do this, air photos were geo-referenced using ARC-View and the fifty-six plot sites were used as discrete, spatial reference data points with which to compare by back-casting differences between successive air photo and satellite surveys. The fifty-six plot sites were revisited (on foot) in 2015 to visibly assess their most recent condition. The sampling protocol for the vegetation survey was both systematic and fairly comprehensive in its coverage of the two watersheds. As such, cumulative changes across the fifty-six points are assumed to be reasonably representative of broader trends in watershed landscape change.

Farmer and Key Informant Interviews

Most interviews with farmers were conducted in 2007 with some follow-up in 2015. In total, thirty-seven smallholders and six estate farmers were interviewed. The small sample size of estate farmers reflects that only a handful of actively farmed estates exist within the study watersheds, even though their cumulative size accounts for about one-quarter of all land area. Interviews were based on a semi-structured format and included questions about farm and farmer characteristics, farming history, recent changes in farming practice and land use, patterns and motivations for tree planting and cutting, and so on. As well, farmers were asked to characterize their lands in terms of estimated amount of forest or bush cover, relative site accessibility (easy, moderate or difficult), steepness (flatter or steeper) and abundance of planted trees. Sampling included farmers from each of the six rural settlements within the two watersheds and either the owner or manager (or both) of each of the six active agricultural estates.

Over thirty key informants were also interviewed in 2007 and 2015. This included government officials, representatives of non-governmental organizations, private land surveyors and developers, private agriculture organization representatives and resident historians. These interviews were also semi-structured but varied widely in topical coverage, depending on the expertise and interests of the persons interviewed.

Government Statistics, Reports and Other Publications

Various statistics and published and unpublished reports were consulted during the course of this research. Among the most useful sources included statistics compiled under the Saint Lucia National Agricultural Census, which has been conducted once per decade since the early 1960s (GOSL 1974, 1987a, 1996a, 2007a). Also of notable value was the *Economic and Social Review,* published annually by the Government of Saint Lucia since the early 1980s. Reports in this series provide succinct and informative snapshots of economic trends and key developments in the country.

It is worth noting that boundaries of administrative districts, the level at which government statistics are typically compiled and reported, do not correspond precisely with study watershed boundaries. That said, each of the study watersheds was encompassed entirely within a distinct district, and so reports from those districts provide a reasonably good indication of watershed-level statistics. Specifically, the Soufrière watershed falls in the centre and dominates (by area and population) the Soufrière District. The Mamiku watershed falls within the centre of what was formerly the Praslin District. District lines have since been redrawn, leaving the Soufrière District essentially unchanged, but resulting in the smaller Praslin District becoming absorbed by a larger Micoud District.

Finally, several key sources were particularly useful for helping to piece together the historical narrative presented in chapter 2. This includes Breen's (1844) classic study of early Saint Lucian history; Harmsen et al.'s (2014) recent monograph, *A History of St Lucia*, and Thomas's (2006) report on the history of slavery in Saint Lucia.

ANALYTICAL METHODOLOGY IN HUMAN-ENVIRONMENT RESEARCH

Human-environment research spans a range of academic disciplines but usually seeks to integrate the methods and insights of more than one (Lambin et al. 2001; Ludeke et al. 2004; Newell et al. 2005; IGBP 2006; Young et al. 2006; Rudel 2008; Holm et al. 2013; Ogden et al. 2013; Palsson et al. 2013; Agnoletti and Rotherham 2015). Such interdisciplinary efforts are typically bedeviled by two key analytical challenges. The first is how to integrate environmental science and social science information coherently and rigorously. This is not a straightforward task given differences in the respective methods, theories and epistemological foundations of the natural and social sciences.

The second challenge is to demonstrate in a compelling way that local environmental changes are, in fact, causally connected to events that may be distant in time or space to those changes (GLP 2005, 3; Turner et al. 2007, 2016; Pooley et al. 2013). For example, it may be fairly straightforward to show how deforestation in a particular place is caused by changes in local farming practices. It is likely more difficult to then show how these changes in local farming practices are themselves possibly caused by political and economic events unfolding far beyond the local farmlands in question. If we want to develop good explanations, however, we need to understand how both local and non-local causes may be relevant.

To address these challenges, my colleague, Andrew Vayda, and I devised a research methodology, based on application of causal-historical analysis, which we call *abductive causal eventism* (Walters and Vayda 2009; Vayda and Walters 2011; Walters 2012a; Walters 2017). In a nutshell, ACE entails constructing causal histories of interrelated social and/or biophysical events backward in time and outward or inward in space through a process of eliminative inference and reasoning from effects to causes, called "abduction". In the following discussion I review and critique three alternative methodological approaches that are commonly used in leading subfields of human-environment research: land change science (LCS), socioecological systems (SES) and political ecology. ACE is then described and contrasted with these.

First, a brief word on terminology. Since the focus of these discussions is methodology, it is useful to distinguish this from methods, theories and hypotheses. Methods are the tools and techniques of research. Methodology is the logic- and justification-guiding deployment of methods and interpretation of research results (Vayda and Walters 2011, 2). Theory has diverse meanings (Abend 2008). For the purposes here, theories are explanations of empirical phenomena that have attained some degree of generalizability by virtue of their prior confirmation elsewhere (theories that attain extremely high levels of confirmation may become established "facts" or "laws"). Hypotheses are conjectured explanations for the case at hand, so they may or may not be recognized theories.

Land Change Science

LCS emerged as a coherent programme of human-environment research during the 1990s, propelled by a series of international research collaborations conducted under the auspices of the International Geosphere-Biosphere Program (Lambin et al. 1999; GLP 2005). In short, LCS entails "the linking of natural, social and geographic information sciences to study land surface changes and their consequences" (IGBP 2006, 29).

A stated priority of LCS is advancing understanding of the causes of land change (Geist et al. 2006, 42). To do this, researchers employ a range of methods and analytical tools but typically approach investigations inductively[1] by search-ing for general patterns within quantitative data sets using inferential statistics and modelling (e.g., Chowdhury and Turner 2005; Mena et al. 2006; Mendoza et al. 2011; Redo et al. 2012; Silva et al. 2016; Turner and Robbins 2008, 6.7–6.8). As empirical findings have multiplied, however, general theories and models have emerged and introduced a more explicitly deductive bent to some LCS work (Verburg et al. 2006, 120). Forest transition theory, which is examined in this book, is perhaps the best known example of this (Mather 1992; Rudel et al. 2005; Turner et al. 2007; Rudel et al. 2010). Most LCS researchers now presume elements of forest transition theory are credible and some design studies, not to explain changes in forest cover *per se*, but rather to test the validity of the theory as it is currently understood (Perz 2007; Barbier et al. 2010; Lambin and Meyfroidt 2010; Costa et al. 2017).

LCS researchers recognize that causes of land use change are often complex and site specific, with both proximate and underlying factors ("drivers") needing to be considered (e.g., Lambin et al. 2001; Geist et al. 2006; Turner et al. 2007; Dalla-Nora et al. 2014; Shaver et al. 2015; Plieninger et al. 2016; Newman et al. 2018). Qualitative methods are not categorically ruled out, but the guiding research strategy for LCS is explicitly founded on the application of quantitative methods and data collection, preferably standardized across case studies (Geist et al. 2006; Lambin et al. 2006). This approach has encouraged use of social science methods common to quantitative sociology and economics, notably regression modelling of discrete variables (i.e., factors) using data derived from national statistics or large sample, prestructured household surveys. Using these methods, LCS studies have shown statistical associations between land use/land-cover changes and various socio-economic and demographic factors.

Such statistical approaches can be severely limiting, however, where explan-ations of change entail multiple, conjunctural causes, as they often do (Ragin 1987; Gaddis 2002; Goba 2008; Yikoski and Kuorikoski 2010; Efroymson et al. 2016). In the absence of in-depth, contextual knowledge of the actual cases under study, such analyses are best viewed as exploratory as they tend to gener-ate findings which beg more questions than they answer about why identified factors *actually* correlate or not with land use decisions, practices or land-cover changes in specific places (Walters and Vayda 2009; Redo et al. 2012, 799–802). Thus, Geist et al. (2006, 45) acknowledge the obstacles created for LCS where factors "crucially important in explaining change in one place may be irrelevant in other nearby places" and where "a given factor may be implicated in opposite land-cover outcomes" (see also Meyfroidt 2015). In fact, this book will present a number of illustrations of this sort of contradictory finding, including the ambiguous influence of land tenure on tree planting and forest conservation practices (see also Walters et al. 1999). As argued below, LCS researchers facing confounding or ambiguous results like this could benefit from adopting a more explicitly, causal-historical approach to their analysis (cf. Freedman 1991; Goba 2008; Ebach et al. 2016).

Socioecological Systems

SES thinking emerged in the late 1990s, the result of collaboration between ecologists and social scientists seeking to bring a more holistic, ecosystem-inspired perspective to research on the human environment (Berkes and Folke 1998; Adger 2000; Gunderson and Holling 2002; Folke 2006). The SES approach is founded on appeals to a loose cluster of conceptual heuristics and theoretical propositions, adapted mostly from systems thinking in the natural sciences (Holling 1996; Turner et al. 2003a; Walker et al. 2006; Liu et al. 2007; Leslie and McCabe 2013). In this respect, SES differs from LCS in being more deductively oriented in its analytical approach, although among researchers there is little consensus regarding the status of "theory" in SES. For some, SES concepts and ideas comprise the building blocks of a solid theoretical foundation (actual or in the making), but others appear to view them as just analytical heuristics (Folke 2006; Walker et al. 2006; Ostrom 2009).

Consider, for example, the SES concept of resilience, which has attained prominence in many academic and policy circles (Downes et al. 2013; Neocleous 2013). Like the concept of sustainable development, resilience serves as a so-called boundary object, drawing to it a variety of scholars seeking to reconcile the social and ecological within an integrated analytical framework (Brand and Jax 2007). Resilience has much normative appeal, but there is little scientific or policy consensus on its actual meaning (Grimm and Wissel 1997; Adger 2000; Brand and Jax 2007; Downes et al. 2013; Baggio et al. 2015). The more widespread its use, the less consistent are the meanings for which it is used (Neocleous 2013). In fact, the conceptual vagueness of resilience, while analytically dubious, is arguably a source for much of its appeal (Brand and Jax 2007; Strunz 2012; Basken 2013).

Another prominent conceptual proposition within SES is the *adaptive cycle*, a model of organic succession whereby ecosystems and social systems (or SES) are thought to pass in sequence through four distinct phases: (1) growth/expansion; (2) conservation; (3) disturbance/collapse; and (4) reorganization, which is then followed by a return to growth, and so forth (Gunderson and Holling 2002; Folke 2006). As with resilience, there are disagreements as to whether the adaptive cycle constitutes a heuristic schema or something more solidly theoretical and explanatory (Walker et al. 2006; Burns and Rudel 2015). Either way, the adaptive cycle has a teleological quality about it and is conceptually vague in that it lacks specific criteria by which to clearly define and demarcate different phases of the cycle (Bunce et al. 2009, 223). What constitutes a system "collapse", "reorganization" and so on thus seems too much in the eyes of the beholder (e.g., Winkel et al. 2016).

SES approaches have also been criticized for their inability to meaningfully incorporate history, politics and other qualitative factors whose influences are difficult to measure discretely and usually originate beyond the temporal or spatial boundaries of the designated "system" (Armitage and Johnson 2006; Nadasdy 2007; Bunce et al. 2009; Fraser and Stringer 2009; Hornborg 2009, 251–55; Davidson 2010; Kirchhoff et al. 2010; Jennings 2011; Watts 2011; Clement 2012; Cote and Nightingale 2012; Widgren 2012a, 2012b; Galaty 2013; Homewood 2013; Leslie and McCabe 2013; Friis and Neilsen 2017). SES also offers little concrete guidance beyond its broad conceptual heuristics and general frameworks for practising researchers. An extensive review of resilience studies found no consistency in research methods or methodology (Downes et al. 2013; Binder et al. 2013).

Arguably, the most explicit articulation of methodology in SES entails the application of a coupled human and natural systems approach, wherein researchers are encouraged to compile empirical data to build models that incorporate natural and social factors so that reciprocal interactions and feedbacks between variables can be mapped and assessed (Turner et al. 2003a; Liu et al. 2007; McConnell et al. 2011; Carter et al. 2014). The coupled human and natural systems approach is to some extent an attempt to synthesize SES principles and frameworks with the formal modelling approaches common to LCS. Yet while it is explicit in recognizing that important interactions often occur between the local and non-local ("across scales"), it remains analytically unfocused and is notable for its lack of clear criteria with which to assess the relative boundedness, frequency and recurrence of specified human-environment relationships. It thus remains unduly arbitrary how systems are bounded and components selected for inclusion or not within them. Also, distinctions are not readily made between genuinely systemic interactions ("couplings") and more contingent interactions that may constitute only singular or irregular (but nonetheless important) causal events (Vayda and Walters 2011, 17).

SES and coupled human and natural systems have heuristic value by virtue of their fostering integrative, interdisciplinary thinking and analysis. They may also be appropriate for research where detailed, descriptive understanding is sought and where resources permit development of complex data sets and models, but such initiatives are costly and complex to implement, and so impractical for most researchers. As the research presented in this book illustrates, they may simply be ill suited for answering explanatory "why" questions where relevant causal information is not meaningfully captured or quantifiable within a systems framework of analysis (Walters 2012a, 2017).

Political Ecology

Political ecology includes a range of theoretical perspectives and analytical approaches that are variously informed by Marxist political economy, dependency theory and poststructuralism (Bryant and Bailey 1997; Watts 2003; Watts and Peet 2004; Zimmerer and Bassett 2003). As such, it views peoples' relationships with the environment as decisively influenced by capitalism and mediated by political structures and socially constructed ideas that reinforce unequal access and control over environmental resources (Robbins 2004; Forsyth 2008; Mann 2009). Political ecology is sceptical of the post-positivist/reductionist view of explanation that underlies LCS and SES, preferring structuralist and constructivist explanatory approaches instead (Turner and Robbins 2008; Aldrich et al. 2012).[2] Quantitative methods and models so central to LCS and SES are also typically eschewed by political ecology in favour of qualitative analysis of case studies (Turner and Robbins 2008). Many political ecology studies are empirically detailed, but their analytical orientation is typically more deductive or theory driven than either LCS or SES.

Political ecology has championed the idea that local environmental changes often need to be understood as the outcome of non-local, political processes, structures and events. Influential early advocates for political ecology (Blaikie and Brookfield 1987) argued explicitly for linking the local with the non-local using nested chains of explanation, albeit this approach has been difficult to operationalize in practice and has been criticized for being overly hierarchical in its explanatory structure (Batterbury and Bebbington 1999; Blaikie 1999, 140; Robbins and Bishop 2008; Walters and Vayda 2009, 546). Political ecologists have since for the most part steered clear of this sort of methodological thinking (but see Shaver et al. 2015). Instead, political ecologists can be roughly divided into those who embrace a fairly general theory of the political economy of the environment and those guided by a more eclectic set of analytic-theoretical perspectives.

Either way, the heavily theoretical character of much political ecology scholarship can be seen as both a strength and weakness. Political ecology views LCS and SES approaches as inadequate for dealing with society and politics, yet research within political ecology has been justly criticized for its inadequate attention to the empirical complexities of environmental change (Vayda and Walters 1999; Walker 2005; Nygren and Rikoon 2008; Pollini 2010). More generally, political ecology's emphasis on politics above all else is a recipe for confirmation bias in causal explanations – that is, the human tendency to seek or interpret evidence "in ways that are partial to existing beliefs, expectations or a hypothesis at hand" (Nickerson 1998, 175; Vayda, 2009, 29–43). One consequence of these shortcomings is that political ecologists have been quick to embrace "revised" narratives about human-environment relationships that are enlightening and yet arguably as oversimplified as the original narratives they replaced (Grossman 1998; Nyerges 2008; Pollini 2010; Behnke and Mortimore 2016).

Abductive Causal Eventism

Scholars have long acknowledged an epistemological kinship between history and the evolutionary sciences (biology, ecology, geology, paleontology, etc.) (Gould 1989; Kelly 2016). These fields have largely advanced by resisting law-like generalities and teleological thinking and, instead, by embracing diversity, contingency and change as fundamental features of the human and natural world (McCullagh 1998; Gaddis 2002; Sagoff 2016). While historians are rarely explicit about their methodologies, insights derived from the causal analysis of historical events are viewed increasingly by philosophers as central more generally to explanations in both the social and natural sciences (Dray 1957,

1964; Scriven 1966, 2008; McCullagh 1984, 1998; Lewis 1986; Hawthorn 1991; Roberts 1996; Vayda and Walters 2011). The implication is that making firm distinctions between historical and supposedly "scientific" explanations is simply unwarranted: all explanations are ultimately causal-historical.

It is therefore not just a matter of scientists adopting a historical perspective or incorporating historical methods and information in their research. Indeed, scholars from a range of academic disciplines have approached studies of land use and forest change historically (e.g., Cronon 1983; Thirgood 1989; Foster 1992; Kummer 1992; Moran 1993; Rudel 1993; Balee 1998; Kirby and Watkins 1998; Agnoletti and Anderson 2000; Reenberg 2001; Williams 2003; Lukas 2014). Historians approach research in different ways, and not all entail causal explanation as a goal (McCullagh 1998; Gaddis 2002). For example, much historical research is primarily descriptive or interpretive. Even where explanatory, it does not always follow the causal-analytic approach described here. The name *abductive causal eventism* was thus adopted to emphasize critical elements of historical analysis that are often, but not always, given priority by historians themselves. But these are elements well suited for the analysis of environmental change.

Specifically, ACE is an explanation-oriented methodology, based on a pragmatic view of research methods and explanation that places at the centre of research inquiry the answering of *why* questions about events, including human actions and environmental changes, rather than evaluating causal theories, models or factors that are thought in advance to influence such changes. ACE entails constructing causal histories of interrelated social and/or biophysical events backward in time and outward or inward in space through a process of eliminative inference and reasoning from effects to causes. Avoiding rigid a priori assumptions about which events (or kinds of events) will do the explaining, the researcher may seek whatever socio-economic and biophysical information is expected to be relevant to answering specific questions of interest. Diverse types of evidence are then effectively integrated by virtue of focus, not on what is prescribed by some general theory or model, but rather on clear, concrete events as possible, situation-specific causes. The approach and underlying rationale for ACE is detailed elsewhere (Vayda 2009; Walters and Vayda 2009; Vayda and Walters 2011; Walters 2012a; Vayda 2013). This section highlights key distinctions between ACE and the aforementioned research approaches.

First, ACE makes *events* the primary, but not exclusive, focus of analysis.

Put simply, an event is something that happens somewhere during a particular interval of time (Lombard 1991; Walters and Vayda 2009, 540–41). The causal analysis of events may entail consideration of particular events or, at a more general level, *events of a given kind* (Lewis 1986; Vayda and Walters 2011, 1–6). More durable structures or conditions may also form parts of explanations, as findings from this research will show, but ACE researchers should where possible identify effects and causes in terms of events. This is because, for explanation, events are generally regarded as more precise analytically and less problematic ontologically than systems, structures or processes. By focusing on events, ACE can readily incorporate the influence of causes that are singular or infrequent (contingent) in their effects, as well as causes that are recurrent and thus possibly indicative of the presence of "systems", "structures", "processes" or "event sequences" (cf. Perramond 2007, 502).

A second distinction is the central place of abductive reasoning in ACE. Many philosophers have long recognized abduction as a form of analytic reasoning distinct from induction and deduction (see especially Peirce 1932), but there has been a revival of interest in it (Hintikka 1998; Thomas 2010; Campos 2011). Abductive reasoning is inference to an explanatory hypothesis: faced with novel and perhaps puzzling observations, a researcher conceives of plausible conjectures to explain these. Abductions may be *habitual* (drawing from conjectures already known to the inquirer) or *creative* (conjectures previously unknown to the inquirer but conceived of in response to puzzling observations). Seemingly mundane, abduction is an act of intellectual insight and arguably the basis for scientific creativity and discovery (Campos 2011, 425–31).

Critical for ACE, abduction entails reasoning from effects to causes (rather than from causes to effects) and thus provides the analytical basis for following chains of event causation backward in time and either outward or inward in space (table 1.1). This stepwise process entails an eliminative strategy whereby alternative plausible hypothesis are first derived abductively to explain an event of interest. Next, these hypotheses are evaluated inductively or deductively using counterfactual reasoning and whatever empirical methods and evidence can be brought to bear on the matter. Less plausible hypotheses are then progressively eliminated in favour of those more plausible (cf. Chamberlin 1965 [orig. 1890]; Scriven 2008, 21–23). This eliminative strategy may reveal singular or multiple converging causes, and it can then be repeated to follow specific chains of event causation further steps backward.

Table 1.1. Examples of questions for human-environment researchers using causes-to-effects reasoning versus effects-to-causes reasoning

Causes-to-Effects Reasoning	Effects-to-Causes Reasoning
How are globalization and population pressure affecting land use decisions and practices? (GLP 2005, 10)	Why did fires in Indonesia's wet tropical forests start but only some of them spread? (Vayda 2006)
Is yam cultivation a major proximate cause of forest cover change in Jamaica's Cockpit Country? (Newman et al. 2018)	Why are Saint Lucia's tropical forests expanding in area? (Walters 2017)
What effects did the collapse of the coffee market have on peasant farmers and the forests in which it is harvested? (Robbins 2004, 5)	Why are the lands north of Binangun, Java, severely degraded (deforested and eroding)? (Lukas 2014)
What effects do land tenure, population density and other factors have on reforestation in Nepal? (Nagendra 2007)	Why are people in the Philippines planting mangroves in some coastal villages but not others? (Walters 2004)
What are the effects of bioenergy policy on land use change? (Efroymson et al. 2016)	Why did the North Atlantic cod population collapse in the early 1990s? (McGuire 1997)

Abduction is indispensable to doing science, so all researchers engage in at least some effects-to-causes reasoning, but for most it is secondary to causes-to-effects reasoning. ACE suggests reversing this emphasis and offers the following advantages for doing so:

ACE is iterative and adaptive. Causal inquiries evolve as evidence is revealed and interrogated; novel or unexpected findings can be readily incorporated and investigations modified accordingly.

ACE is unbounded and scale independent. Causal chains can be traced backwards to proximate and/or distant origins as interest and evidence warrants. That is, researchers follow causal chains where they lead, not to predetermined boundaries, levels or scales of analysis (Walters and Vayda 2009, 543–45). As such, ACE avoids reification of "systems" and "scale" and escapes the hierarchical, causal determinism that is found, for example, in Blaikie and Brookfield's (1987) "chains of explanation" approach (Robbins 2004, 210; Rangan and Kull 2009).

ACE is interdisciplinary. Events and their causes may be sociocultural, political, economic or biophysical in nature, but regardless, focusing on events encourages analytical clarity and precision, which fosters cross-disciplinary communication. Likewise, both qualitative and quantitative empirical evidence can be drawn upon to evaluate the plausibility of causal connections between events. This encourages an eclectic use of methods, models and theoretical ideas, as well as fostering integrative, interdisciplinary analysis without being committed to either a reductionist-analytical paradigm or to systems as ontological entities or to specific holistic analytical frameworks.

CHAPTER SUMMARY

This research applied a variety of natural and social science methods to study changes in land use and forests in Saint Lucia and to understand the causes of these changes. This included vegetation surveys, interviews of farmers and other key informants, time-series air photo assessments and extensive use of archival materials and government statistics. Field research and air photo assessments focused on two representative watersheds in Saint Lucia (Soufrière and Mamiku), but this local information was complemented by national records and statistics.

The analytical approach used here to integrate diverse sources of information into a coherent causal narrative is based on application of causal-historical reasoning, or what Brad Walters and Andrew Vayda refer to as "abductive causal eventism" (Walters and Vayda 2009; Walters 2017). This approach is qualitatively different and has analytical advantages over other commonly used approaches in human-environment research, including LCS, SES and political ecology. With ACE, one seeks to answer "why" questions about environmental changes of interest by constructing causal histories of interrelated social and/or biophysical events backward in time and outward or inward in space through a process of eliminative inference and effects-to-causes reasoning, called "abduction". This study presents the first comprehensive analysis of land use and forest change using ACE.

CHAPTER 2

BEFORE BANANAS

The history of primary exports from the West Indies is a record of advances and declines brought about by developments in consuming countries in Europe and the North American continent, and by agreements to which the West Indies were seldom signatories but which nevertheless influenced the level and direction of exports for particular commodities.

—McFarlane (1964, 81)

SAINT LUCIA'S ECONOMIC AND ENVIRONMENTAL HISTORY ARE INEXTRICABLY bound to its agricultural history. Cultivation of exportable commodities like cotton, sugar and cocoa formed the backbone of the island's early development, and its landscapes were massively transformed over time in the service of growing these and other crops for export and local consumption. Changes associated with the post–World War II rise and fall of bananas are a major focus of this book. Before getting to that, it is worth reviewing the island's earlier settlement and agricultural history to establish some context for the emergence and development of the banana industry. A study of Saint Lucia's earlier history also enables us to consider notable parallels between long-past and more recent experiences. For example, this chapter will show that booms and busts in agriculture are recurring events in Saint Lucia's history. The recent experience with bananas is thereby neither as unique nor perhaps as significant as it seems.

EARLY SETTLEMENT AND AGRICULTURAL DEVELOPMENT

The Windward Islands were colonized by Island Arawak (Taino) and then Kalinago (Carib) Indians from South America over a thousand years ago. They fished, foraged and hunted, and cultivated a variety of plants, some still commonly grown in Saint Lucia, including manioc (cassava), sweet potato, arrow-root, squash, maize, beans and allspice (*pimenta*) (Mintz 1985; Kimber 1988; Harmsen et al. 2014). As for European colonization, it and the development of Saint Lucia was slow compared to its island neighbors. Barbados was settled by the British and Martinique by the French in the early seventeenth century, and their extensive flatlands were rapidly transformed into sugar plantations. By contrast, Saint Lucia's rugged terrain made it less appealing for agriculture, and its relatively impenetrable interior was inhabited by Amerindians hostile to colonists. Colonial governments nonetheless viewed Saint Lucia as strategically valuable because of its sheltered bays and one especially deep, sheltered harbour, now the port of Castries (Breen 1844; Harmsen et al. 2014).

Early attempts to settle Saint Lucia by English colonists were rebuffed by Carib aggression (Harmsen et al. 2014). The first permanent settlement was established in 1651 by parties from Martinique who planted cotton, ginger, tobacco and ground provisions. These remained the principle crops until the early 1700s, when coffee and cocoa became widely planted (Breen 1844). But colonization proceeded slowly for decades because of violent resistance from resident Caribs and ongoing political jostling between the French and English for control of the island (Thomas 2006; Harmsen et al. 2014).

The first civil authority in Saint Lucia was established by the French in 1744, whereupon official town plans and land surveys were completed and land concessions granted to settlers. This initiated a period of significant growth in population and agriculture. Estimates vary but suggest a resident population in 1760 of about a thousand whites and four thousand blacks (slaves plus free people of colour) (Thomas 2006). Cotton became widely cultivated, especially on the newly granted estates on the drier east side of the island, including the area covered by the Mamiku watershed (figure 1.1). Coffee and cocoa plantings also expanded into the uplands, especially on the wetter and more fertile soils of the west side of the island around Soufrière, which emerged around this time as a centre of plantation agriculture (Harmsen et al. 2014).

ASCENDENCY OF THE SUGAR PLANTATION (1763–1847)

England retook Saint Lucia in 1762, but it was returned to France in the Treaty of Paris in 1763. Around the same time, sugar cultivation was introduced, and its subsequent spread dramatically transformed the island's economy and landscape

(Williams 2001). By 1773 sugar had replaced cotton on many large estates, and its cultivation occupied almost triple the land area. Sugar production is labour intensive, so its growth depended on a huge expansion of slavery. From 1764 to 1784 the island slave population tripled to eighteen thousand, while the non-slave population grew by only one-third, to around three thousand (Harmsen et al. 2014). Many of the new slaves came to Saint Lucia with French planters who migrated from Martinique and other nearby islands (Grenada, Saint Vincent) following their restitution to the British in the Treaty of Paris (Breen 1844).

Sugar's astonishing growth was halted in 1780 by a powerful hurricane that caused widespread damage, death and escaping of slaves. Some 300 plantations were abandoned in its wake (Breen 1844; Thomas 2006; Harmsen et al. 2014). According to Breen (1844), from 1756 to 1831 Saint Lucia was "laid waste" by six hurricanes, the worst being in 1780, which was "probably the most destructive that has ever been experienced in this hemisphere" (136). This storm was estimated to have killed an astounding twenty-two thousand people across Saint Lucia, Barbados, Saint Vincent and Martinique.

Many estates quickly recovered, however, and by 1784 land area under sugar cultivation (3,271 carres,[1] or about 10,800 acres) far exceeded the area of land under all other export crops combined. A detailed, island-wide survey of land-holdings and agriculture was conducted in 1784 by the island's chief surveyor, Lefort de Latour (table 2.1). The preserved map and accompanying notes offer the first clear picture of land use across the island, including Mamiku and Soufrière watersheds (de Latour 1883; Bruneau-Latouche 1989). Based on these, the entire Soufrière watershed and about 90 per cent of Mamiku had been demarcated into plantations, ranging in size from 4 to 390 carres (13 to 1,300 acres).[2] De Latour's notes on primary crops show, first, that sugar dominated the large, valley-bottom plantations in both Mamiku and Soufrière. Second, coffee and cocoa were especially common in Soufrière, where they were usually grown

Table 2.1. Summary of plantations with primary land use in Soufrière and Mamiku watersheds in 1787

	Sugar	Cocoa	Coffee	Cotton	Abandoned
Soufrière (n = 33)	7	20	17	–	6
Mamiku (n = 7)	2	–	3	1	1

Source: de Latour (1883) and Bruneau-Latouche (1989).

together on smaller plantations located on hilly, upland terrain. Third, cotton was farmed on only one plantation, which occupied the extensive tract of dry, flatlands abutting the sea in Mamiku. Finally, seven of the forty plantations surveyed by de Latour were identified by him as "abandoned", and all of these were located in relatively remote uplands of the two watersheds.

The de Latour survey reveals the main crops grown on each estate, but it does not specify the area of land under cultivation of these crops or in other uses, including forest and bush. This point was recognized later by Breen (1844, 292) who observed of earlier land use surveys, "In those days every garden that displayed a coffee bush was dignified with the name of a coffee plantation". This distinction matters because some analysts have cited de Latour's survey as providing evidence of early, widespread deforestation and estate-crop cultivation throughout Saint Lucia's uplands, but was this, in fact, the case? Saint Lucia's upland terrain is extremely varied and characterized by steep slopes and many sites that are difficult to access. Given this, it seems likely that upland estates in de Latour's day concentrated cultivation on the relatively flatter and more accessible portions of their properties, leaving the remaining lands either in forest or under bush fallow for use by slaves for growing provisions (Walters and Hansen 2013).

In any case, the continuities between de Latour's early observations and the more recent situation are worth highlighting. For one, although coffee is long gone, Soufrière has remained the island epicentre of cocoa agroforestry (Walters 2016b). Second, the de Latour survey reveals that abandoned plantations were more common on remote sites, a pattern consistent with evidence presented in chapter 4 that shows a clear tendency for remoter sites to be abandoned first by farmers downsizing their production.

The 1787 de Latour survey indicates a relatively diverse agricultural economy, but over time Saint Lucia became, like so many Caribbean colonies, largely dominated by its plantation sugar industry. War returned between the French and British, and French Revolution–inspired slave revolts began in 1792 and led to a protracted conflict on the island from 1794 to 1798, the so-called Brigands Wars. These events motivated an exodus of French planters and widespread abandonment of plantations (Williams 2001; Harmsen et al. 2014). From 1790 to 1799 the resident slave population declined by more than one-quarter, from 18,400 to 13,400.

The British reclaimed Saint Lucia for the last time in 1802, and there followed

Table 2.2. Number of agricultural estates by primary crop in Saint Lucia, 1787–1834

	1787	1815	1819	1834
Cocoa	150	49	27	13
Coffee	313	110	89	94
Cotton	459	19	14	2
Sugar cane	73	112	110	95
Provisions	0	25	30	90
Total	**1,000**	**315**	**270**	**294**

Source: Thomas (2006, 36, table 12).

a modest influx of British planters, although the new colonial administrators sought to accommodate French planters willing to stay.[3] Still, the preceding period of turmoil had severely impacted agriculture. Statistics reveal huge declines from 1787 to 1815 in the number of estates growing cocoa, coffee and especially cotton. Only sugar expanded during this period (table 2.2). Not only were there more sugar estates by 1815, but these were usually much larger than other estates and were concentrated on the island's best farmlands. The relative dominance of sugar in the agricultural export economy was thus firmly established and would remain so despite setbacks for over a century (Thomas 2006). To put this in perspective, exports of sugar from Saint Lucia in 1934 were 7 million pounds, 30 times the weight of coffee and 110 times the weight of cocoa exports. In addition to these raw sugar exports, Saint Lucia exported abundant sugar-based products that year, including 194,000 gallons of molasses and 8,500 gallons of rum (Thomas 2006).

These general trends notwithstanding, changes unfolded differently across the island during this turbulent period. Soufrière District, in particular, fared relatively well, experiencing a much smaller decline (25 per cent) in the number of estates from 1787 to 1812, as compared to an island-wide decline rate of nearly 70 per cent and a Praslin District (where Mamiku watershed is found) decline rate of 80 per cent. This in part reflects the near total collapse of cotton farming, which was especially widespread on the dry, easternmost coastlands. In fact, Breen (1844, 289) specifically notes that extensive former cotton lands in the Praslin area, which includes the coastal lowlands of Mamiku, had reverted back to native "wilds", although this was offset in places by expansions of sugar cultivation. By contrast, Soufrière District stands apart in the early 1800s as an epicentre of plantation agriculture in Saint Lucia, leading all other districts in terms of the number of active sugar, coffee and cocoa estates, as well as total number of slaves, with double that of any other district (2,664 or 25 per cent of the island slave population in 1834) (Thomas 2006).

The slave trade was ended in 1807 and full emancipation achieved across the British West Indies by 1838. A devastating hurricane in 1831 and loss of slave labour led to financial ruin for many Saint Lucian estates. Many estates were sold, others abandoned outright. Country-wide exports of sugar, molasses, coffee and cocoa each declined by about 50 per cent, while cotton exports ended entirely (Breen 1844, 319). Desperate planters responded to labour shortages by widely adopting the métayage system, a form of sharecropping (Lowenthal 1972; Williams 2001; Moberg 2008). With métayage, peasants grew the cane and split profits with the mill owners. Métayage may well have prevented a total collapse of the sugar industry in the wake of emancipation (Harmsen et al. 2014). Based on export statistics provided by Breen (1844), after a sharp initial decline from 1831 to 1836, sugar production stabilized at about half its former level. At the time of writing, Breen (1844) estimated 5,245 acres of land were under sugar cane cultivation, 460 under coffee, 275 in cocoa, 3,920 in provisions (food crops) and 3,000 acres in pasture.

SUGAR'S SLOW, STAGGERED DECLINE (1848–1957)

During the second half of the nineteenth century, it become increasingly common to fill labour shortages in the plantation sector with indentured workers. From 1862 to 1893 some five thousand indentured labourers – 85 per cent of Indian origin – came to Saint Lucia, and most worked in the sugar industry (Roberts and Byrne 1966; Harmsen et al. 2014). Still, declining market prices for sugar emerged during this period as the critical challenge for the Saint Lucian industry. This began with the passage of the UK Equalization Act in 1848, which eliminated tariffs that had protected West Indian sugar and opened up competition with sugar cane producers from the Dominican Republic, Mauritius, Cuba, Brazil, Java and Queensland (Lowenthal 1972; Moberg 2008). The much larger British colonies of Trinidad and Guiana were also expanding their acreage under cane cultivation. Things then went from bad to worse in the early 1880s when subsidized European beet sugar flooded the British market (Cox 1897; Brassey 1898). In response to growing price pressures in the 1870s and 1880s, four of Saint Lucia's larger sugar estates built modern, centralized factories in Cul de Sac, Vieux Fort, Roseau and Dennery (Harmsen et al. 2014).

Despite these developments, an abrupt crash in the price of muscovado sugar in 1884 precipitated widespread bankruptcy among sugar estates. Muscovado is lower-grade, brown sugar, commonly used in rum-making and molasses. It fetches a lower market price than the more refined *usine* sugar, which central-ized mills typically produced (WIRC 1897). In response to market challenges, marginal sugar estates either sought to diversify into limes, livestock, coffee and cocoa or were abandoned (Williams 2001; Harmsen et al. 2014). From 1882 to 1896 the value of the island's sugar exports declined by 70 per cent, while that of cocoa grew by 250 per cent. Only 38 of 75 sugar estates from two decades earlier remained in sugar, with 25 selling cane to one of the four centralized mills and the rest producing muscovado sugar on a smaller scale in conjunc-tion with other industries like rum, cocoa and livestock. Of the thirty-seven estates no longer in sugar, ten moved heavily into cocoa, while the rest lapsed "back into bush" (WIRC 1897).

The decline of sugar brought such hardship to plantation economies and their workers that the British government appointed a royal commission to study the problem and offer recommendations ("Jamaica's Sugar Industry: Threatened with Ruin by the Bounty System", *New York Times*, 17 January 1897; WIRC 1897; Richardson 2007). Notably, the so-called Norman Commission on the West Indian Sugar Industry learned that smallholder farmers were faring better than plantations and recommended support for resettlement of unemployed plantation workers onto holdings of their own. In fact, the collapse of sugar had already motived the breakup and resale of estate lands to smallholders in the uplands of Soufrière, notably around Ravine Claire, Diamond, the Pearle and Fond Saint Jacques (WIRC 1897). These areas include some of the most productive smallholder farmlands in the Soufrière watershed today.

Despite these troubles, the sugar industry in Saint Lucia persisted through consolidation and mechanization on the few, largest estates and by diversifica-tion on some of the smaller ones. In fact, some of these estates were among the first to adopt commercial banana cultivation in the 1920s and 1930s. However, the world recession of the 1930s drove sugar prices down further and brought crisis again to the industry. Political turmoil erupted, driven by pro–labour union activism that challenged the country's elite planter and merchant class. In response, the British government dispatched in 1939 another Royal Commission to the West Indies, headed by Lord Moyne. War eased domestic political tensions and delayed release of the Moyne Report until 1945, but its main recommendations echoed sentiments expressed by the earlier Norman Commission in calling for land reform and resettlement of landless plantation workers (Axline 1986; Myers 2004). The Saint Lucian sugar industry barely survived the war, concentrated now in only three large river valleys: Roseau, Cul-de-Sac and Mabouya. Labour strife returned the following decade, however, with strikes that crippled the industry in 1957 and precipitated its final demise a few years later (Welch 1994; Reynolds 2006).

PLANTATIONS AND SMALLHOLDERS

Plantations dominated Saint Lucian agriculture for most of its colonial history, yet as we shall see in chapter 4, through the course of the second half of the twentieth century, smallholder or "peasant" farmers grew to relative dominance in their role as banana producers. The origins of this dynamic peasant economy warrant brief consideration.

Before emancipation, it was common practice on West Indian plantations to allocate small plots of land – typically on marginal, hillside lands of the estate – to enable slaves to grow their own food. In some cases, estates even encouraged slaves to grow and market their surplus, which enabled some to later buy themselves out of bondage. Many slaves also cultivated fruit trees, spices and vegetables adjacent to their living quarters. These so-called provision grounds, along with home gardens, enabled slaves to share knowledge and develop farming skills that proved critical to their success as independent farmers following emancipation (Mintz 1974, 1985; Hills and Iton 2000).

Escaped slaves, called "Maroons", survived in large numbers in Saint Lucia by subsistence farming on remote interior lands. Following emancipation, many Maroons and freed slaves established usufruct claims by squatting on Crown lands or abandoned estates. Many estates also permitted former slaves to continue to farm their provision grounds in exchange for rent (Lowenthal 1972). Others purchased land outright. As already described, for some decades following emancipation, estates depended on sharecropping arrangements with former slaves (métayage) to maintain adequate supply of canes for sugar production. Through métayage or other occupational activities, former slaves and their descendants saved money to buy land when it became available, for example, through the break-up and resale of bankrupt or abandoned estates (Harmsen et al. 2014). Lands were also sometimes purchased by cooperative groups, often aided by churches or missions, to form *free villages* (Lowenthal 1972; Mintz 1974). Over time, these various smallholders and their descendants became the numerically dominant agriculturalists across much of the rural countryside (Mintz 1985; Wiley 2008). The esteemed Caribbean anthropologist, Sidney Mintz, termed this emergent class of smallholder farmers a "reconstituted peasantry" (Mintz 1974, 1985).

This peasantry typically grew a diversity of root, vegetable and tree crops, in part to reduce risk but also because much of what they grew was consumed by the household (Innes 1961; Beckford 1966; Hills and Iton 2000). To raise cash, they sold some of their produce to local food markets or cultivated portions of their land in crops like sugar, coffee, cocoa or spices that could be sold onto markets destined for export (Marshall 1968; Mintz 1974). Many smallholders worked as seasonal or occasional labour on the estates or pursued other occupations (carpentry, fishing, buy and sell, etc.) to complement farming (Mintz 1985). When opportunities presented themselves, many also sought seasonal or longer-term work out of country (Walters 2016a). In fact, this widely shared propensity to innovate, adapt and diversify occupational pursuits has been recognized as a defining cultural trait of West Indian peasants (Carnegie 1982; Momsen 1986), one that made them well suited to the requirements of banana farming.

CHAPTER SUMMARY

Indigenous peoples altered the lands and forests of Saint Lucia for centuries before contact, but introduction of intensive crop cultivation for export by Europeans in the seventeenth and eighteenth centuries massively transformed the island environment and resulted in the loss of much of its native forests. In particular, cotton and then sugar cane dominated agriculture on the lowlands and near the coast, where they were grown mostly on large agricultural estates. By contrast, farming on hillsides and interior lands was more diverse and typically included mixed food crops ("provisons") and tree crops (coffee, cocoa, coconuts, spices, citrus, etc.) grown by smallholders. Emancipation and growing commercial competition in the sugar industry gradually eroded the estate farming sector while smallholder, peasant farming expanded in importance. After nearly two centuries of relative dominance, the sugar industry came to its final end in the wake of World War II, just as bananas entered the picture as a commercially viable export crop. The smallholder farming sector in Saint Lucia was especially well-positioned to exploit the opportunity presented by a nascent banana industry.

CHAPTER 3

POST-WAR CHANGES IN
FORESTS AND LAND USE

SAINT LUCIA'S LANDSCAPE HAS CHANGED DRAMATICALLY IN RECENT decades. To explain *why* it has changed, one must first determine with some precision *how* it has changed. This is the focus of this chapter, which is organized in four parts. The first presents findings from the watershed-vegetation surveys and air photo interpretation to show how rural landscapes of Saint Lucia have changed over the past five decades and what their current ecological characteristics are like. The second part examines how patterns of change reflect local topographic conditions of slope, altitude and proximity to roads. In the third and fourth parts, findings from the vegetation survey and air photo analysis are considered in light of farmer opinions and select government statistics about changing land use and cultivation practices.

This chapter is especially data-rich with quantitative information summarized in a dozen tables and two figures, each one described in the accompanying text where particularly notable details are also highlighted. The most important overall findings are then recapped in the chapter summary.

MORE FORESTS, LESS FARMING

The vegetation surveys sampled a large variety of natural and human-dominated habitats, including coastal mangrove forest, coastal dry scrub forest, mixed wet-dry tropical forest, wet tropical forest, agroforest, annual crop agriculture, pasture land, residential yard, grassy field, and the rock caldera and grassy emission-plume field of a semi-active volcano. The landscapes of both watersheds were dominated by forested habitats, including mature forests, early-succession forests, and planted agroforests. Specifically, 82 per cent of vegetation plots (forty-six of fifty-six) fell in forested habitats, of which nearly half were post-agricultural forests under varying stages of natural succession. For analytical purposes, plot vegetation was classed into one of four major habitat types: annual crop agriculture, including pasture (six plots), agroforest (nineteen plots), secondary forest (thirteen plots) and mature forest (fourteen plots). Of the remaining plots, two fell within residential areas and two on volcanic terrain. Comparing watersheds, Soufrière had significantly more plots fall in agroforest habitats, whereas Mamiku had more plots fall within natural forest (table 3.1).

Selected measures of tree species richness and vegetation structure are summarized in table 3.2. Vegetation plots averaged 6.3 tree species per plot, with approximately 70 per cent of this richness accounted for by natural and 30 per cent by planted tree species. Basal area measures (which estimate the standing tree volume of an area) mirrored this with 71 per cent of basal area accounted for by natural trees. Three general measures of forest structure – basal area, canopy height and canopy openness – provide further indication of the dominance of trees in the vegetation of both watersheds. In particular, mean canopy openness, which measures the percentage of land not directly overtopped by tree canopy, was only 26.1 per cent for Mamiku and 18.5 per cent for Soufrière.

Table 3.1. Summary of major habitat types by sampling plot frequency and watershed

	Number of Vegetation Plots		
Habitat Type	Mamiku Watershed	Soufriére Watershed	Combined Watersheds
Agroforest	2	17[b]	19
Mature forest	8	6	14
Secondary forest	8	5	13
mature + secondary forest	*(16)*[a]	*(11)*	*(27)*
Annual crops	4	2	6
Permanent grass	0	2	2
Volcanic rock surface	0	1	1
Residential yard	0	1	1
Total	**22**	**34**	**56**

[a]Two of twenty-two plots vs seventeen of thirty-four plots, $\chi^2 = 6.63$, p < 0.01.

[b]Sixteen of twenty-two plots vs eleven of thirty-four plots, $\chi^2 = 4.52$, p < 0.05.

Table 3.2. Summary of select tree measures of vegetation plots, comparing mean values (and standard deviations) between Mamiku and Soufrière watersheds

Tree Measures	Mamiku (n = 22 plots)	Soufrière (n = 34 plots)	Total (n = 56 plots)	F-values (df = 1,54)
Species richness:				
All trees	5.9 (4.9)	6.5 (4.6)	6.3 (4.7)	0.21
Natural trees	5.4 (4.9)	4.4 (5.5)	4.8 (5.2)	1.13
Planted trees	0.5 (0.7)	2.1 (2.4)	1.45 (2.0)	7.18*
Basal Area (m2/ha):				
All trees	37.6 (36.9)	41.4 (29.5)	39.9 (32.3)	0.18
Natural trees	35.0 (38.4)	24.2 (33.4)	28.5 (35.5)	3.87
Planted trees	2.6 (4.7)	17.2 (21.9)	11.5 (18.7)	9.46**
Canopy structure:				
Canopy height (m)	15.5 (6.3)	12.5 (6.7)	13.7 (6.7)	2.77
Canopy openness (%)	26.1 (35.3)	18.5 (34.5)	21.5 (34.7)	0.45

*p < .01

**p < .005

To put this in perspective, pure stands of mature tropical forest commonly have canopy openness measures ranging from 5 to 15 per cent.

With habitats so varied and trees so abundant, it is not surprising that many different tree species were identified across the fifty-six vegetation plots. Species counts for individual sample plots (100 m^2) ranged from 0 to 18, with cumulative counts across all plots (a sample area of 5,600 m^2) totaling 125 species (table 3.3).[1] Of these, twenty-six were planted tree species and ninety-nine were natural tree species. Not surprisingly, most planted species were found in agroforests and, to lesser extent, within annual crop habitats where it is common to find individual trees growing here and there within or on the perimeter of cultivated fields. Three planted species (mango, coconut and glory cedar, *Gliriciida sepium*) were also identified in natural forest plots. These were most likely remnant, planted trees that survived despite the site being long abandoned and now regrown in natural forest. However, natural seeding cannot be ruled out, given that all three

Table 3.3. Cumulative species richness of natural and planted trees in vegetation plots by primary habitat type

Habitat	No. of Plots	Tree Species Richness (Cumulative)		
		Planted Trees	Natural Trees	All Trees
Annual crops	6	3	1	4
Agroforest/agro-secondary[a]	19	25	19	44
Secondary forest	13	3	69	72
Mature forest	14	0	57	57
Other	4	0	0	0
All habitats	56	26	99	125

[a]Includes both.

of these species (as well as other commonly cultivated tree species like mahogany and guava) are now considered "naturalized" to the island (Graveson, 2005).

More striking is the large number of natural tree species (n = 19) that were found within agroforest habitats (table 3.3). In many cases, this reflected natural recolonization of forest tree species into agroforest stands that were no longer being managed intensively, if at all. It is also not uncommon to find natural tree species co-mingled with planted species in actively managed agroforests. This is because farmers will sometimes maintain natural trees within their agroforests to protect against soil erosion or serve as cover for shade-grown species like cocoa. It may also reflect less intensive management whereby the farmer simply tolerates a certain presence of non-cultivated tree species in the midst of other species that are intentionally being cultivated.

The wider landscape consequences of these and other changing land use practices is revealed by time-series analysis of air photos. These reveal a striking increase in forests and decline in agriculture (both agroforests and annual crops), especially from 1977 to 2004. However, these trends appear to have significantly moderated between 2004 and 2015 (figure 3.1). Overall, the net change is still striking. In 1966 thirty-three of fifty-six plot sites were under cultivation, while twenty-one were in forest. In 2015 these numbers were essentially reversed, with thirty-five under forest and fifteen being actively farmed.

Farmer interviews from 2007 confirm the trend of increased forest in the

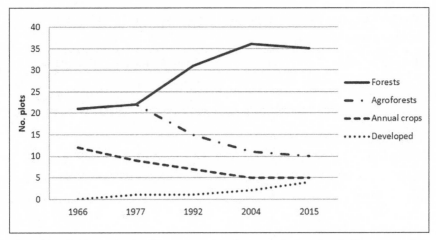

Figure 3.1. Back-casting land use on census plots over time, using field census and air photos (data from Soufrière and Mamiku watersheds combined)

landscape. All but one farmer (thirty-six of thirty-seven) cited having at least *some* forest or bush on their land. Of these, 80.6 per cent (twenty-nine of thirty-six) said the amount of their lands under forest or bush had increased in recent years, with no apparent difference in responses between watersheds or between estate and smallholder farmers (table 3.4). Farmland abandonment was by far the most commonly cited reason for the presence of forest or bush on a farmer's land (table 3.5).

Another change detected with the air photo analysis and worth highlighting is the increase in "developed" land (figure 3.1). Of four plots identified as developed in 2015, three entailed conversion of agroforests in the lower watershed of Soufrière to residential housing and public infrastructure (a new school).

Table 3.4. Recent changes to the area of land under forest/bush as cited by farmers in 2007, comparing watersheds and type of farmer

| | Watershed | | Type of Farmer | | |
	Mamiku (n = 14)	Soufriére n = 22)	Estate (n = 6)	Smallholder (n = 30)	Total (n = 36)
More forest	11	18	4	25	29
No change	3	2	1	4	5
Less forest	0	2	1	1	2

Table 3.5. Reasons cited by farmers in 2007 for the presence of forest or bush on their lands

	Estate Farmer (n = 6)	Smallholder Farmer (n = 30)	Total (n = 36)
Land abandoned from farming	3	21	24
Land too steep to farm	3	5	8
Environmental protection	5	1	6
Tourism opportunities	3	–	3
Swidden fallow	–	2	2
Landowner retired	–	2	2
Land too inaccessible	–	1	1

The fourth involved the clearing of natural forest along a lower slope of the Mamiku watershed to accommodate a new roadway for a planned residential housing development.

LANDSCAPE TOPOGRAPHY MATTERS

Both the Soufrière and Mamiku watersheds are characterized by extremely varied terrain: relatively flat and undulating near the coast, but grading quickly into hills and then steep slopes as one moves inland. Soufrière is especially rugged, with slopes commonly exceeding 30° or even 40° in steepness. The fifty-six vegetation plots were sampled from sea level to 646 metres in altitude (mean = 239.8 m, SD = 159.3) and on slopes that ranged from flat (0°) to very steep (47°), with a mean of 18.9° (SD = 14.2). The mean altitude of vegetation plots was significantly higher in Soufrière at 286.4 metres (SD = 166.3), compared to Mamiku at 167.6 metres (SD = 118.3) ($p < 0.005$, $F = 8.44$, $df = 1,54$). However, mean slope and distance to the nearest road of vegetation plots were roughly similar between the two watersheds.

The key finding from the topographic analysis is that, compared to farmed areas, forests are usually found at higher altitudes, on steeper slopes and more distant from roads (Walters and Hansen 2013, 216–17). These patterns mostly reflect access constraints and land use decisions by farmers and the national government. Specifically, it is commonplace for individual farm holdings to

Table 3.6. Summary of watershed vegetation survey comparing currently farmed versus recently abandoned plots by mean (with standard deviation) of altitude, slope and distance from nearest road

	Farmed Plots **(n = 20)**	**Abandoned Plots** **(n = 20)**	**t-value** **(d.f. = 38)**
Altitude (m)	182.4	300.9	2.40*
	(115.4)	(187.7)	
Slope (degrees)	12.7	26.4	–3.60**
	(11.2)	(12.8)	
Distance to road (m)	114.4	286.0	–2.08*
	(117.4)	(299.4)	

*p < .05

**p < .005

include a mix of flatter and steeper lands at varied distances from roads. Some farmers maintain portions of their land under more-or-less permanent forest cover, especially on steep slopes that are difficult to farm and at high risk of erosion and landslides. Economic considerations may influence whether such marginal lands are brought under cultivation. Given market turmoil in bananas and other broader challenges facing the agricultural sector, farmers have tended to downsize their production by abandoning cultivation on more marginal sites first. For example, 38.5 per cent (10 of 26) of farmers who had reduced their land area under cultivation specifically cited having abandoned the steeper and/or more remote lands on their respective holdings. Confirming this, vegetation plots on abandoned farmland were found to be at significantly higher altitude, on steeper slopes and more distant from roads than vegetation plots on lands still being farmed (table 3.6).

DECLINING CULTIVATION

Evidence from farmer interviews and government statistics confirm the main findings of the vegetation survey and air photo analysis. In particular, when asked about recent changes to the area of their land under cultivation, 74.3 per cent of farmers, or twenty-six of thirty-five, cited a net overall reduction,

Table 3.7. Recent changes to the area of land under cultivation as cited by farmers in 2007, comparing watersheds and type of farmer

	Watershed		Type of Farmer		
	Mamiku (n = 14)	Soufrière (n = 21)	Estate (n = 6)	Smallholder (n = 29)	Total (n = 35)
Reduced	10	16	4	22	26
No change	4	3	1	6	7
Increased	0	2	1	1	2

whereas only 5.7 per cent (two of thirty-five) cited an increase (table 3.7). These trends were consistent between watersheds and for both smallholder and estate farmers. They are also consistent with government statistics from 1974 to 2007 that show broad trends of reduced cultivation nationwide and in the districts of Soufrière and Micoud, where Mamiku is found (figure 3.2).

Farmers cited a variety of reasons for their reducing cultivation, including declining farm-gate prices for crops, especially bananas (46 per cent); growing cost/scarcity of farm labour (42 per cent); ageing (23 per cent); and increased cost of farm inputs like fertilizers and pesticides (19 per cent). Key informants echoed the same causes, but included the loss of farmland to residential and tourism development, improved enforcement against illegal farming in forest

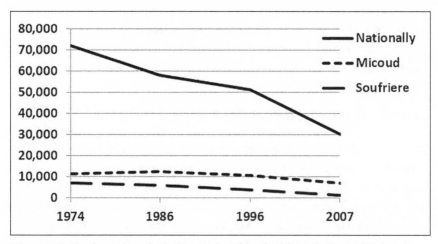

Figure 3.2. Total area (acres) of all agricultural landholdings (1974–2007) nationwide and in Soufrière and Micoud Districts (GOSL 1974, 1987a, 1996a, 2007a)

Table 3.8. Primary reasons cited in 2007 for decline in farming in Saint Lucia, according to farmers and key informants

	Farmers (n = 26)	Key Informants (n = 25)
Declining farm-gate prices	12	14
Growing shortage of farm labour	11	16
Ageing of farmer population	6	5
Increased cost of farm inputs	5	6
Loss of farmland to residential and tourism development	–	9
Improved enforcement against illegal farming in forest reserves	–	7
Uncertain tenure over family lands	–	6
Absentee ownership of farmlands	–	1

reserves and uncertainties over land tenure (table 3.8). In fact, government has also reinforced the shift from farming to forests by strategically targeting selected areas deemed critical for watershed protection, in some cases acquiring lands outright from private owners through purchase or land swaps, but more generally by encouraging tree planting on steep-sloped private lands and by stepping up enforcement against illegal farming of forest reserve land. While not trivial, the cumulative effect on the landscape of these various government initiatives is relatively small compared to that of voluntary farmland abandonment. In any case, explanations for farmland decline and increasing forests are complex and the subject of forthcoming chapters.

SHIFTING CULTIVATION PRACTICES

There has no doubt been a massive, net decline in area of land under cultivation, but evidence points to significant *qualitative* changes in cultivation in recent years as well. When farmers were asked to specify whether they had shifted their production of different crops, more than half indicated that they had reduced cultivation of bananas, yet none had increased it (table 3.9). Most estate farmers, in particular, also cited reducing their cultivation of coconuts, which they farm primarily to extract copra. This particular change helps account for the

Table 3.9. Recent changes to crop cultivation as cited by farmers in 2007

	Estates (n = 6)	Smallholders (n = 28)	Total (n = 34)
Reductions in cultivation			
Bananas	3	15	18
Coconuts	5	1	6
Provisions (root crops)	1	4	5
Cocoa	1	2	3
Fruit crops	0	2	2
Increases in cultivation			
Vegetables	3	7	10
Provisions (root crops)	0	8	8
Fruit crops	1	4	5
Ornamentals (cut flowers)	4	0	4
Cocoa	2	0	2

sharp decline in agroforests (and concomitant increase in forests) from 1977 to 1992 (see figure 3.1) because one especially large estate landowner in Mamiku abandoned an expanse of coconut land in the early 1980s equal in area to about 20 per cent of the entire watershed.

Most farmers lamented having downsized their cultivation, especially of bananas. Yet, some had increased their cultivation of other crops, especially mixed vegetables, but also root crops (provisions), fruits and cut flowers (table 3.9). National statistics on crop cultivation are broadly consistent with these findings, which suggests changes detected in Soufrière and Mamiku are accurate and not unique to those areas. For example, agricultural census data on tree-crop planting from 1973 to 2007 show a growing percentage of farmers cultivating various fruit trees, cinnamon and cocoa, although less are growing coffee (table 3.10). These data are consistent with findings from 2007 interviews that show many different tree species to be commonly cultivated on farms in Soufrière and Mamiku. Among these include a variety of fruit, spice, and timber and shade trees (table 3.11).

Among those still farming, vegetable cultivation is also sharply on the rise, even if not yet practised by a majority of farmers (table 3.12). Trends in root crop

Table 3.10. Percentage of agricultural holdings growing common tree crops in Saint Lucia, 1974–2007

	1973/1934 (n = 10,436)	1986 (n = 10,071)	1996 (n = 11,642)	2007 (n = 9,448)
Coconuts	–	78.1	82.8	80.6
Mangoes	–	65.2	73.2	73.2
Breadfruit	49.5	63.9	65.7	65.1
Grapefruit	20.1	35.5	49.2	54.0
Limes	14.5	31.4	38.7	53.3
Avocadoes	30.1	43.5	51.3	52.3
Oranges (sweet)	27.5	40.1	46.1	44.4
Cocoa	15.0	31.9	31.5	27.9
Cinnamon	–	0.8	17.0	23.3
Tangeriness	–	0.3	19.0	20.9
Coffee	16.7	26.4	18.1	0.0

Source: National Agricultural Census (GOSL 1974, 1987a, 1996a, 2007a).

Table 3.11. Percentage of farmers interviewed in 2007 (n = 43) who cultivate selected tree species (smallholders and estate farmers combined)

	Fruit Trees	Spice Trees	Timber and Shade Trees
Most Common: >50% of farmers	Oranges (sweet) (78%)	Cocoa (50%)	Mahogany (61%)
	Mango (75%)		
	Grapefruit (64%)		
	Breadfruit (61%)		
	Coconut (60%)		
	Avocado (55%)		
	Lime (55%)		
Common: 10–25% of farmers	Cashew (25%)	Cinnamon (16%)	Gloricida (23%)
	Papaya (22%)	Nutmeg (16%)	Blue maho (16%)
	Apple (golden) (16%)		Immortel (16%)
	Tangerine (16%)		Red cedar (13%)
	Soursop (13%)		Native spp. (13%)

Table 3.11 continues

Table 3.11. Percentage of farmers interviewed in 2007 (n = 43) who cultivate selected tree species (smallholders and estate farmers combined) (*cont'd*)

	Fruit Trees	Spice Trees	Timber and Shade Trees
Rare: 1–9% of farmers	Passion fruit (9%)	Bay leaf (9%)	White cedar (6%)
	Mandarin (9%)	Coffee (9%)	Pine (3%)
	Apple (star) (6%)		Teak (3%)
	Apple (sugar) (6%)		Gmelina (3%)
	Carambola (6%)		
	Guava (6%)		
	Orange (sour) (6%)		
	Akee (3%)		
	Almond (3%)		
	Apple (wax) (3%)		
	Calabass (3%)		
	Cherry (3%)		
	Lemon (3%)		
	Pomegranate (3%)		
	Tamarind (3%)		

cultivation show relatively little change (table 3.13). Lastly, since the interviews and agricultural census data were last collected (2007), a significant turnaround in the fortunes of the cocoa industry has encouraged more farmers to restore existing cocoa groves or establish new ones.

Evidence of growth in the cultivation of crops like vegetables, fruits, cocoa and cut flowers provides some optimism for an otherwise struggling agricultural sector. Expansion of these crops may also largely account for the apparent stabilization of farming and stalling of reforestation since 2007 (figure 3.1). Growth in these diverse crops remains relatively modest in scale by historical standards and does not yet come close to offsetting the area of land lost to cultivation from the collapse of the banana industry. For decades, bananas utterly dominated farming across much of Saint Lucia, and the island's landscapes remain very much in banana's shadow. We turn to this crucial part of the story in the following chapter.

Table 3.12. Percentage of agricultural holdings growing common vegetable crops in Saint Lucia, 1974–2007

	1973–1974 (n = 10,436)	1986 (n = 10,071)	1996 (n = 11,642)	2007 (n = 9,448)
Pumpkins	3.0	–	25.8	36.2
Cucumbers	2.3	–	32.1	29.8
Sweet peppers	0.2	–	21.2	26.1
Tomatoes	3.6	–	18.2	23.4
Celery	–	–	14.7	19.3
Christophene	0.2	–	13.2	16.3
Spinach	–	–	8.8	15.5
Lettuce	1.3	–	10.4	13.5
Watermelons	–	–	6.3	11.7
Cabbages	3.0	–	11.2	11.1
Carrots	1.5	–	8.9	7.0
Eggplants	1.5	–	2.9	4.7
Cantaloupes	0.7	–	2.4	3.5
Ginger	5.2	–	9.8	16.7

Note: Vegetables were not covered in the 1986 census.

Source: National Agricultural Census (GOSL 1974, 1996a, 2007a).

Table 3.13. Percentage of agricultural holdings growing common root crops in Saint Lucia, 1974–2007

	1973/1974 (n = 10,436)	1986 (n = 10,071)	1996 (n = 11,642)	2007 (n = 9,448)
Dasheen	88.6[a]	–	59.4	62.1
Yams	66.9	–	58.7	57.3
Tannia	–	–	–	48.9
Sweet potatoes	46.5	–	33.0	33.8
Cassava	25.2	–	13.6	13.9

[a]Figure includes dasheen + tannia.

Note: Root crops were not covered in the 1986 census.

Source: National Agricultural Census (GOSL 1974, 1996a, 2007a).

CHAPTER SUMMARY

Evidence from vegetation surveys, farmer interviews and air photo analysis confirm widespread reforestation across the rural landscapes of both watersheds in recent decades, and this trend appears mirrored island wide. Watershed landscapes include diverse habitats that are rich in both natural and planted tree species. Reforestation was more common on lands on steeper slopes, at higher altitude and more distant from roads. Farmers confirmed that these patterns reflect widespread abandonment of cultivation, especially of lands that are deemed marginal for farming. Agroforests remain common, especially in Soufrière, but some of these are returning to natural forest because of lack of upkeep. Intensive crop cultivation continues but is now concentrated on the best-quality farmlands only and has shifted away from conventional crops like bananas and coconuts to more diversified production of mixed vegetables, fruits and cut flowers. In fact, reforestation of the Saint Lucian landscape may have reached its apogee as agriculture is experiencing some recovery and "hard" development (residential housing, tourism infrastructure, etc.) encroaches onto farm and forest lands. Overall, long-term trends reveal a profound shift in human impacts away from uplands to lowlands, especially near the coast.

With these findings in hand, we now have a pretty clear picture of the environmental characteristics and changes in the landscape, including those changes (events) that are especially interesting and significant (i.e., widespread reforestation, downsizing and shifts in cultivation) and thus most worthy of explanatory attention. We also have some idea already about the influence of certain proximate causes, notably topographic features of the landscape like slope, altitude and road distance. Attaining this level of clarity and precision about events of interest makes the subsequent work of causal explanation more straightforward and compelling because it enables better analytic focus. As we shall see, explaining the causes of such things as changing cultivation practices and reforestation of the landscape can be a complex matter, one that entails consideration of diverse kinds of evidence and evaluation of alternative, sometimes competing hypotheses. If we are not reasonably clear and precise at the outset about what it is we want to explain, then our search for explanations (using ACE or any other approach) is likely to be muddled from the start.

CHAPTER 4

BANANA BOOMS AND BUSTS

THE ECONOMIC AND POLITICAL TURMOIL WROUGHT BY SUGAR'S demise, described in chapter 2, helped set the stage in the 1950s for emergence of a new agricultural industry based on the production and export of bananas. The growing of bananas offered smallholders, in particular, an unprecedented opportunity to participate and benefit directly from a lucrative export market. In so doing, however, it fostered an unparalleled expansion of farming and deforestation into the country's rural interior. In fact, no other development in the second half of the twentieth century has proven to be so consequential for the island's rural economy and landscapes. The extraordinary rise and equally stunning fall of the banana industry is a remarkable story, one that found Saint Lucia and its Windward Island neighbors at the centre of international diplomatic intrigue and conflict over global trade policy. The story is complex and so worth recounting in some detail and from the beginning. This chapter examines the banana industry's nine-decade history in Saint Lucia, with a particular emphasis on understanding the causes of industry expansions and declines because these are crucial for explaining changes in rural land use and forests on the island.

ORIGINS OF THE WEST INDIAN BANANA TRADE

Bananas originated in South East Asia but had spread widely throughout the Pacific, South Asia and Africa by the time of Columbus. Portuguese traders introduced bananas and plantains from Africa to the Canary Islands in the late fifteenth century. They were introduced from there to the Caribbean in 1516 (McFarlane 1964; Robinson 1996). Banana cultivation spread to Jamaica and later the Windward Islands, where both sweeter varieties and starchier plantains were planted for food by smallholders and slaves on their provision grounds (McFarlane 1964a; Soluri 2003).[1] A modest commercial trade in bananas

Table 4.1. Key trade-related policies and their impact on Windward Island banana production and export

Year	Event	Impact on Windward Island (WI) Bananas
1932	UK Import Duties Act passed.	WI market access protections enhanced by enacting tariffs on UK imports of non-Commonwealth bananas
1956	UK import tariffs increased.	WI market protections enhanced by increased tariffs on non-Common-wealth bananas from UK$2.50–7.50/ton
1959	UK import quotas established.	WI imports further favoured following establishment of a tariff-free quota (4,000 tonnes) for non-Common-wealth bananas
Late 1960s–1970s	Dollar banana imports increased by UK permits.	Competition with WI imports is heightened by slumping WI production leading to growing imports of dollar bananas
1972	Treaty of Rome exemption for bananas received by UK.	UK$7.50/ton by 20% ad valorem tariff rate replaced, securing continued protection of WI imports
1975	Lomé Convention signed between EC and Africa, Caribbean, Pacific (ACP) group.	Favoured trading nation status with ACP formalized; WI import protections continued by Lomé-Banana Protocol
1980	Lomé II signed.	Continued WI import protections
1985	Lomé III signed.	Continued WI import protections
1990	Lomé IV signed.	Continued WI import protections
1992	European Union (EU) Single Market created.	Threat to UK–WI import protections magnified by formal entry of UK into EU
1993	EU Banana Protocol (BP) signed.	Mixed quota-tariff system established; core WI import protections maintained

Table 4.1 continues

Table 4.1. Key trade-related policies and their impact on Windward Island banana production and export (*cont'd*)

Year	Event	Impact on Windward Island (WI) Bananas
1993	GATT complaint filed vs EU-BP.	WI import protections threatened
1995	EU-Banana Framework Agreement (BFA) signed.	WI import protections weakened by quota change and tariff reduction
1995	WTO complaint filed vs BFA.	WI import protections threatened
1999	BFA revised by BFA.	Competition within ACP opened up by shift from country-to global-ACP quota, weakening WI import protections
1999	WTO complaint filed vs revised BFA.	WI import protections threatened.
2000	Cotonou Agreement signed.	More WTO-friendly policies towards ACP promised by post Lomé Agreement, potentially threatening WI import protections
2001	Shift to single tariff (EU-ST) trade regime agreed to by EU	WI import protections eroded by phased-in replacement of BFA by tariff-only regime
2006	EU-ST enacted	BFA replaced by single tariff (€174/tonne) on non-ACP bananas, weakening WI import protections
2007	WTO complaint filed vs EU-ST	WI import protections threatened
2008	EU-Caribbean (CARIFORUM) Economic Partnership Agreement signed	Secures Cotonou commitments to single tariff regime secured
2010	ST lowered by EU	Single tariff on non-ACP bananas lowered from €176–148/tonne, further weakening WI import protections
2017	ST to be lowered further by EU	Single tariff on non-ACP bananas to be lowered to €114/tonne, further weakening WI import protections

from Jamaica to ports on the US East Coast emerged in the late 1860s but grew dramatically a few decades later with the transition from schooners to faster steamships, which greatly reduced spoilage (Soluri 2003; Myers 2004). In particular, the Boston Fruit Company (founded in 1885) and its successor, the United Fruit Company (UFC), led development of the industry by establishing from the 1880s to the 1920s a vast network of plantations of Gros Michel bananas in Central America and Jamaica (Myers 2004).[2] Exports of Jamaican bananas to England began in 1895 but grew quickly after 1901, with establishment of fortnightly shipments there. These shipments were initiated by the newly founded UK-based company Elders and Fyffe. However, within a year after founding, Elders and Fyffe was partially bought by UFC, and in 1913 it became a wholly owned subsidiary of UFC (Clegg 2002a).

The UK government was at the time sensitive to the growing economic turmoil facing its West Indian colonies in light of their struggling sugar industries (WIRC 1897; Clegg 2002a). Bananas were a bright light in an otherwise bleak picture. By the early 1920s Jamaica was exporting about 137,000 tonnes,[3] much of this still to the United States (McFarlane 1964). Yet there was growing concern within the industry that Jamaican bananas could be displaced by growing production from Latin America.[4] These concerns were heightened by the global recession of the 1930s, which ushered in a wave of anti-immigration policy and trade protectionism (Walters 2016a). In response, the UK Import Duties Act of 1932 established Imperial Preference by using tariffs to curtail imports of non-Commonwealth goods, including bananas (table 4.1). This provided a huge boost for West Indian banana producers: Jamaican imports to the United Kingdom soared, and by 1937 constituted 90 per cent of the UK banana market (McFarlane 1964). This colonial preference set an important precedent that would subsequently structure the UK–West Indian banana trade for six decades (Clegg 2002a).

EARLY EXPANSIONS AND COLLAPSES (1923–1942)

Banana plants are fragile and vulnerable to damage from drought, storms and disease. In particular, the scourge of the Gros Michel banana, Panama disease, first struck Jamaican plantations in 1911 and leaf spot followed in 1936 (McFarlane 1964). Panama disease (Fusarium wilt) is caused by a soil-borne, fungal pathogen, *Fusarium oxysporum*, which infects the plant's roots and kills it. The disease first became epidemic in 1890 in banana plantations in Panama and spread quickly thereafter, devastating commercial plantations throughout Latin America and the Caribbean (Robinson 1996). No effective control has been found, thereby necessitating the industry's total conversion during the 1950s/early 1960s from Gros Michel to Panama disease-resistant varieties, especially the Cavendish (Soluri 2003). "Leaf spot" may refer to several airborne fungal pathogens, including black Sigatoka (*Mycosphaerella fijiensis*), yellow Sigatoka (*M. musicola*) and Cardana (*Cardana musae*). These diseases weaken banana plants and reduce production, but they can be controlled with an application of fungicides, albeit treatments are expensive (Robinson 1996).

With a fast-growing UK market for bananas, production shortfalls in Jamaica from disease outbreaks and bad weather encouraged importers to search for alternative sources. But the British government was sceptical of increasing banana imports from Latin America, where there might be potential for increased supplies from the colonies. In 1926, the Imperial Economic Committee published an influential report on fruit production in the British Empire and recommended that the government support development of a Windward Island banana industry to supply bananas for the UK market (Welch 1994; Grossman 2003; Myers 2004; Mathurin 2012).

Banana cultivation was already commonplace on the Windward Islands, where it was frequently interplanted with other crops for food and as a cover crop. The broad leaves and fast growth of bananas make them valuable as a cover crop for shade-tolerant seedlings of coffee, cocoa and vanilla (Hoy 1962; personal observation). There was also a small inter-island trade in bananas, mostly to Barbados (Hoy 1962; McFarlane 1964). In 1923 the Swift Banana Company, a UFC-subsidiary, initiated the first exports of Windward Island bananas to the United Kingdom (table 4.2).[5] Exports grew to 578 tonnes in 1926, but the company encountered financial difficulties and shuttered its Saint Lucia operations in 1927 (Mathurin 2012). Conventional wisdom is that the Swift Banana Company's departure from Saint Lucia was a response to banana production shortfalls resulting from Panama disease outbreaks (see McFarlane 1964; Moberg 2008). However, Mathurin (2012) makes a compelling case that financial difficulties facing the company, not problems of product supply, were the primary cause.

Interest was nonetheless revived in 1934 when the Canadian Buying Company, another UFC subsidiary, initiated shipments to Montreal, Canada, under

Table 4.2. Early banana exports (tonnes) from Saint Lucia, 1924–1950

Year	Exports (tonnes)
1924	52[a]
1926	578
1934	275
1935	755[a]
1936	1,358[a]
1937	1,587[a]
1938	1,262[a]
1939	931[a]
1941	725[a]
1942	28
1946	1
1950	26

[a]Figures derived from number of exported stems, where 80 stems = 1 tonne.

Source: McFarlane (1964, 90), Welch (1994), Mathurin (2012, table 2), Harmsen et al. (2014).

a five-year, contracted agreement that banana grower associations be formed on each of the Windward Islands (Saint Lucia, Dominica, Saint Vincent and Grenada) to coordinate collection and loading of bananas onto ships (Romalis 1975; Welch 1993, 1994; Torgerson 2010).[6] The Saint Lucia Banana Growers Association (SLBGA) was thereby founded in 1934, and it entered into an exclusive marketing arrangement with the Canadian Buying Company, which promised to purchase all bananas delivered dockside. By 1937, 914 acres of land were under banana cultivation and 1,587 tonnes exported, making bananas a close competitor with cocoa as the island's third largest export crop (after sugar and limes) (Harmsen et al. 2014).

The rapid growth of the industry created unanticipated problems, however. For one, clearing of forests and cultivation of hillside lands to grow bananas was blamed for deadly landslides in 1938. The most notorious among these occurred on November 22, 1938, when a series of landslides near Ravine Poisson (upper Cul de Sac River) killed a hundred people and rendered seven hundred homeless. These landslides were triggered by high rainfall but linked to intensive banana cultivation on steep slopes (Harmsen et al. 2014). As well, the industry expanded faster than available marine shipping could accommodate, resulting in oversupply and growing product wastage. The Company responded by adopting more rigorous product quality standards that led to high rates of rejection of bananas, which discouraged many farmers from continuing to plant them (Mathurin 2012). War-related curtailments of shipping ended exports entirely by 1942 (McFarlane 1964; Moberg 2008; Wiley 2008).

The collapse of banana exports in 1941 might lead one to expect that Saint Lucia experienced a significant decline in cultivation and uptick in reforestation during the war, but there are reasons to believe that this, in fact, did not happen. First, the banana industry grew quickly, but its cumulative, pre-war impact on the Saint Lucian landscape was never that large, even if localized impacts were significant. Second, these early developments in the banana industry unfolded during a period when the country experienced a sharp increase in population, from 51,505 (1921) to 70,113 (1946), the combined result of restrictive immigration policies elsewhere and declining infant mortality rates in Saint Lucia (figure 6.1; Walters 2016a). There were many extra mouths to feed and, aside from military base construction work, few jobs to be had. Added to this was the wartime curtailment on shipping that forced Saint Lucia to become largely food self-sufficient for several years (Axline 1986; Timms 2008). These factors suggest that a considerable expansion of cultivation occurred during the war to meet subsistence and larger domestic food demands. In fact, elderly residents recounted that currently forested hillsides in Soufrière were then cleared of natural vegetation to grow food crops like yams and manioc, and air photo evidence from this period supports these claims. Specifically, the earliest recorded air photos of Saint Lucia were taken in 1940–1941 by the US military, but these were limited in coverage to only the northern and southern ends of the island in preparation for eventual construction of US military bases there (see Harmsen et al. 2014). The air photos of the southern part of the island, in particular, reveal extensive hillside lands under smallholder cultivation that are today under dry-scrub forest or residential development.

POST-WAR GROWTH, DECLINE AND CONSOLIDATION (1948–1981)

The British government established tight controls over the import and export of goods by ship during the war. These controls were gradually lifted in the late

1940s, prompting renewed interest in the prospects of an expanded West Indian banana trade. In addition, the war had left the United Kingdom desperately short of hard currency, and civil unrest had re-emerged in its West Indian sugar colonies. Emboldened by having received, in 1955, a General Agreement on Trades and Tariffs (GATT) waiver in the case of protecting vital agricultural interests in its colonies, the UK government responded by strengthening its policy of Imperial Preference by tripling existing tariffs in 1956 and implementing quota controls in 1959 on non-Commonwealth bananas (Grossman 1994; Clegg 2002a; Myers 2004; Torgerson 2010). This created highly favourable market conditions for a nascent banana industry in the Windward Islands.

The Irish-owned Antilles Products Limited introduced Panama disease-resistant Lacatan and then Cavendish banana varieties in 1948 to Dominica and Saint Lucia (Clegg 2002b; Moberg 2008). Then, in 1949, in partnership with the Belgium Fruit Line Co., the company began shipping bananas to ports in Ireland and Belgium, and then to Holland and Sweden. However, Antilles Products quickly ran into financial difficulties, whereupon entrepreneur John van Geest, a major horticultural distributor in the United Kingdom, intervened in 1952 to buy controlling interest in the company. He assumed its directorship and then changed its name in 1954 to Geest Industries (BWI), Limited (Clegg 2002a). Geest negotiated ten-year agreements with the four Windward Islands to purchase all export-quality bananas they could produce for export to the UK market (Myers 2004). With these commitments in place and a desire to prevent Fyffes, a UFC-subsidiary, from expanding into the region, the British government stepped up with financing to support industry development by purchasing fertilizers and establishing nurseries and extension services (Clegg 2002a; Wiley 2008).

With a protected British market and backing from both a major company and the British government, the Windward Island banana industry firmly took root, and production soared. This was aided by drought- and disease-related production shortfalls in Jamaica, which opened the door for greater Windward Island imports, growing from 11 per cent (1956) to 45 per cent (1966) of total UK banana imports (Clegg 2002a, 187/8). During this same period, Saint Lucian exports (the largest of the Windward Islands) grew from 10,000 to 83,000 tonnes (figure 4.1) (Welch 1996a). By the mid-1960s bananas were representing a remarkable 90 per cent of the value of all Saint Lucian exports (Romalis 1975).

Some of this increased production came from estates as they diversified away

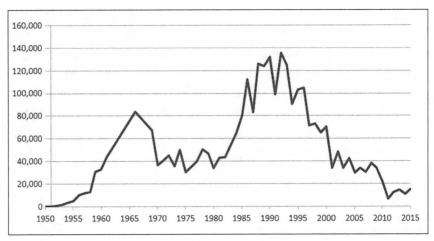

Figure 4.1. Saint Lucia banana exports (tonnes), 1950–2015 (McFarlane 1964; World Bank 1979; GOSL 1991a, 2002, 2012a, 2016)

from sugar and other crops. Most significantly, in 1960/1961 Geest acquired and then planted in bananas the extensive valley properties of two of the last producing sugar estates (Roseau and Cul-de-Sac). Still, the majority of production increases came not from estates but from smallholders, to whom bananas were close to an ideal crop. While mechanization of agricultural production, distribution and marketing tends to favour large producers, small farms can have the advantage where labour costs represent a significant part of total costs because family farms supervise themselves and provide flexible labour as needed (Hazell et al. 2010; Wiggins et al. 2010). Banana cultivation is indeed labour intensive, and the quick-maturing fruit grows all year round where local conditions permit (as they do in most of the country). With a guaranteed market, farmers could anticipate a steady, profitable income from cultivation of a modest area of land (O'Neil 1964; Rojas 1984). Not surprisingly, Saint Lucian small farmers embraced bananas enthusiastically. Barbara Welch, citing fellow geographer Janet Momsen's 1965 survey of banana farming in Saint Lucia, estimated there were 13,000 hectares of bananas cultivated in pure or mixed stands by 12,479 registered growers. In short, "Practically every farmer in Dominica and Saint Lucia with land capable of growing bananas was involved in the industry. The crop covered a greater area than at any time before or since, and exports attained levels not surpassed until the late 1980s" (1994, 130).

As the industry grew, so did its formal organizational structure and coordination. The early banana growers' associations were dominated by larger producers. Political pressures to support expansion of smallholder farming led to their restructuring in 1953, as more democratically responsive organizations, wherein any farmer with thirty or more banana plants could join. This led to massively increased membership and increased responsiveness to the needs of small farmers (Romalis 1975; Grossman 2003). Originally created as statutory bodies, banana growers' associations were responsible for coordinating purchase, inspection and dockside delivery of bananas; bulk purchase and importing of agrochemicals and other inputs for resale to farmers; coordinating pest control; and providing extension services and credit to members (Romalis 1975; Grossman 1994, 2003; Wiley 2008). In 1958 the four island banana growers' associations joined to form the Windward Island Banana Growers Association, an umbrella body that assumed responsibility for contract and price negotiations with Geest Industries, Limited, bulk purchase of fertilizer and administration of a crop insurance scheme to compensate farmers for severe weather-induced losses (Grossman 1994, 2003).

These various supports were enormously beneficial to farmers and arguably encouraged industry expansion beyond sustainable levels. For example, at its peak the SLBGA operated 159 packing sheds across the island, enabling market access to marginal producers and encouraging deforestation and cultivation of ever-remoter sites (Welch 1996a). By the mid-1960s, combined exports from the Windward Islands and Jamaica had grown so large they overshot UK demand, causing a sharp decline in price (Clegg 2002a). This initiated a relatively short-lived banana war between Jamaican and Windward Island producers that was resolved in 1966 with negotiation of the Banana Marketing Agreement, which allocated 48 per cent of the market to Windward Island producers and 52 per cent to Jamaican (Clegg 2002a). A different set of market problems then emerged in 1967, following the steep devaluation of British Sterling (to which the value of local $EC currency was then tied). This had the effect of driving up the costs of imported fertilizer and pesticides, which in turn led to reductions in their use by farmers and consequent declines in banana production and quality (Clegg 2002a). By the early 1970s these market-related challenges had combined with ongoing high cost of administrative overhead to drive the SLBGA deeply into debt (Romalis 1975). With these problems compounding, pessimism grew within the industry, and many farmers left to pursue alternative employment in Saint Lucia's emerging tourism and service sectors or outmigrated for work elsewhere (Grossman 1994; Walters 2016a). National statistics reveal 20 per cent fewer

Table 4.3. Selected population and agricultural statistics, 1961–2007

	Census Year				
	1961	**1973/ 1974**	**1986**	**1996**	**2007**
Population living in farm households (% of National)	–	52,283 (48.6%)	58,000 (47%)	51,553 (37%)	32,919 (21%)
Soufriére District only	–	4,522	–	2,684	1,460
Micoud District only	–	3,670	–	9,919	6,742
Total no. farmers		10,772	11,501	13,052	9,800
Full-time farming[a]		6,960	7,455	7,625	5,723
Part-time farming[a]		3,812	4,046	5,427	4,077
Median age of farmers		45.0	43.8	46.0	50.3
Total no. farm holdings	13,008	10,938	11,551	13,366	9,972
Soufriére District only		999	855	792	455
Micoud District only		1,086	1,693	2,462	2,008
Cumulative area of farm holdings (acres)	87,375	72,001	58,017	51,323	30,204
Soufriére District only		6,953	5,988.2	3,784.3	1,490
Micoud District only		11,301	12,416.4	10,810.7	7,047

[a]"Full-time" are farmers whose primary income source is farming; otherwise, they are considered "part-time".

Source: National Agricultural Census (GOSL 1974, 1987a, 1996a, 2007a).

farm holdings in 1973/1974 than in 1961 (table 4.3). Banana exports continued to stagnate through the 1970s, at roughly half their mid-sixties peak (figure 4.1).

To make up for production shortfalls from the West Indies, the United Kingdom permitted what was presumed at the time to be a temporary increase in imports from Latin American and other sources (Ivory Coast, Martinique, Suriname). These other suppliers had in place by then more advanced quality-control methods (discussed below), so the entry of their bananas onto the UK market created downward price pressures on West Indian fruit because of their perceived inferior quality (Grossman 1994). This quality issue became a growing concern for the UK government, given its ascension in 1972 to the European Economic Community, where it now faced growing political pressure from fellow Community members to justify its policies of Colonial Preference. In response, the Commonwealth Banana Growers Association was established in 1972 with support from the United Kingdom and West Indian governments to facilitate rationalization efforts in the predominantly small-farmer, banana sector (Clegg 2002a). Central to this were commitments by the United Kingdom to guarantee market access and fair price in exchange for commitments by producers to improve quality and efficiency.[7]

The United Kingdom was able to achieve continued formal trade protection of West Indian banana imports through a complex series of negotiations leading to the signing of the Lomé Convention in 1975. Lomé provided formal legal recognition from the European Economic Community that enabled Britain, France and Italy to maintain favoured trading status with their former colonies in Africa, the Caribbean and Pacific, the so-called ACP group (Myers 2004; ACP 2005; European Commission 2009a). In particular, the "Banana Protocol" of Lomé stipulated continued duty-free access to the UK market for ACP producers based on historical patterns of banana export (Clegg 2002a).[8] Even with Lomé in place, however, exports from the Windward Islands continued to founder, as a series of droughts and cost challenges associated with the energy crisis and inflation added to the industry's woes (Grossman 2003; Myers 2004; World Bank 1979). By the mid-1970s it was apparent to many that the Windward Island banana industry needed a significant makeover.

With mounting outside pressure, the Saint Lucian government reasserted statutory control over the SLBGA and forced upon it cost-cutting measures that entailed, for example, a drastic reduction in the number of buying depots (Romalis 1975). These changes were particularly hard on small, marginal producers, many of whom subsequently left the industry. Added to this, beginning in the mid-1970s, were a series of large, aid-funded projects that fostered restructuring and modernization of the industry (Grossman 1994).

Notable among these was the Banana Development Programme (1977–1982), which coordinated the widespread adoption of the so-called field-pack method among growers. The Cavendish variety of banana is highly susceptible to bruising, especially during transport from field to storage. In hilly terrain like Saint Lucia's, bruising of fruit was a common problem and often precluded farming in places where access by road or foot was too rough. Field packing entailed sorting and boxing bananas at the farm site rather than at centralized depots. This innovation had been widely adopted by the early 1960s on Latin American plantations to reduce fruit damage and spoilage (Soluri 2003). West Indian bananas were put at competitive disadvantage when large quantities of these blemish-free fruit entered the UK market in the late 1960s.

Another major development entailed an ambitious land redistribution scheme targeting smallholder banana producers (Rojas 1984; Rojas and Meganck 1987; Moberg 2008). By the early 1970s, Geest owned 5,880 acres of prime farmland, but the company then began to divest itself from its banana production assets to focus exclusively on shipping and marketing. Under the auspices of the Saint Lucia Model Farms Limited, a joint project financed by Geest, the Government of Saint Lucia, the EU Development Fund and Commonwealth Development Corporation, 1,444 acres of Geest's former Roseau estate were subdivided into 175 smallholder farms: 115 valley-bottom farms of 5 acres each for pure banana cultivation and 60 hillside farms of 12 acres each for mixed banana-tree crop cultivation (OAS 1986). These "model farms" were given intensive technical support and soon achieved banana production levels double the national average (GOSL 1987b).[9]

Lastly, significant aid funds were disbursed to support rapid recovery of the industry from the devastation caused by hurricanes David in 1979 and Allen in 1980, and to subsidize purchase of fertilizers whose costs had been driven up by the energy crisis in 1982 (Grossman 1994).

THE BIG BANANA BOOM (1982–1992)

The restructuring efforts of the 1970s and early 1980s put the banana industry on a stronger footing. In particular, widespread use of better agronomic practices and adoption of field packing of nearly 100 per cent substantially improved both production and quality (GOSL 1986). By the mid-1980s the same quantity of bananas was being produced as in the mid-1960s, but by half as many farmers cultivating less than half as much land (Welch 1996a). Also, the series of targeted investments in post-hurricane recovery and bulk purchase of high-cost fertilizer may well have kept the struggling industry from collapsing entirely in the early 1980s (GOSL 1984; Grossman 1994).

Subsequent developments on the trade front became critical to growth of the industry in the mid-1980s. The Lomé Convention was renegotiated in 1980 and then again in 1985, with trade protections for bananas essentially kept intact (Clegg 2002a). With a protected market still in place, rising prices caused a surge in production (figure 4.1). Prices rose because the Commonwealth States of the Eastern Caribbean had in 1976 tied their currency to the US dollar, rather than UK sterling, while the contract price for bananas continued to be negotiated in sterling. This change initially proved a hindrance to growth (World Bank 1985), but it paid huge dividends in the mid-1980s, when the value of the UK sterling appreciated 29 per cent versus US$ (Welch 1994). This combined with strong growth in demand from UK consumers to drive up the real price of bananas by 38 per cent from 1984 to 1988 (World Bank 1990; Clegg 2002a).

This mix of highly favourable conditions resulted in a staggering, nearly threefold increase in banana production from 1982 to 1986 (figure 4.1). With parallels to the late 1950s/early 1960s, existing farmers expanded their plantings and many new ones got into bananas, especially as part-time farmers. Smallholder resettlement schemes also continued. The large (1,057 ha) Dennery-Farmco Estate in the Mabouya Valley was bought in 1978 from the owner by Saint Lucia's government. With financial assistance from the European Development Fund (under Lomé III), under the guise of the Mabouya Development Project, many of these lands were subsequently distributed in the late 1980s for settlement by smallholders for banana and other crop cultivation (Moberg 2008; OAS 1991).

Industry growth was further aided by the SLBGA, which – as it had done in the early 1960s – expanded its support structure for smaller farmers by subsidizing agrochemicals and establishing a network of twenty inland buying depots (GOSL 1985, 1987b). In another parallel, a crop insurance scheme – WINCROP – was introduced by the Windward Islands Banana Growers Association to compensate banana growers from weather-related losses. According to GOSL (1989, 3), the introduction of WINCROP provided a particularly strong inducement to enter banana farming.

Cultivation of marginal sites further from roads and on steeper slopes became increasingly common again, as did incidences of deforestation, soil erosion and landslides (World Bank 1985; Harmsen et al. 2014).[10] The total number of farmers and farm holdings grew nationally by 20 per cent from 1974 to 1996, although this was uneven across the island. In particular, the number of farm holdings actually declined slightly over this period in the Soufrière District on the west coast, while it more than doubled in the Micoud (Mamiku) area on the east coast (table 4.3). These differences were attributed by Welch (1996a) to deteriorating road conditions in Soufrière and improved roads in Micoud. Total banana exports peaked at 135,000 tonnes in 1992 and otherwise remained robust and in excess of 100,000 tonnes for most years between 1986 and 1996 (figure 4.1). This decade-long boom in bananas, the product of more than ten thousand mostly smallholder farmers, delivered an unprecedented level of prosperity to the rural countryside of Saint Lucia (Moberg 2008; Reynolds 2006).

TRADE TURMOIL AND THE BIG BUST (1993–2000)

> First to go out of production were the steepest hillside farms, established in the 1980s when all available lands in the valley itself had already been brought under cultivation. Now, as the hillsides are gradually reforested with lush secondary growth, even some farms on prime bottomlands with well-drained top soils are being abandoned.
> —Mark Moberg (2008, 141) on the Mabouya Valley, Saint Lucia

The prospect for an end to the protected market that Saint Lucia had so long enjoyed had been acknowledged for years in government reports (e.g., GOSL 1985, 1989, 1990; World Bank 1988) and academic articles (Welch 1968), yet its arrival still came as a shock to many. The convoluted trade disputes that gradually undermined the United Kingdom's protected market for Windward Island bananas have been well documented (e.g., Read 1994; McQueen et al. 1997; Clegg 2002a; Myers 2004; Alter and Meunirer 2006; Wiley 2008; Fridell 2011). Only a summary is presented here.

The United Kingdom had managed to forestall efforts within the European Community to dismantle its preferential trade relationships with its former colonies, principally by formalizing these within the Lomé Convention, which had been renewed in 1990 (Lomé IV) for another 10 years (Wiley 2008). The commitment to Britain's former colonies was evident in the declarations of both leading political parties at the time (Myers 2004). Even Margaret Thatcher, that otherwise staunch free trader, remained a strong advocate for colonial preference when it came to bananas (Clegg 2002a). The United Kingdom's official entry into the newly formed European Union in 1992 required it to reconcile these trade preferences with the otherwise free flow of goods within the Common Market. Resolving the issue proved challenging given the pre-1992 patchwork of country-specific trade rules regarding banana imports, ranging from highly regulated trade based on post-colonial preference (Britain, France and Italy) to essentially free trade (e.g., Germany). The resulting 1993 Banana Protocol achieved a significant victory for the advocates of colonial preference. In short, the European Union agreed to a tariff-free quota of 857,000 tonnes for ACP and European Community members, divided up by country based on historical levels of imports, with non-ACP banana imports subject to a tariff of ECU100[11] per tonne (approx. 20 per cent) for the first 2 million tonnes and ECU850 per tonne beyond that (Clegg 2002a; Myers 2004).[12] Because Saint Lucia's tariff-free quota was based on recent high exports, its access to the UK market remained essentially protected (GOSL 1993; McQueen et al. 1997).

This should in theory have settled the matter, but in fact the negotiation of the Banana Protocol set in motion a series of events that would progressively under-mine the Windward Island banana industry. Most immediately, anticipating greater harmonization of trade under the impending formation of the European Union, multinational banana companies sought to gain relative advantage by deliberately flooding the European market, beginning in 1992. This had the effect of driving banana prices down sharply and triggering panic in the West Indies about the future of the industry, even as the European Union worked out its new version of protections for it (Read 1994; Moberg 2008). According to GOSL (1994), farmers received on average 18 per cent less for their bananas in 1993 compared to 1992. However, Moberg (2008) notes that prices dropped particularly sharply (70 per cent) during the fall of that year. At their lowest, prices were well below the break-even point for most farmers. In response, on 4 October 1993, banana farmers conducted an island-wide strike that resulted in the tragic shooting deaths of two farmers (Harmsen et al. 2014).

The second, more lasting consequence was the Banana Protocol's immediate triggering of a formal GATT complaint by five Latin American producer coun-tries (Costa Rica, Colombia, Venezuela, Nicaragua and Guatemala) (Clegg 2002a). The ensuing GATT panel ruled against the Protocol, forcing EU officials back to the table, whereupon they agreed to lower the tariff (to ECU75 per tonne) and raise the quota (to 2.2 million tonnes) for non-ACP bananas beginning in 1995 (Myers 2004). But this new, so-called Framework Agreement only antagonized other Latin American producer countries and the United States, who in 1995 filed a complaint to the newly formed World Trade Organization (WTO).[13] A WTO panel ruled against the EU Framework Agreement and instructed it to bring its commitments to the ACP (under Lomé) more into line with GATT trade principles. But subsequent EU revisions were still viewed as unsatisfac-tory, instigating yet another round of formal complaint by the United States and

Ecuador to the WTO, which in 1999 again ruled against the European Union (Clegg 2002a).[14] This time, retaliatory sanctions against the European Union were authorized (Barkham 1999). This added pressure induced substantial changes to the Banana Protocol, including a reduction in the ACP tariff-free quota by 100,000 tonnes to 750,000 tonnes in 2001 and a commitment by the European Union to move to a tariff-only system by 2006 (Clegg 2002a).

These various developments eroded what confidence there might have been in the new EU protections. Things were made worse by domestic developments in the UK retail market, where oversupply of bananas triggered a series of price wars between leading supermarket chains, further driving-down prices (Joseph 2004). According to Myers (2004), the retail price of bananas sold in UK super-markets declined by 60 per cent (in real terms) from 1990 to 2000. Meanwhile, in Saint Lucia the indebted SLBGA was forced to reduce its support to farmers, including closing many of its inland buying depots in 1997 (GOSL 1998a). The SLBGA's debt was absorbed by government and the organization restructured in 1998 as a private company, the Saint Lucia Banana Corporation, with shares allocated based on production volumes. Infighting ensued, however, and led to the splintering-off and formation of four other rival companies (GOSL 1999; Moberg 2008; Wiley 2008). Uncertainties plagued the industry and contributed to the exodus of several thousand farmers even as significant market protections still (officially) remained in place (GOSL 1998a; Clegg 2002a; Moberg 2008).

Interviews of farmers in Soufrière and Mamiku in 2007 provide a snapshot of these changes on-the-ground. When farmers were asked about significant changes they had made to farming in recent years, by far the mostly commonly cited response was reduced cultivation of bananas (table 3.9). In fact, many had exited bananas altogether. These findings were especially striking among farm-ers in Mamiku, an area noted above (and by Welch 1996a and Moberg 2008) as having been a front of banana farming expansion a decade earlier, but where only pockets of banana cultivation now remained. Yet, when queried about why cultivation had been reduced, roughly equal numbers of farmers cited labour scarcity and declining prices as causes (table 3.8). Several cited the rising cost of inputs (agrochemicals, etc.) and increased age. Key informants roughly echoed these responses, but added a few more causal factors, including loss of farmland to development and strengthened enforcement against farming on forest reserve lands (table 3.8). A number of these points will be examined in depth in later chapters.

"FAIR" AND REGIONAL TRADE IN BANANAS (2001–2016)

Repeated trade challenges revealed that the trade preferences enshrined in Lomé were no longer tenable in a world increasingly ruled by the imperatives of free trade. The successor to Lomé IV, the Cotonou Agreement, is a twenty-year agreement that is like Lomé in its intention to foster development through partnerships based on aid, trade and other forms of cooperation. Unlike Lomé, however, Cotonou explicitly embraces trade development that is consistent with WTO principles (Myers 2004; Wiley 2008). Central to this is the negotiation of Economic Partnership Agreements between the European Union and regional free-trade groupings of ACP states. The first of such agreements was signed in 2009 between the European Union and 14 ACP member states in the Caribbean, the CARIFORUM Group (including Saint Lucia and the other three Windward Island states). This secured their special treatment under the new banana regime (European Commission 2009b).

Adoption of a tariff-only structure for the new banana regime was consistent with this strategic imperative, but posed a serious threat to the Saint Lucian banana industry because one set high enough to actually protect ACP growers would unlikely be politically acceptable (McQueen et al. 1997). The single tariff for non-ACP bananas (and ACP bananas above 775,000 tonnes) was in 2006 set at €176 per tonne, arguably too low to ensure viability of the industry (Wiley 2008; ACP-EU 2009). Yet even this amount was viewed by dollar-banana competitors as too high and thus subject to further WTO challenge. In the latest settlement (2009), the European Union agreed to lower its single tariff to €$148 in 2010 and then to €114 by 2017, a level few believe will protect a viable Windward Island industry (Porter 2009; Fridell 2011).

To lessen the impact of revisions to the Lomé Banana Protocol, in 1998 the European Union established the Banana Production Recovery Plan, a ten-year programme of aid to assist ACP producers to adapt to new market conditions and improve their competitiveness (Clegg 2002a; Myers 2004). In Saint Lucia, this was coordinated in part through creation in 2001 of the Banana Emergency Recovery Unit in the Ministry of Agriculture (Moberg 2008). A main focus of these efforts was to support restructuring and the subsequent transition made to fair trade. Fair trade is a worldwide movement that seeks to foster more ethical trade relationships by linking southern producers with northern consumers through independent farmer certification, product labelling and more remunerative pricing arrangements for producers (Raynolds 2000; Fridell 2004).[15] The United Kingdom has been on the vanguard of fair-trade activism since the mid-1990s, and bananas were an obvious target, given the fruit's high consumer profile and Britain's close cultural and historical ties to the West Indies (Lamb 2008).[16] It was also recognized that converting smallholder banana farmers in the Windward Islands to fair-trade production would be relatively straightforward, because their existing conditions and practices were already consistent with many fair trade requirements (Raynolds 2003). For example, it was well known that many of the production advantages held by larger banana plantations were gained through environmentally damaging and exploitative labour practices. In this regard, the small-scale, owner-operated farms that dominated the Windward Island banana industry came much closer to the ideal being sought by fair trade advocates.

The Windward Islands Farmers Association[17] began working with the Fair-Trade Labelling Organization in the late 1990s, and it became a registered fair-trade banana producer, overseeing the first shipments of Saint Lucian fair-trade bananas in 2000 (Fairtrade Foundation 2003). Initial scepticism by the industry and government gave way to enthusiasm, as it became apparent that fair trade offered perhaps the last, best hope for preserving the industry (Moberg 2005; Lamb 2008; Torgerson 2010). In public comments addressed to the president of UK-based Sainsburys Company, following their commitment to buy 100 per cent fair-trade bananas, the prime minister of Saint Lucia, John Compton, exclaimed, "You have saved the banana farmers of Saint Lucia!" (Vidal 2007). While the industry continued to struggle with declining exports and a shrinking farmer population, the Saint Lucia Banana Corporation, with support from government, mobilized nationwide to promote farmer certification. By 2007 there were twelve fair-trade groups with over thirteen hundred members, representing over 90 per cent of Saint Lucia's banana farmers. All exports destined for the United Kingdom were labelled as fair trade, with the remainder of production being sold onto domestic and regional markets (Fingal 2008; GOSL 2008a).

To be fair-trade certified, farmers are required to adhere to a range of labour and environmental standards, including adherence to international labour laws and standards (e.g., freedom to unionize, no forced child labour, etc.), maintenance of vegetated buffer zones adjacent to streams, tightly controlled and/or restricted use of pesticides and replacement of herbicide with mechanical weed control (FAO 1998; Moberg 2008). Farmers are also required to join and participate regularly in meetings of their local fair-trade producer group. In exchange, farmers receive a guaranteed minimum set price[18] for their bananas; in addition, they share in a social premium (US$1.75 per box) that is allocated to respective producer groups for investment in community projects.[19] Experience from Saint Lucia and elsewhere shows that certification delivers significant benefits in terms of higher prices, a more secure market and community development (Moberg 2008; Smith 2010; Torgerson 2010).[20]

That said, the additional costs – primarily for added labour – and hassles associated with meeting fair-trade standards discouraged many, especially older farmers, from participating. Plus fair-trade standards are not the only ones that banana farmers have been required to meet in recent years to continue participation in the industry. For example, a consortium of European grocery retailers established a code of practice in 2003 meant to improve sanitary and phytosanitary standards in response to growing food safety concerns among EU consumers (Frundt 2009). The so-called EUREP-GAP (Euro-Retailer Produce Good Agricultural Practices) standards were implemented in the early 2000s, with financial support from the European Union through the Banana Production Recovery Plan (GOSL 1999; Moberg 2008).

As with conventional bananas, the viability of fair trade ultimately depends on the consumer market. Consumption of fair-trade bananas soared in the United Kingdom through the mid-2000s, bolstered in large part by activist promotional campaigns and the commitments of major supermarket chains to sell fair-trade bananas. Bananas are the largest selling fruit in the United Kingdom, for which they have long been a marquee product, one subject to frequent market and price competition between leading grocery retailers. Fair-trade activists played on this, encouraging individual supermarket chains to lead the pack by marketing fair-trade bananas (Lamb 2008). The Co-Op, Sainsburys and then Tesco were first to retail fair-trade bananas (BBC 2000), but Sainsbury's made history when it committed to selling 100 per cent fair-trade bananas in all its stores by 2006 (Sainsbury's 2007). Waitrose followed soon after with a similar commitment (Butler 2006). By 2006, 25 per cent of all bananas sold on the UK market were labelled fair trade, with a significant amount of these sourced from the Windward Islands. This led to stabilization of Saint Lucian exports at around 35,000 tonnes between 2002 and 2009, in the midst of continued decline (eventually to zero) of conventional banana exports to the United Kingdom (figure 4.1).

Yet, it remains unclear whether Saint Lucian fair-trade bananas will survive, in light of growing competition from lower-cost fair-trade producers and continued reductions in the tariff on non-ACP bananas. Furthermore, Moberg (2008) suggests that breakdown of the field coordination that followed from the splitting up of the banana producer organizations in the late 1990s contributed to the return of leaf spot (yellow Sigatoka) outbreaks beginning in 2002. Recent events are ominous: severe weather (drought, tropical storms) and outbreaks of black leaf spot disease between 2010 and 2014 knocked back Saint Lucian production and exports to levels not seen since the mid-1950s (figure 4.1; GOSL 2012a, 2015). Government statistics indicate only 501 banana farmers traded onto the export market in 2014 (GOSL 2015), which constitutes a roughly 95 per cent decline from peak numbers in the 1990s.

Faced with so many challenges in the European export market, efforts have shifted towards the development of regional (Caribbean) markets. Such exports have probably long occurred, but until 2013 they were insufficient in size (apparently) to warrant inclusion in national export totals. About 2,000 tonnes of bananas were exported regionally – most to Barbados – in each of 2013 and 2014. This number jumped the following year to over 6,300 tonnes with a surge in exports to Trinidad (GOSL 2016). Regional exports thus constituted 43 per cent of total (14,786 tonnes) banana exports in 2015. Given ongoing uncertainties and onerous quality control standards associated with UK/European markets, it would not be surprising were Saint Lucian banana growers to shift more production to regional export markets, assuming there is growth potential there.

Either way, it seems extremely unlikely that bananas will return to former prominence as a dominant industry on the island. As this chapter has shown, market challenges abound, and the bottom line is that Saint Lucian producers cannot readily compete in the global marketplace with producers in other countries that have access to vastly greater areas of prime farmland and lower-cost labour. Furthermore, reduced access to increasingly competitive export markets is only one (albeit central) part of the story of agricultural decline in Saint Lucia. Other social and economic changes have reinforced the post-agrarian shift now well underway across the country. Before exploring these, however, I turn in the next chapter to the thorny issue of land tenure and the influence this might have had on the land use and forest changes explored in this book.

CHAPTER SUMMARY

Bananas have long been cultivated as a food and shade crop in Saint Lucia. Early efforts in the 1920s and 1930s to develop commercial banana production on the island were short lived. However, the collapse of sugar following World War II brought renewed urgency to efforts aimed at developing commercially viable alternatives in agriculture. A favourable alignment between colonial government and private sector interests led in the 1950s to the successful founding of an export-oriented banana industry in Saint Lucia and neighboring Windward Islands. Unlike sugar, bananas were widely adopted by smallholders, leading to dramatic agricultural expansion and deforestation into the rural interior. Structural problems plagued the industry in the 1970s, but it returned to growth in the 1980s with production peaking in the early 1990s. A series of WTO decisions then ruled against the United Kingdom's preferential market for West Indian bananas, precipitating an 80 per cent decline in industry exports over the following decade. Recent attempts to rescue the industry through adoption of fair trade certification met with some initial success, but challenges continue and the industries' future remains highly uncertain.

The utility of ACE as a research methodology is well illustrated by the study of the rise and fall of the banana industry in Saint Lucia. This is because precise chains of event causation can be followed from the local change of interest (e.g., reforestation) to proximate causes (farmers choosing to abandon banana cultivation) to causes further back in time and outward in space (WTO rulings against the United Kingdom's policy of Imperial Preference). Political ecologists would likely applaud this analysis and these findings because they highlight the central influence of politics in agricultural and environmental change and illustrate how decisions made in the centres of power can have major consequences for local people half a world away (Grossman 1993, 1998; Bryant and Bailey 1997; Watts and Peet 2004). Political ecology analysis, however, has a common tendency to draw gross generalizations about political-economic influences without paying careful attention to the empirical details of the cases at hand (Vayda and Walters 1999). By contrast, the strength of this analysis using ACE is its analytic focus: causal connections between local and distant changes are precisely established, and so explanations are clear and compelling.

This kind of causal-historical clarity would also not be achievable using the statistical approaches of conventional LCS alone, although multifactor analysis of land use change might have helped to identify key relationships for further causal-historical inquiry. Likewise, SES approaches are typically ill-equipped to deal with a case like this where key causes, like the WTO rulings, are contingent and originate well beyond the boundaries of the watershed or island "system" (but see Friis and Neilsen 2017).

CHAPTER 5

LAND TENURE, TREE PLANTING AND FOREST CONSERVATION

LAND TENURE HAS LONG BEEN AN ISSUE OF concern and controversy in the Caribbean. This reflects in part the historical predominance of the plantation sector and the social and economic inequalities it engendered. Smallholder land tenure is also surprisingly varied and complex, a reflection of unique histories and socio-economic circumstances on each island. For example, in addition to the more conventional categories of land tenure (i.e., smallholder private, estate private and public) extensive lands in Saint Lucia fall under a form of kin-based, communal ownership known as *family land*. For over a century, researchers and policymakers interested in Saint Lucia's development have debated the merits of existing land tenure arrangements and often argued for their reform (e.g., WIRC 1897; Clarke 1953; OAS 1986; Dujon 2000; Walters 2012b). Yet, almost no attention has been paid to the question of whether there are environmental consequences associated with these different forms of land tenure.

This study presented an excellent opportunity to examine this question in light of the wider effort to explain the causes of land use and forest change. Specifically, has the type of land tenure influenced how people use their land and does this have consequences for trees and forests on those lands? In this chapter I explore these questions by comparing land use, tree-planting practices and vegetation characteristics on government, estate private, smallholder private and family lands within the two study watersheds.

THEORETICAL CONTEXT

The topic of property rights is often prominent in discussions about natural resources management and environmental conservation (McCay and Acheson 1987; Feeny et al. 1990; Ostrom 1990; Campbell 2007; Robinson et al. 2014; Yin

2016). At the centre of this are debates about which forms of tenure (public, private, communal, etc.) are more or less likely to encourage environmentally sustainable outcomes (McCay and Jentoft 1998; Mansfield 2004; Walters 2012b). Views on these matters are often heavily polarized because they reflect competing assumptions about human motivation and behavior (Walters 2007, 141–43). On one hand, economists and business interests typically advocate for privatization of resources because they assume people usually act rationally and out of self-interest, and privatization is the most efficient way to harness these tendencies. In contrast, those with a cultural or sociological perspective often advocate common/collective forms of resource ownership because they presume peoples' behavior is heavily situational and shaped by community norms and social contexts. Both privatization and common property advocates tend to view public (state) ownership with scepticism – necessary only when more decentralized tenure arrangements are either impractical or unattainable.

Unfortunately, this polarization in perspective has encouraged researchers and policymakers to idealize and overgeneralize the relative merits of one or another form of tenure. In short, many fail to recognize that on-the-ground realities often entail a varied commingling of individual and collective rights that may change as circumstances do (Castro 1991; McCay and Jentoft 1998; Campbell et al. 2001; Giordano 2003; Young 2001; Johnson 2004; Tanner 2007). For example, *common* lands may be subject to varied and changing rules of access at both collective and individual levels, depending on such factors as the season; ecological characteristics of the resources; population pressures; available technology; social, gender and kinship relations; and external markets and policies. Trees in particular may be subject to different tenure arrangements than the land upon which they are planted or grow naturally (Fortmann 1985; Raintree 1987; Wilson 1989; Castro 1991; Walters 2004).

Arguably, embedded in much of this critique is an even more basic question: to what extent or under what circumstances do property rights even matter for resource management and environmental outcomes? Within many circles it is now an article of faith that sustainable resource management and environmental conservation depend on our getting the property rights *right* (Agrawal and Gibson 1999). Yet, rigorous empirical evidence of the causal influence of property rights on resource and environmental outcomes is surprisingly difficult to find (Rudel 1995; Tucker 1999; Walters 2004; Nagendra 2007; Tanner 2007;

Larson et al. 2010; Agrawal and Benson 2011; Walters 2012a; Bonilla-Moheno et al. 2013; Yin et al. 2016).

For forests in particular, the influence of property rights is surprisingly ambiguous (Bonilla-Moheno et al. 2013). On the one hand, deforestation has been frequently associated with weak or absent property rights, especially on public lands in frontier, colonization zones (Rudel 1995, 2005, 38–39; Dolisca et al. 2007; Oliveira 2008; Wannasai and Shrestha 2008). Likewise, it has been widely reported that tree planting is positively correlated with secure property rights (Simmons et al. 2002; Pattanayak et al. 2003). Yet a careful reading of the literature suggests the influence of property rights on forest protection and tree planting is often ambiguous or eclipsed in significance by other factors (Godoy 1992; Tucker 1999; Degrande et al. 2006; Gonzalez-Insuasti et al. 2008; Place 2009; Larson et al. 2010; Agrawal and Benson 2011; Casse and Milhoj 2011; Robinson et al. 2014; Shi et al. 2016).

Secure property rights – be these private or communal in character – are no guarantee that land users will protect existing forests (Acheson and McCloskey 2008; Ludewigs et al. 2009). Furthermore, the causal relationship between land tenure and tree planting cuts both ways: secure tenure may provide motivation for some people to plant trees, but others may be motivated to plant trees in order to strengthen their otherwise insecure claims to land (Fortmann 1985; Castro 1991; Dewees and Saxena 1997, 211; Walters et al. 1999; Angelsen and Kaimowitz 2004; Walters 2004; Wannasai and Shrestha 2008). *Whether* and, if so, *how* property rights matter often depends on other local and non-local factors (Campbell et al. 2001; Tucker et al. 2007; Walters and Vayda 2009; Larson et al. 2010; Jones 2012; Bottazzi and Dao 2013; Robinson et al. 2014; Shi et al. 2016).

FAMILY LAND AND PROPERTY RIGHTS IN THE CARIBBEAN

Under colonial rule, lands throughout the West Indies were mostly privatized in the form of agricultural estates, with ownership typically concentrated in the hands of a small minority of individuals. As described in earlier chapters, smallholder farming has always coexisted with plantation agriculture, and since at least the days of the Norman Commission in the late 1800s (WIRC 1897), researchers and policymakers in the West Indies have debated the relative merits of large (estate) farms versus smallholders for agricultural development. Many have since attributed the region's agricultural decline – characterized by underinvestment and land abandonment – to underlying patterns of land-ownership and tenure (e.g., Finkel 1964; Welch 1968; Rubenstein 1975; Rojas 1984; Brierley 1985a, 1985b). In the face of recurrent crisis, the lands of many failed estates were either subdivided into smallholdings or acquired by governments and returned to the public domain as crown lands.

The smallholder sector is far from homogeneous, however. It includes a variety of land tenure arrangements, and individual farmers may engage in more than one of these. Tenant and share-cropping arrangements, such as métayage, were once very common, although are much less so in light of wider declines in estate landownership and subsistence farming. In Saint Lucia, smallholders today usually farm their own private land or cultivate plots on common family lands.

The origins and consequences of family land have perplexed Caribbean scholars and policymakers for decades (Clarke 1953; Smith 1955; Smith 1956; Marshall 1971; Zuvekas 1979; Walters 2012b). Family land (*te famiy*) is a form of communal land tenure common to Afro-Caribbean peasantries (Besson and Momsen 1987; Barrow 1992). It is based on a system of unrestricted cognatic descent, whereby holdings of land are bilaterally inherited by all descendents of the original owner. The land is not partitioned by heirs but is, rather, held in common with all rightful heirs maintaining a shared claim to the overall parcel. Co-owners of family land are entitled to use and/or occupy a portion of the land and to bequeath it to their children in turn, but they cannot sell or otherwise dispose of it (Le Franc 1979; Barrow 1992, 1). Such use rights typically include space to build a permanent residence and, contingent on availability, space to farm individual plots within the larger family holding.

Coheirs of family land are entitled in principle to equal shares of ownership, but in practice they do not usually hold equal rights of use. Various factors may influence who among heirs establishes actual use rights, including the availability of land; land use history and prior claims to land; size of the inheritance group; the location of coheirs' residences; priority accorded to the deceased person's proximate kin; assessment of the relative needs of the coheirs for land in relation to the availability of other land or the possibility of non-agricultural employment, and so on (OAS 1991, app. B).

Research and policy analysis of family land has focused on its economic and cultural significance and has generated polarized opinion about its value that parallels the wider theoretical disagreements described above. Sympathetic researchers have highlighted both the symbolic-cultural value of family land as an institution and the crucial role it serves ensuring a degree of livelihood security in communities historically fraught with hardship and uncertainty (Lowenthal 1961; Bruce 1983; Besson 1987; OAS 1991; Barrow 1992; Dujon 1997, 2000; Vargas and Stanfield 2003a, 2003b; Mycoo 2005a; Mills 2007). By contrast, "official" opinion has typically characterized family land in negative terms: as antiquated, inefficient, a barrier to agricultural innovation and development, and an obstacle to modernization in general (e.g., Lowenthal 1961, 5, 1972, 103–4; Finkel 1964, 171–72; Mathurin 1967, cited in Besson 1987, 37; Braithwaite 1968; Welch 1968; Momsen 1972, 104, cited in Besson 1987, 31; Rubenstein 1975; Rojas 1984, 41; OAS 1986; Harrington 1987, 127; Alleyne 1994, 61; Cole 1994; GOSL 1998b, 43; Griffith-Charles 2011).[1] In fact, the land tenure specialist R.A. Foreman went so far as to declare family land in Saint Lucia to be "the greatest single factor responsible for the unsatisfactory state of the island economy" (cited in OAS 1986, 21).

Despite all this attention, the potential implications of family land for environmental conservation have been largely overlooked. Observations in this regard have been few but seemingly paradoxical. On the one hand, some researchers have claimed that tenure uncertainties associated with family land encourage short-term cropping strategies at the expense of long-term investments like tree planting and soil conservation (e.g., Edwards 1961, 112, cited in Besson 1987, 31; Lowenthal 1961; Mathurin 1967, 141–42, cited in Barrow 1992, 6; O'Loughlin 1968, 42; Finkel 1971, 299). By contrast, others have specifically noted an abundance of planted fruit and other trees on family land, the legacy of prior generations of family landowners (Lowenthal 1961, 5; Besson 1987, 15–16; Barrow 1992, 45).

LAND TENURE IN SOUFRIÈRE AND MAMIKU WATERSHEDS

Smallholder farming in Saint Lucia historically developed adjacent to the estates, on nearby slopes, ridgetops and interior lands. Over time, estates that fell into decline were also sometimes subdivided into smallholdings. Family land is widespread in these areas today because it was common for original owners to pass on property to heirs without formally subdividing it. The result is that Saint Lucia is thought to have among the highest incidence of family land in the Caribbean (Barrow 1992; Cole 1994). According to the 2007 Census of Agriculture, 46.6 per cent of all agricultural parcels and 41.9 per cent of agricultural land area were held under family ownership (GOSL 2007a). Consistent with this, data from site-specific research within Saint Lucia indicate about one-third of smallholders farm on family lands (Shearer et al. 1991; Cole 1994; Vargas and Stanfield 2003a; Bloch et al. 2005).

For this study, information about specific land tenure and landholding size was obtained from farmer interviews and official land registry maps. These revealed that family land was, indeed, common in both Soufrière and Mamiku. Other common forms of tenure included private land (either estate or smallholder owned) and public land, which was concentrated in the uppermost reaches of each watershed where it constituted, in the case of Mamiku, part of the National Forest Reserve and in Soufrière a designated watershed protection zone. We can gain a sense of the relative commonness of different land tenure types by grouping the watershed vegetation plots by tenure category. Based on this, the proportion of land under different categories of tenure is roughly equal and similar between the two watersheds, with the notable exception that there were twice as many vegetation plots on family land than on any other tenure type (table 5.1). No plots fell on land currently under tenant or squatting cultivation. Interviews confirmed that squatting and tenant farming still occur but are far less common than they used to be.

Estate lands were mostly concentrated in the lower part of each watershed, government lands near the top and smallholder farms (private and family) between these. Although site-to-site variations were large, vegetation plots on family and government lands were more likely to be found at higher elevations and on steeper slopes, compared to plots on private estate and private smallholder

Table 5.1. Summary of vegetation plot samples by land tenure category and watershed

Watershed	Private Estate	Private Smallholder	Family Smallholder	Government	Total
Soufriére	6	8	15	5	34
Mamiku	6	2	8	6	22
Total	12	10	23	11	56

Land Tenure (spanning header over Private Estate, Private Smallholder, Family Smallholder, Government)

Table 5.2. Measured elevation and slope of vegetation plots comparing means (and standard deviations) by land tenure category (n = no. of vegetation plots)

	Land Tenure				
	Private Estate (n = 12)	Private Smallholder (n = 10)	Family Smallholder (n = 23)	Govern-ment (n = 11)	F/t-values
Elevation (m)	180.1	183.8	278.3	275.3	F = 1.66
	(160.7)	(118.7)	(188.0)	(91.9)	(df = 3,52)
Slope (degrees)	11.4	14.5	24.0	20.3	F = 2.70*
	(12.9)	(13.3)	(12.9)	(15.8)	(df = 3.52)

*$p < .05$

lands, findings echoed by interviews with farmers (table 5.2; see also Walters 2012b, tables 6 and 7). These findings point clearly to the relative inferiority of family and government lands in terms of agricultural potential.

Table 5.3 summarizes the type of tenure and landholding size among farmers who were interviewed. Most farmers were smallholders (thirty-seven of forty-three), and among these the majority (twenty-four of thirty-seven) farmed exclusively on family land. Only six of thirty-seven smallholders farmed exclusively on private holdings. There was huge variation in the size of landholdings, from 0.2 to 450 acres, and estate properties were on average far larger than the others (table 5.3). The data also suggest that private smallholder properties

Table 5.3. Summary of farmer landholding sizes (acres) by category of land tenure, based on farmer interviews (n = no. of farmers)

	Land Tenure					
	Private Estate (n = 6)	Private Smallholder (n = 6)	Family Smallholder (n = 24)	Tenant Smallholder (n = 4)	Mixed Smallholder (n = 3)	Total (n = 43)
Mean size (acres)	216.5	31.4	4.1	2.6	2.0	37.3
Range (acres)	21.0– 450.0	0.5– 115.0	0.2– 30.0	0.5– 5.0	1.0– 3.0	0.2– 450.0

Note: The "mixed" group includes farmers with parcels of mixed tenure, including private + family or family + rented land.

were larger than other smallholders, but this is misleading because it reflects one private smallholder who owned 115 acres but farmed only a fraction of this area. The remaining seven smallholders included four tenants who farmed on rented parcels and three who had some mix of holdings (e.g., private + family, family + rented, etc.). Because there were so few, the mixed-holding farmers were excluded from most of the comparative analysis.

LAND TENURE AND WATERSHED VEGETATION

Findings presented in chapter 3 show that the landscapes of both watersheds were dominated by diverse natural and planted forests with smaller areas under intensive (annual) crop cultivation or hard development (i.e., housing, infrastructure, etc.) (tables 3.1, 3.2, 3.3; figure 3.1). Is there evidence that either the abundance or type of trees on the land vary in relation to the type of land tenure? Looking first at the distribution of general habitat types, there are few clear patterns associated with tenure. Each type of tenure included a wide range and roughly similar mix of habitat types, with two notable exceptions (table 5.4). First, government lands were significantly more likely than other lands to have mature forest ($p < 0.05$), and family lands were more likely than others to be under annual crop cultivation ($p < 0.05$), although such cultivation only constituted a small minority of family land plots (5 of 23).

Table 5.4. Summary of vegetation plots comparing land tenure by primary habitat (n = no. of vegetation plots)

	Land Tenure				
Primary Habitat	Private Estate (n = 12)	Private Smallholder (n = 10)	Family Smallholder (n = 23)	Government n = 11)	Total (n = 56)
Annual crops	1	0	5*	0	6
Agroforest	4	7	7	1	19
Forest (mature)	4	2	6	1	13
Forest (mature)	3	0	5	6*	14
Other	0	1	0	3	4

*p < .05

Table 5.5. Summary of selected ecological characteristics measured in vegetation plots, comparing mean values (and standard deviations) by land tenure (n = no. of vegetation plots)

Tree Measures	Private Estate (n = 12)	Private Smallholder (n = 10)	Family Smallholder (n = 23)	Government (n = 11)	Total (n = 56)	F-values (df = 3,52)
Species richness						
All trees	6.5 (5.0)	6.2 (2.7)	6.1 (5.5)	6.4 (4.7)	6.3 (4.7)	0.02
Natural trees only	5.3 (5.2)	2.5 (3.7)	4.9 (6.1)	6.3 (4.7)	4.8 (5.2)	1.1
Planted trees only	1.3 (1.1)	3.7 (2.8)	1.2 (1.7)	0.1 (0.3)	1.5 (2.0)	7.52**
Basal area (m²/ha)						
Live trees	36.0 (25.1)	39.8 (24.1)	39.8 (32.1)	44.8 (47.0)	39.9 (32.3)	0.35
Natural trees only	26.6 (30.2)	12.8 (23.1)	29.9 (34.9)	41.8 (48.2)	28.5 (35.5)	1.17
Planted trees only	9.4 (12.8)	27.0 (25.0)	9.9 (18.4)	2.9 (9.7)	11.5 (18.7)	4.82*
Canopy structure						
Canopy height (m)	14.9 (2.2)	13.0 (6.1)	13.0 (6.3)	14.3 (10.8)	13.7 (6.7)	0.29
Canopy openness (%)	11.3 (27.4)	9.5 (15.9)	27.4 (38.1)	31.4 (43.7)	21.5 (34.7)	0.75

*$p < .005$; **$p < .001$

A more detailed assessment of plot vegetation also reveals few major differences between types of tenure. Natural and total tree-species richness, tree basal area and canopy structure were all similar across the four types of tenure (table 5.5; see also Walters 2012b, table 4). The notable exception is that planted trees were significantly more abundant and species rich on private smallholder lands but were almost entirely absent from government lands.

LAND TENURE AND LAND USE

We have learned that the most significant and widespread recent change in land use is reduced cultivation, especially of bananas. Further analysis revealed that land abandonment was more likely to have happened on topographically marginal lands (table 3.6). The previous vegetation analysis suggests tenure may have influenced tree-planting practices but has otherwise been unimportant (tables 5.4, 5.5). Analysis of land use based on vegetation plots confirms tenure's limited impact. When the prevailing land use of vegetation plot sites is considered, it was found that the proportion of sites that were either "farmed" or "abandoned" is almost identical between the different tenure categories (private estate, private smallholder and family smallholder) (table 5.6). The exception to this pattern is that government lands were significantly more likely to be "protected" than lands in the other three tenure categories (p < 0.001). Ten of eleven government sites were under protection, whereas only one was developed (a public schoolyard). None of the plot sites on government land were being farmed or had been recently farmed (i.e., abandoned).

Interviews of farmers further confirm tenure's limited effect on land use. Nearly identical percentages of farmers on both private and family land cited having reduced their land area under cultivation (80 per cent and 78 per cent, respectively). Identical percentages of farmers on private and family lands (70 per cent) likewise reported having either "all" or "much" of their land in forest or "bush" (Walters 2012b, table 5). In fact, land tenure was never specifically

Table 5.6. Summary of vegetation plots comparing land tenure by land use (n = no. of vegetation plots)

	Land Tenure				
Land Use	Private Estate (n = 12)	Private Smallholder (n = 10)	Family Smallholder (n = 23)	Government (n = 11)	Total (n = 56)
Farmed	5	5	10	0	20
Abandoned/idle	4	4	12	0	20
Protected	3*	0	1	10**	14
Developed	0	1	0	1	2

*p < .05

**p < .001

cited by farmers as a factor influencing their decision to increase, decrease or abandon cultivation.

LAND TENURE AND TREE PLANTING

Results of the vegetation analysis suggest that tree planting is widespread but may be most common on private smallholder lands (table 5.5). Interview findings are ambiguous on this point but suggest that tree planting is common under all forms of tenure except where land is being rented or is publicly owned. Specifically, farmers typically concentrate most of their cultivation on one or a few commercial crops, but it is common practice for them to diversify and cultivate a variety of other plants, including different types of fruit, spice and timber trees (see table 3.11). For example, only one of thirty-seven farmers interviewed did not grow tree crops of any kind, yet only one of thirty-seven grew tree crops exclusively (table 5.7).

Cultivating trees was common on family and private lands (smallholder and estate), but there were some notable variations (table 5.7). First, estate farmers were significantly more likely compared to other farmers to have planted "many" or "exclusively" tree crops (six of six vs nine of thirty-one, $\chi^2 = 6.25$, df = 1, p < 0.025). Smallholder farmers on private lands were only somewhat more likely than smallholders on family lands to have cited planting "many" trees (three of five vs five of twenty-two, $\chi^2 = 1.91$, df = 1, p < 0.025). By contrast, farmers who rented land, while few in number, were significantly more likely than other

Table 5.7. Tree crop abundance on farms by land tenure category, based on qualitative farmer estimates (n = no. of farmers)

	Land Tenure				
Tree Crops	Private Estate (n = 6)	Private Smallholder (n = 5)	Family Smallholder (n = 22)	Tenant Smallholder (n = 4)	Total (n = 37)
Exclusively	1	0	0	0	1
Many	5	3	5	1	14
Some	0	2	12	0	14
Few	0	0	5	2	7
None	0	0	0	1	1

farmers (on private or family lands) to have cultivated "few" or "no" trees (three of four versus five of thirty-three, $\chi^2 = 7.70$, df = 1, p < 0.01).

Farmers cited few barriers to tree planting (table 5.8). Specifically, the majority said no when asked if they faced any barriers to planting trees. Only four of thirty-four farmers cited insecure tenure as a problem, and three of these were tenant farming. Most family-land farmers did not express concern about tenure security when considering to plant trees, but a few did raise the issue, and one in particular stated emphatically that tenure insecurity discouraged him from planting trees. The key here appears to be the existence of a clear and respected decision-making mechanism within the family to allocate lands for use by individuals. This often takes the form of an elder patriarch or matriarch (sometimes more than one) who is empowered to make decisions on behalf of the family regarding who can farm where, and so on. Where understandings are clear, there is unlikely to be significant disincentive to planting trees or other crops.

Considering the abundance of planted trees under different types of tenure, we should also consider the flip side: whether tenure influences the likelihood of existing planted trees being cut. Pressures to cut trees are sometimes intense, as they were during the banana booms of the 1960s and 1980/1990s,

Table 5.8. Farmers' perceived barriers to tree planting by land tenure category, based on farmer interviews (n = no. of farmers)

| Barriers to Tree Planting | Land Tenure | | | | |
	Private Estate (n = 6)	Private Smallholder (n = 5)	Family Smallholder (n = 19)	Tenant Smallholder (n = 4)	Total (n = 34)
No perceived barriers	6	4	10	1	21
Insecure land tenure	0	0	1	3	4
Uninterested in planting	0	0	4	0	4
Inadequate land	0	0	3	0	3
Inadequate gov't support	0	0	1	0	1
Payback too long	0	1	0	0	1

when thousands of planted trees were cut to clear additional space for bananas. Yet there are economic and cultural reasons why farmers often refrain from cutting trees even when faced with appealing alternatives like bananas. Most obviously, trees add value to the land in the form of harvestable products, shade cover, windbreak and erosion protection. Unlike bananas, trees also represent a long-term investment that tends to increase in value as the tree grows. In this respect, farmers often view planted trees as contributing to livelihood *security*, not just immediate economic gain.

Related to this are cultural prohibitions that discourage the cutting of planted trees, especially on family lands. For example, many farmers believe that they *cannot* cut trees planted by their forefathers because these trees are assumed to be property of all heirs to the family land. Similarly, some farmers feel that, even if they *could* cut such trees, they still *should not* cut them because these have been bestowed to them from past generations. Some such farmers expressed the desire to plant trees themselves in part to reciprocate this obligation to future generations.

LAND TENURE AND REAL ESTATE DEVELOPMENT

An unexpected way that tenure was found to influence land use was through the real estate market. Recall that hard development (housing, infrastructure, etc.) has expanded significantly, even though it still constitutes a small percentage of the land area of each watershed (figure 3.1). This phenomenon will be examined in detail in chapters 6 and 7. Worth noting here is that family ownership of land, in particular, poses a major impediment to sale onto the formal real estate market by virtue of complex and costly legal requirements to obtain shared agreement and compensation for sale among multiple co-owners. In fact, two land developers in Soufrière who were interviewed said they avoid family lands altogether in their business dealings. This stands in stark contrast to private estate lands, where extensive subdivision, sale and residential and/or commercial development have occurred in recent years.

It is nonetheless difficult to estimate how significant the family land "effect" has been in terms of constraining hard development overall, in part because there are confounding factors. Estate lands are not only legally but also location-wise more attractive for development because they are concentrated in the lowlands and near the coast, whereas family lands are typically inland and on more rugged, inaccessible terrain (table 5.2). That said, there are some sizeable tracts of undeveloped, forested family land in both Mamiku and Soufrière that are located in attractive real estate locations near the coast (personal observation). It seems plausible that these properties would have been sold and developed by now were they not under family ownership.

DO PROPERTY RIGHTS MATTER FOR CONSERVATION?

"What you see in the landscape is a product of our parents and grandparents."
—Senior forester, Government of Saint Lucia

Public lands clearly stood apart from the others in being dominated by mature forests and natural trees. For the most part, public lands occupy relatively inaccessible and rugged terrain in both watersheds and efforts to protect them from illegal hunting, wood cutting and farming have been notably strengthened since the late 1980s. These factors, combined with broader agricultural decline that has undercut demand for squatting on public lands, have created a situation where most state-owned forests are now well protected, with the notable exception that there is some illegal growing of ganja in small, scattered patches.

Beyond public lands, recent trends of agricultural decline and reforestation in Saint Lucia need to be situated in a historical context in which low investment and underutilization of land have long plagued the region's agriculture (WIRC 1897; Finkel 1964; Braithewaite 1968; Welch 1968; Rubenstein 1975; Brierley 1985a, 1992; Besson 1987; Harrington 1987; Rojas and Meganck 1987; Cole 1994; Bloch et al. 2005). The reasons for this have been much debated, but many experts have suggested that landownership and tenure patterns have played a central role (e.g., WIRC 1897; Finkel 1964; Welch 1968; Rubenstein 1975; Rojas 1984; Brierley 1985a). In particular, estates and family land properties have often been singled out as unproductive.

There are indeed confirmed cases of family lands being underutilized because of tenure conflicts and uncertainties, but the assumption that family lands are categorically more susceptible to underutilization has been challenged by several researchers (Rubenstein 1987; Crichlow 1994; Le Franc 1994; Vargas and Stanfield 2003b; Bloch et al. 2005), as well as by the findings here. In short, this study found no consistent pattern and otherwise little evidence to indicate a causal link between land tenure and land underutilization or farmland abandonment. There has in recent years been widespread abandonment of cultivation on each of private estate, private smallholder and family smallholder lands in Saint Lucia. The specific reasons for this are complex and discussed in other chapters, but briefly they involve commodity and labour market changes that have especially impacted the previously dominant banana sector.

Local geographical factors have also influenced land use and abandonment (table 3.6). Possessing relatively better lands (flatter, more accessible) has not necessarily made farmers immune from the need to downsize production, but where necessary it has usually involved abandonment of relatively steeper and/or less accessible portions of farm holdings (Walters and Hansen 2013). Compared to private lands, family lands are more likely to be on steeper and higher-elevation terrain (table 5.2). This has surely contributed in cases to their being abandoned during periods of production downsizing, and it likely accounts for the relatively high measures of second-growth forest (table 5.4) and natural trees (table 5.5) on family versus private smallholder lands. But there is little evidence that tenure per se was a significant factor influencing farmer decisions to abandon particular lands.

The finding that land tenure was relatively unimportant as a cause of land abandonment and reforestation was unexpected, given that literature on West Indian land use has often emphasized its significance (Rubenstein 1975; Rojas 1984; Besson and Momsen 1987; Rojas and Meganck 1987; Barrow 1992; Brierley 1992; Dujon 1997; see also Robinson et al. 2014). We saw in chapter 2, for example, how collapse of the sugar industry in the late 1800s and again in the 1930s/1940s hit the estate farm sector especially hard and led to calls for land redistribution and more support of smallholder farming as a viable alternative (WIRC 1897; Harmsen et al. 2014). These apparently contradictory findings suggest either that tenure's significance for land use in the West Indies has generally been overestimated or its influence is highly context-specific. Salient here are observations made of Saint Lucia by land tenure specialist David Stanfield (1987, 29; see also Le Franc 1994, 59):

> Agriculture production is a function of a complex array of factors: soil quality, rainfall, temperature, prices and availability of inputs. Why should we believe that the constraint of ownership insecurity is the most important constraint, overshadowing all others? Rules which define property rights play an important role in farm management decisions, but the web of factors which fashion their decision is highly complex and the importance of any one factor varies from situation to situation.

The influence of tenure on tree-planting practices was more apparent but still rather ambiguous. The wider literature reveals that people who lack secure tenure over land are less likely to practise tree planting unless doing so serves to strengthen their tenure claim (Blaut et al. 1959; Fortmann 1985; Grossman 1997; Davis-Morrison 1998; Walters et al. 1999; Vargas and Stanfield 2003b; Walters 2004; Bloch et al. 2005; Degrande et al. 2006; Wannasai and Shrestha 2008). The sample size of tenant farmers in this study was small, but they clearly stood apart in being the only group to consistently express reluctance to plant trees because of tenure insecurity, but tenant and squatter farming has declined sharply over the past few decades, so their cumulative impact on the landscape is now small. For example, each of the two largest estates in the study supported more than twenty tenant farmers in the early 1990s but had fewer than five in 2007. Lands used for tenant farming are often marginal, so it is not surprising that these were abandoned during the period of sharp agricultural decline. In addition, several of the estates now actively discourage tenant farming as they reposition themselves as ecotourism destinations (see chapter 7).

Tree planting on family lands is particularly interesting. Drawing largely from anecdotal evidence or limited qualitative observation, early researchers were quick to condemn family lands as discouraging investment like tree planting, even as these same researchers sometimes acknowledged an abundance of planted trees on those very lands (Lowenthal 1961, 5; Besson 1987, 15–16; Barrow 1992, 45)! This apparent contradiction has since been clarified by recent, more in-depth research revealing that farmers on family lands usually perceive their tenure claims to be secure (Barrow 1992; Le Franc 1994; Bloch et al. 2005). Findings presented here likewise show that planted trees are abundant on family lands (tables 5.4, 5.7) and also that most farmers using family land are not discouraged from planting trees because of perceived insecurity of tenure (table 5.8). In other words, farmers can in most cases plant trees on family land with the confidence that they will enjoy the fruits of their labour (Dujon 1997, 1533).

The presence of "legacy" trees also helps to explain the relative ubiquity of planted trees in the rural landscape. The value of land is enhanced by the presence of productive trees (for fruit, spice, timber, etc.). Farmers are reluctant to cut such trees without good reason, given the time invested in their growth. Yet there is more at stake than economic calculation. On family lands, in particular, just as there is a collective prohibition against subdivision and sale of land without full agreement among shared heirs, there is also an understood prohibition against cutting trees that were planted by previous generations because these, too, are viewed as commonly owned and their fruits thus available to all heirs (Besson 1987; Barrow 1992).

Finally, it was learned that the legal hurdles associated with the formal sale of family land are usually so onerous that such lands are largely shut out from the formal real estate market (OAS 1986; Shearer et al. 1991; Liverpool 1994; Dujon 1997; Mycoo 2005a; but see Crichlow 1994, 89–90, and Mills 2007). Reforms under the Land Registration and Land Adjudication Acts of 1984 sought to remedy legal barriers associated with the sale of property in Saint Lucia, including family lands, by creating a formal property registry and a "trust of sale" mechanism that vests the power to sell family land parcels in the hands of a designated family trustee or a limited number of trustees (OAS 1991, app. C). While this may have facilitated the sale of some lands, recent literature (e.g., Dujon 1997, 2000; Bloch et al. 2005; Mycoo 2005a; Mills 2007) plus findings here suggest that significant legal and customary barriers to the sale of family land remain. As such, the issue of family land will likely draw continued policy attention because pressures for development are unabated, yet family-owned property increasingly dominates the remaining stock of undeveloped lands (Bloch et al. 2005; GOSL 2007a, 18). According to the Saint Lucia Census for Agriculture, between 1986 and 2007 the proportion of total agricultural lands that are held under family ownership has grown from 24 to 42 per cent, while lands under private ownership have shrunk from 60 to 40 per cent (GOSL 2007a). Family lands may play an increasingly important role in preserving forests and agricultural land in Saint Lucia.

CHAPTER SUMMARY

The Soufrière and Mamiku watersheds include a mix of public, private estate, private smallholder and communal "family" lands. Tenant farming also occurs but is relatively uncommon by comparison. The main finding of the analysis is that land tenure had surprisingly little influence over land use and tree planting. Tree planting and abandonment of cultivation (with ensuing reforestation) were commonplace under all types of land tenure. The effects of land tenure were for the most part swamped by other causal factors, including local topography and changing commodity and labour markets. A notable exception to this trend is that for legal and cultural reasons, family lands are less likely to be subdivided and sold onto the formal real estate market. Family land tenure is thus a disincentive to commercial development but otherwise has little influence on agricultural land use.

In the search for causal-historical explanations, the land tenure question nicely illustrates the process of eliminative inference: how alternative explanations (hypotheses) are formulated, evaluated and either confirmed or refuted. In short, because so much had been written about Caribbean land tenure and its significance for land use and development, it seemed quite plausible that the changes in land use and land cover documented in this study might be influenced by land tenure. Its causal significance was thus rigorously evaluated – and largely rejected – by compiling and then assessing various sources of empirical information.

It is worth noting that land tenure, the hypothesized cause in this case, is structural in form, not event-like. The same can be said about topographic characteristics like slope and altitude, whose causal influences were evaluated and confirmed in chapter 3. The point to make here is that, while events have certain ontological advantages and so are typically preferred in causal-historical analysis (Vayda and Walters 2011), not all causes can be readily conceived of in event terms. As such, it can still be meaningful to consider specific "structures" or "conditions" as having causal influence, albeit the more clear and precise their specification, the better.

CHAPTER 6

MIGRATION, LABOUR AND LAND USE CHANGE

DECLINES IN SAINT LUCIAN AGRICULTURE HAVE BEEN CAUSED in significant part by changes in agricultural commodity markets. Yet the story is more complicated than this because the negative impacts of trade disruptions have been compounded by changes in the domestic labour market. In short, falling commodity prices have coincided with rising production costs as farm labour becomes increasingly scarce. This is happening because rural families are having fewer children and most young adults are leaving farming and outmigrating from the rural countryside to urban destinations in Saint Lucia and elsewhere.

Migration of people to and from the countryside has had profound consequences for rural populations, farming practices, land use and the ecological character of small islands across the region, throughout history (e.g., Lowenthal and Comitas 1962; Rubenstein 1975; Marshall 1982; Kimber 1988). Yet the environment typically occupies little more than background in the vast majority of Caribbean studies of human migration. This chapter remedies this by examining how migration has influenced land use and forest change in Saint Lucia and the wider West Indies. This is challenging, because migration can be both a cause and an effect of agricultural decline and its influence is confounded by other factors. Nonetheless, the topic merits serious attention because it undoubtedly plays an important part in the larger story being presented in this book. Saint Lucia's experience needs first to be situated in the wider history of West Indian migration.

WEST INDIAN MIGRATION

"A man must always be ready to move!"
—An elderly Saint Lucian, quoted by Carnegie (1982, 11)

Human migration has long been a prominent, arguably *defining* feature of Caribbean societies (Tobias 1980; Carnegie 1982; Marshall 1982; Richardson 1983, 1992, 2004; Momsen 1986, 50; Watts 1987; Thomas-Hope 1992, 160; Conway 1999/2000). The population of the West Indies was built on immigration. Amerindian Tainos (formerly referred to as "Island Arawaks") and then Caribs (Kalinago) migrating from South America colonized and settled the Antillian archipelago centuries before European discovery (Kimber 1988; Harmsen et al. 2014). European colonization in the sixteenth century and after brought waves of settlers from different parts of western Europe. These numbers were eventually dwarfed by the millions of African slaves and half-million indentured Indian labourers who were brought to work on agricultural plantations throughout the region (Roberts and Byrne 1966; Laurence 1971; Lowenthal 1972).

Emancipation in the 1830s triggered widespread departure of former slaves from their resident plantations. Many of them relocated to free villages or to unclaimed lands, where they established as smallholders (Lowenthal 1972; Harmsen et al. 2014). Thousands more outmigrated in the mid- and late 1800s from the smaller islands to Trinidad and Guyana and later to Cuba and the Dominican Republic, where fast-growing sugar industries offered better wages (Roberts 1955; Byron 1994). Others migrated to work in the goldfields of French Guiana or to banana plantations and railroad construction projects in Central America (WIRC 1897; McElroy and de Albuquerque 1988; Thomas-Hope 1992). Most significantly, an estimated 130,000 West Indians worked on construction of the Panama Canal, including 5,000 Saint Lucians in its first phase (1883–85) and 14,000 in its second (1903–5) (Abenaty 2000). These outmigrations were large enough to significantly reduce population growth between the 1880s and 1920 in Saint Lucia (figure 6.1) and other West Indian islands (Byrne 1969; Rubenstein 1977; Marshall 1982).

Completion of the Panama Canal in 1914, a crash in world sugar prices in 1921, curtailment of legal immigration to the United States in 1924 and onset of the Great Depression in 1929 combined to sharply reduce outmigration from the West Indies, while encouraging many abroad to return home (Marshall 1982). Economic hardships wrought by the Great Depression were exacerbated

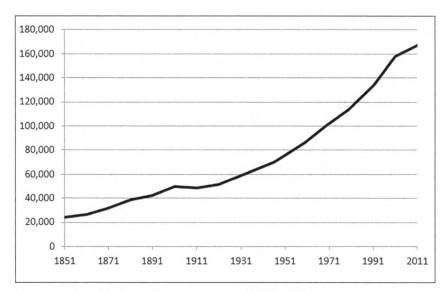

Figure 6.1. Saint Lucia population, 1851–2011 (GOSL 2012b)

by growing domestic populations that now had little opportunity or incentive to outmigrate. These developments created conditions that led to a sharp rise in political and labour unrest that, in turn, hastened decline of an already struggling sugar industry (Roberts 1958a; Richardson 1992, 2004; Harmsen et al. 2014).

Economic conditions shifted again with the onset of World War II. In response, the Americans initiated development of a cluster of military installations in the region that created substantial employment in construction and maintenance for local populations. Among these were two major projects in Saint Lucia: an air force base in the south of the island at Vieux Fort and a naval air station in the north at Gros Islet (Harmsen et al. 2014). The war also presented new opportunities for outmigration. Many West Indians migrated to the United Kingdom, where they worked in munitions factories or enlisted and served in the military (Byron and Condon 2008).

Opportunities to migrate to the United Kingdom continued following the war. In response to soaring demand for construction and factory labour, the British government in 1948 "conferred unrestricted entry and the right to live and work in the United Kingdom upon all citizens of the United Kingdom and colonies and citizens of the Commonwealth" (Byron 1994, 81). West Indians responded to this opportunity and migrated in huge numbers until the Commonwealth Immigration Act tightened restrictions in 1962 (Peach 1965). In sum, about 450,000 West Indians – the vast majority young adults – migrated to the United Kingdom from 1946 to 1966, a hugely significant migration event in demographic terms (Peach 1967; Thomas-Hope 1992; Byron and Condon 1996). Among these migrants were an estimated 10,000 Saint Lucians or about one in nine island residents; entire villages were literally emptied out of their young adult populations (Midgett 1977; Abenaty 2000). Unlike earlier migrations, most who moved to the United Kingdom during this period settled there for the long term.

Curtailment of migration to the United Kingdom after 1962 was partly offset during the 1960s, 1970s and 1980s by sizeable migrations to the United States and Canada, where strong economies and less restrictive immigration made them appealing destinations (Palmer 1974; Strachan 1983; Richardson 1992). As well, the economies of a number of Caribbean islands began to modernize and then grew rapidly in the decades after the war. Urbanization, major infrastructure projects and tourism development created significant employment opportunities and encouraged within-country movements of people and sizeable inter-regional migrations to the Bahamas, Barbados, Martinique, US Virgin Islands, and Saint Kitts and Nevis (Clark 1974; Rubenstein 1977; McElroy and de Albuquerque 1988; Potter 1993, 1995).

In particular, many Saint Lucians moved to nearby Martinique, Barbados and the US Virgin Islands to avail themselves of new employment opportunities created by these modernizing island economies (Momsen 1986; Byron 2000). West Indians also continued to migrate to North America as students, seasonal and contract workers, and longer-term/permanent residents (Wood and McCoy 1985). While the cumulative numbers were large, migrant streams to North America were more occupationally and educationally selective, less male dominated and smaller in size (per capita) than the massive post–World War II migration to the United Kingdom and so did not have as significant a demographic impact back home (Ebanks et al. 1979; Gmelch 1992; Thomas-Hope 1992; Byron 1994; Castellani 2007).

MIGRATION, LAND USE AND FORESTS

The social science literature on human migration is vast (Thomas 1954; Kearney 1986; Gmelch 1992; Massey et al. 1993; Byron and Condon 2008; Piguet 2013; Clemens et al. 2014), but the relationship between migration, land use and forests has until recently received little attention (Carr 2009; Adamo and Izazola 2010). Early research of this kind focused on rural in-migration as a primary cause of frontier forest clearance in Southeast Asia and Latin America (e.g., Rudel 1993; Kummer and Turner 1994), but recent attention has shifted to the reverse phenomenon: rural outmigration as a cause of agricultural land abandonment and reforestation (Rudel 1998; Rudel et al. 2005). This outmigration typically entails the movement of younger adults to urban centres in search of better employment and lifestyle opportunities. For rural areas, this loss of young adults creates both short-term scarcities in farm labour plus longer-term trends in farm downsizing, as older cohorts retire out of farming and are not replaced by their now absentee offspring. The consequences include net farmland abandonment and reforestation, especially of marginal sites, as these usually require more labour and other costs to farm (Klooster 2003; Aide and Grau 2004; Gellrich and Zimmermann 2007; Schmook and Radel 2008).

Empirical evidence of this kind of outmigration-driven reforestation has been found in a variety of countries, including Puerto Rico (Grau et al. 2003), El Salvador (Hecht et al. 2005; Hecht 2010), central Mexico (Lopez et al. 2006; Robson and Berkes 2011), Costa Rica (Kull et al. 2007) and southern Brazil (Baptista 2008). At a region-wide level, the percentage of rural people in Latin America and the Caribbean declined from 50 to 25 per cent between 1960 and 2002, with a net loss of 20 million rural inhabitants between 1980 and 2002, which suggests reduced farming pressure (Aide and Grau 2004). In fact, a meta-analysis of published literature worldwide concluded that rural to urban migration in response to new economic opportunities was the most common driver of agricultural land abandonment (Benayas et al. 2007).

Yet some research suggests that rural outmigration does not always lead to reforestation. Outmigrants may leave, but later return with cash savings to reinvest in the farms or they may send cash home while away ("remittances") that is used to hire farm labour in their absence. For example, Gray and Bilsborrow (2014) found that rural outmigration in Ecuador led to net expansion in cultivation. Likewise, Sloan (2007) and Fearnside (2008) have argued that rural depopulation may simply reflect a "hollowing-out" of the frontier in which smallholders are gradually replaced by fewer but larger consolidated landholdings devoted to less labour-intensive farming like cattle ranching or industrial agriculture. This kind of dynamic has occurred in parts of Brazil, Panama, Guatemala and Indonesia (Sunderlin and Resosudarmo 1999; Sloan 2007).

MIGRATION AND LAND USE IN THE WEST INDIES

The relationship between migration and forests has been barely studied in the West Indies, but some patterns can be inferred from research into migration's impact on agriculture and land use. The historical transformation of the West Indies into a significant agricultural-export region was made possible by the massive in-migration of people who proceeded to clear these islands of existing forest and replace them with cultivated crops (Watts 1987; Kimber 1988; Harmsen et al. 2014). Early European settlers initiated this trend, but labour scarcity was a recurring constraint to agricultural expansion and became the primary justification for the ensuing migrations of slaves and indentured labour (Laurence 1971).

The land use effects of outmigration are less clear, however. For example, early research on the Barbados sugar industry found that adoption of labour-saving technologies offset declines in the labour force that resulted from outmigration of farm workers to Panama (1891–1921) (Roberts 1955). By contrast, Roberts's (1958b) detailed study of post-war emigration from Jamaica to the United Kingdom suggests that the sugar industry there suffered from the departure of skilled and unskilled farm workers, although it is unclear how this impacted land use specifically.

Lowenthal and Comitas (1962) were among the first Caribbean scholars to make explicit the connection between outmigration, farmland abandonment and reforestation. In their classic study of Montserrat, an island subject to extreme rates (30 per cent) of post-war emigration to the United Kingdom, they observed that "pasture succeeds tillage, and wilderness, pasture; more than half of the arable acreage now lies idle" (206). Similarly, Rubenstein's (1975, 1977) study of land use in Saint Vincent revealed persistent, widespread under-utilization of land. Outmigration contributed to this in two ways. First, much of the private land was owned by absentee landlords and often not cultivated as intensively by remaining caretakers. Second, heavy outmigration of younger men created a chronic shortage of farm labour. Subsequent research in Saint Vincent (Rubenstein 1983a, 1983b), Jamaica (Thomas-Hope 1993), and Saint Kitts and Nevis (Byron 2007) further revealed that remittance income enabled recipients to purchase food (and other things), and so they had less incentive themselves to farm. Lands purchased using remittance income were typically not farmed, yet their purchase inflated local land prices, making it more difficult for those who actually wanted to farm to acquire land (Rubenstein 1983a, 1983b; World Bank 1975).

REMITTANCE INCOME, RETURN MIGRATION AND URBANIZATION

> In the small British Caribbean islands nearly every shop, taxi or house of any substance may be traced to the owner or family members having traveled away earlier to a destination where wages were higher and more reliable than at home.
> —Richardson (1992, 151)

The Caribbean includes some of the highest per capita source countries for migration remittance income in the world (Castellani 2007), but the effects of remittances on land use have changed over time. Caribbean studies of pre–World War II migration to countries such as Panama suggest that remittance income was often reinvested in agriculture, particularly the purchase of farmland (Momsen 1986). By contrast, research on post-war migration shows that such income was usually spent on housing, consumer goods and education (Wood and McCoy 1985; Conway 1993; Byron 2007; but see Thomas-Hope 1993, Byron 1994). This is consistent with studies from elsewhere showing that remittances usually encourage a transition out of farming, rather than reinvestment in it (Klooster 2003; Hecht et al. 2005; Hecht 2010; Davis et al. 2010).

Exceptions to this were more likely where farming was an economically viable sector and outmigration was seasonal or short term (Schmook and Radel 2008; Hecht 2010; Moran-Taylor and Taylor 2010). On this point, research findings for the West Indies are mixed. Thomas-Hope (1993) found that many rural Jamaicans engaged in seasonal labour migration used remittances to purchase land back home, although she did not examine the actual use of these lands. However, Wood and McCoy (1985) found most remittance income from seasonal farm-worker migrants to Florida (among them many Saint Lucians) was spent on housing and consumer goods.

These trends also hold for Caribbean return migrants. Gmelch's (1980) review found that most outmigrants originate from farming communities, but few long-term migrants go back to farming when they return (see also Strachan 1983). Likewise, Byron (1994) found that among migrants in Nevis, those absent for longer periods were far less likely to return to serious (as opposed to hobby) farming. Migrants often return with significant capital, but their expenditures are primarily consumptive in nature. Where they do buy land, it usually sits idle or is used as a home site. They often build large, modern homes that serve as status symbols as much as their owners' requirements (Gmelch 1980; Byron 1994, 2007).

This dynamic largely accounts for the residential housing boom across the region (Byron 2000). In particular, the huge outmigration to the United Kingdom in the late 1950s and early 1960s reversed itself in the late 1980s and 1990s as a growing stream of retirees returned home with generous UK pension incomes and sizeable savings, often earned from the sale of their UK homes (Byron and Condon 1996; Abenaty 2000; Mills 2007). This trend has continued with the return of migrants from Canada and the United States. Their return has impacted landscapes throughout the Caribbean, as former agricultural lands have been subdivided and developed into extensive housing estates. At the same time, this housing boom has generated much local work in construction and services and so has drawn more labour out of farming, further contributing to reduced cultivation and subsequent reforestation in mostly upland environments (Walters 2016a, 2016b).

As nations across the Caribbean urbanize/suburbanize and their economies become increasingly dominated by the service and industrial sectors, within-country, rural-to-urban migration becomes increasingly important (Adams 1969; Clark 1974; Hope 1986b; Richardson 1992). By Caribbean standards, the Windward Island states were comparatively late to urbanize, with only 15 to 20 per cent of the population of Saint Lucia urban-based by 1970 (Clarke 1974). Saint Lucia emulated other Caribbean countries during the era of "enclave industrialization" (Potter 1995, 338) by enticing branch plants of multinationals to the island in the 1980s using tax holidays and other incentives (Kelly 1986; Potter 1993). The embrace of tourism as a key pillar of economic development has proven even more significant. Substantial movement of labour from agriculture to tourism-related occupations has contributed to the decline of farming and spread of "idle lands" on many islands (Potter 1995; Walters 2016b).

Finally, it is also possible that labour scarcity due to outmigration results not in outright abandonment of cultivation but rather in a shift to less labour-intensive farm production (Davis et al. 2010). For example, a shift from crops to pastured livestock in households where members had outmigrated has been documented in Bolivia (Preston 1998), Ecuador (Rudel et al. 2002) and Yucatan, Mexico (Radel et al. 2010). Tree farming can also reduce the demand for labour in such situations (Schmook and Radel 2008). In fact, Momsen (1986) found that farms in Saint Lucia with migrant owners grew more tree crops and fewer root crops, suggesting a shift to less labour-intensive crops, although it is unclear if this led to a net change in land under cultivation.

POST-WAR OUTMIGRATION AND LAND USE IN SAINT LUCIA

"Today, everyone wants a white collar job. . . . In ten years, I don't know how Saint Lucia is going to feed itself!"
—Chris, elderly farmer and retired civil servant

The status of Saint Lucian agriculture and land use pre-1960 is difficult to discern because the first comprehensive agricultural census was completed in 1961 and island-wide air photo coverage only began in the 1960s. However, several lines of evidence suggest that subsistence cultivation, in particular, expanded dramatically on the island in the 1930s and 1940s. As described earlier, reduced opportunities for outmigration combined with declining mortality rates caused a surge in domestic population and unemployment which contributed to widespread labour unrest and civil strife (Harmsen et al. 2014). Many turned to subsistence farming to survive, a trend further encouraged by wartime curtailments of shipping that increased the need for more food self-sufficiency. Air photo coverage was limited during this period, but photos from 1940 of the south of the island show extensive lowlands under sugar monoculture and adjacent hillsides covered by a dense patchwork of smallholder plots that have long since been abandoned. Elderly farmers in Soufrière likewise recalled during their youth seeing widespread cultivation of food crops on nearby mountain slopes that have long since returned to forest.

The island's labour surplus turned to a deficit in the late 1950s with the massive exodus of young adults to the United Kingdom. Agricultural census statistics reveal a sharp drop in total number of farm holdings and area under cultivation from 1961 to 1974 (table 4.3), changes attributed to rural depopulation resulting from outmigration to the United Kingdom and to abandonment of unprofitable farming enterprises, notably a sharp downturn in the late 1960s to the emerging banana industry (GOSL 1974; Welch 1994, 1996a). Bananas eventually recovered, however, and extraordinary growth during the 1980s established them as the island's dominant crop (figure 4.1). Total number of farmers and farm holdings increased from 1974 to 1996, even as the amount of land under cultivation declined by 30 per cent (table 4.3), a paradox explained by the fact that most growth in banana production was concentrated in the smallholder sector. By contrast, the estate farming sector, which had struggled for decades in the face of sugar's gradual demise, continued to decline: extensive areas of land fell idle; other lands were sold off and redistributed to smallholders privately or under government-sponsored redistribution schemes or developed into residential subdivisions and tourism facilities (GOSL 1974, 2; GOSL 1986, 1996b; World Bank 1979; Rojas and Meganck 1987). From 1974 to 1986 cumulative area in farms greater than 25 acres declined from 48,333 to 30,100 acres, whereas farms less than 25 acres increased from 23,668 to 27,915 acres, with the largest gain (2,146 acres) made for farms less than 5 acres (GOSL 1987a). Farmland in holdings greater than 500 acres shrunk from 26,900 acres in 1974 (37 per cent of total) to 5,500 acres in 1996 (10.7 per cent of total) (GOSL 1996a, 6). These divergent patterns are visible comparing the growth in farming in the District of Micoud, a major smallholder, banana-growing area, with its contraction in Soufrière District, an area poorly suited for growing bananas and with a prominent, estate farm sector (table 4.3).

As trade challenges emerged in the late 1980s as a significant concern for the banana sector, the Government of Saint Lucia identified as an added threat the looming shortage of farm labour caused by the departure of workers:

> One important factor which contributes to Saint Lucia being a high cost producer of bananas and which mitigates against our ability to effectively compete in the European market, is the high wages which currently prevail in the industry. The drift of unskilled labour from agriculture to other competing sectors such as construction has contributed to the steep increase in wages for unskilled labour in the banana industry. . . . The average wage of unskilled labour in the banana industry increased by about 130 per cent from an average of $10 per day in 1980 to about $23 per day in 1989. . . . production in SL is labour-intensive with labour cost accounting for approximately 68 per cent of total cost of production. (GOSL 1990, 6)

In fact, this drift of labour from agriculture to construction and other employment in Saint Lucia was noted by policymakers as early as the late 1970s (e.g., World Bank 1980), but it was not until the late 1980s and early 1990s that government began to express serious concern about its impacts on the agricultural sector (GOSL 1990, 6; GOSL 1991b, 1991c). Subsequent GOSL assessments identify the departure of three thousand smallholder banana farmers between 1992 and 1996 as the primary cause of a 45 per cent decline in banana production, with rising costs and market price volatilities and uncertainties cited as major reasons for this exodus (GOSL 1996b, 1998a, 2007b). In fact, labour shortage was cited as frequently in interviews by farmers and key informants, as was lower commodity prices to explain Saint Lucia's agricultural decline (table 3.8).

Furthermore, government statistics and interviews reveal that the active farmer population is both declining in numbers *and* aging. These trends were especially notable following the collapse of bananas in the mid-1990s, with total population living in farm households dropping 36 per cent nationwide from 1996 to 2007 and percentage of farm holdings managed by persons under thirty-five years of age falling by half (from 24 to 12 per cent) during the same period (table 6.1).

Interview findings were consistent with national statistics: most interviewed farmers were older than fifty years and few were under forty years of age (mean = 58.1, n = 43). Some were already semi-retired, farming only part-time and doing other work like construction or retail concurrently or seasonally. Many relied on seasonal or occasional hired labour, especially during harvest, which entails carrying heavy bunches of bananas or sacks of tubers, fruit or vegetables from field to roadside, often across rugged terrain. Such tasks are physically challenging, so hiring labour is that much more critical for older farmers. Yet a common lament from them is that younger people are uninterested in farming because they lack the work ethic or the patience, preferring instead to make "fast money". Under these circumstances, farmers have strong incentive to down-size cultivation, especially on remote, difficult-to-access sites, as was indeed confirmed by watershed assessments (table 3.6).

Table 6.1. Age structure (per cent of total) of Saint Lucian farmer population, 1996 and 2007

Age (years)	1996 (% total)	2007 (% total)
<35	24	12
35–54	43	46
>54	33	42
Total	100	100

Source: GOSL (2007a, chart 24).

Ironically, farmers who complained about lack of young people to assist them were just as likely to admit having discouraged their own children from pursuing farming as an occupation. Interviewed farmers had on average 5.4 children, yet almost half of these children (46.4 per cent) were not at the time residing in Saint Lucia and only 5.8 per cent were actively farming. In fact, one-third of smallholder farmers (nine of twenty-seven) and half of estate farmers (three of six) had themselves previously lived abroad for a period.

When farmers outmigrate or die in the absence of family members or heirs to replace them, lands typically fall idle, often for long periods, sometimes permanently. This kind of scenario was documented for many sites in Soufrière and Mamiku. For example, several elderly farmers had recently downsized or retired altogether from farming, but they indicated that their formerly culti-vated lands were now going back to "bush" because no one in the family was interested in farming them. In some cases lands had been abandoned recently, but there were also extensive hillside lands that exist today in secondary forests and have not been farmed for decades (Walters and Hansen 2013). The former farmers of these lands are long gone, and their heirs are either overseas or living on the island but are not interested in farming because they have other sources of livelihood and the land in question is viewed as not sufficiently profitable to farm. In some cases, local caretakers acting on behalf of absentee owners are permitted to farm portions of these lands, but often their primary role is to discourage others from farming or cutting wood from it.

For young men with relatively little education, there are opportunities to outmigrate for seasonal farm work in the United States and Canada or for construction work on neighboring islands.[1] In recent years, however, the most ready route out of farming is to remain on island and work either in construc-tion or for one of the hotels or related tourism services, doing landscaping, maintenance or security. For example, one prominent developer in Soufrière suggested that most of his twenty employees were either former or would-be farmers. Driving a taxi or working in minibus transport is even more lucrative but usually requires a capital outlay for purchase of a vehicle and taxi licence that only return migrants with savings can usually afford. Service work in hotels, restaurants and retail are especially common options for women.

These various employment options typically pay better than agricultural labour, but equally important is the regularity and predictability of wages.[2] By contrast, farm work varies seasonally, and given the vagaries of market and

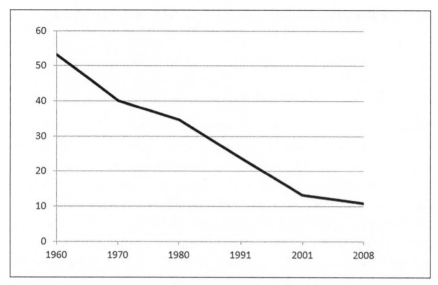

Figure 6.2. Working population (per cent of total) in agriculture in Saint Lucia, 1960–2008 (Abdulah 1977, 52–53; GOSL 2006b, table 4.1; GOSL 2012b, 42)

weather, payback is slow and unpredictable. Better-educated young people tend to outmigrate (often for more education), although many return to fill the growing number of white-collar jobs in tourism and related services industries and in government. The scope of these changes is captured by national labour statistics, which show a continuous decline in percentage of the active workforce in agriculture from 1960 (53 per cent) to 2008 (11 per cent), a decline slowed but not halted by the banana boom (figure 6.2).

Outmigration of labour also appears in cases to have favoured less labour-intensive farming like agroforestry. Most tree crops require only modest tending to remain productive, and they may be left unattended for several years and still be brought back into production with relative ease. Thus, whether intentional or by default, agroforests often persist in the landscape where intensive cultivation no longer exists. For example, extensive cocoa agroforests have been rehabilitated in recent years on both small and estate farms in response to improved market prospects. Similarly, some estates have recently reconfigured themselves as tourism destinations and have rehabilitated orchards to provide fresh fruit and spices for visiting tourists. These well-tended groves of mixed fruit trees offer the benefits of fresh food and pleasing aesthetics yet require only modest ongoing maintenance.

RETURN MIGRATION AND LAND USE CHANGE IN SAINT LUCIA

"You can always tell which houses are owned by return migrants: it says UK pound
sterling all over it!"
    —Ricki, former agricultural extension officer and senator

Construction emerged as a major sector of employment in Saint Lucia during the 1970s (World Bank 1979, 1980). It further surged after the mid-1980s,
drawing more labour out of farming and contributing to agriculture's decline.
Year-to-year changes in the construction sector are volatile and may reflect the
onset and completion of large tourism and public works projects (e.g., World
Bank 1982; GOSL 1987b, 11). Arguably more significant than these big projects
has been a sustained surge in residential house construction, financed in large
part by a steady stream of Saint Lucians returning after long periods abroad in
the United Kingdom, United States and Canada.

The most detailed information on these migrants can be found in Abenaty's
(2000) study of long-term migrants from Saint Lucia to the United Kingdom
This revealed that most of these had migrated to the United Kingdom at twenty
to twenty-nine years of age (only one of twenty-eight was older than forty-five)
and had lived there on average for twenty-seven years before returning permanently to Saint Lucia. Forty per cent of those who returned had inherited
land or purchased it in advance, and more bought land after returning. While
many engaged in home gardening and hobby farming, only two of twenty-eight
farmed seriously upon return.

Unfortunately, it is difficult to gain a clear, broader picture of Saint Lucian
return migrants and their impact on such things as construction investment and
land acquisition because nationals can come and go without a formal immigration record, and many have long done so – for example, making seasonal holiday
visits for years before relocating permanently back to the island. Similarly, the
transfer of funds from abroad back to Saint Lucia takes many forms and may
include occasional gifts to relatives, ongoing wire transfer deposits from abroad
to local savings accounts, regular pension deposits through international banks
and so on. As such, the purchase of land and subsequent construction of a new
home may occur in steps spanning many years, and it is common for homes to
remain only partially finished and underoccupied for long periods (Abenaty
2000; Byron and Condon 2008).

Table 6.2. Estimated number of private households by select district, 2001 and 2010

Districts	2001	2010	% Change
Soufrière	2,252	2,875	27.7
Micoud	4,588	5,601	22.1
Castries and Gros Islet	26,493	33,076	24.8
Other	14,208	17,339	22.0
Total	47,541	58,891	23.9

Note: Micoud District encompasses Mamiku and several other towns and watersheds.
Source: GOSL (2011).

Explicit policy discussion of residential housing construction being a major source of economic growth in Saint Lucia appeared in the mid-1980s (GOSL 1986). Its visible effects were increasingly apparent in the 1990s with the onset of multiple large residential developments (GOSL 1995, 1997). For example, extensive tracts of prime agricultural estate land east of Soufrière Town were converted into a sprawling subdivision (the "New Development"), nearly doubling the size of the town's built area. Homes financed by return migrants are also now commonplace in virtually every small village and on the outskirts of every town across the island. The scale of this can be inferred from government statistics showing an island-wide increase of 24 per cent in the number of private dwellings from 2001 to 2010, with Soufrière District leading at 27.7 per cent (table 6.2).

This boom in residential construction has had dramatic, direct effects on watershed landscapes across the island. For example, since the early 1990s about half of the agricultural estates in Soufrière and Mamiku had sold off sizeable portions of their property for residential development, which now extends considerable distance up each watershed. Subdivided lots are often large and consume sizeable land area for the population settled. They are usually concentrated on lowlands and near the coast, surrounding historical population centres. They have encroached into many natural forests (especially the coastal dry forests), but more often they replace existing or formerly farmed land, including much prime agricultural land. New homes are also common in remoter mountain villages in Soufrière and elsewhere, but these are typically built on smaller lots on family lands, close to existing roads and within previously settled village areas, and so have modest impact on surrounding forest and agricultural land.

MIGRATION AND FOREST CHANGE IN SAINT LUCIA

"In thirty years there will be no land left for agriculture!"
—Senior land surveyor, Saint Lucia

Drawing clear causal links between migration and land use/forest change is challenging because its influence is confounded by other factors (Gray and Bilsborrow 2014; Walters 2017). In chapter 4, for example, we saw how the erosion of protected market status for bananas in the 1990s triggered price declines that caused the industry's collapse and led to widespread farmland abandonment and reforestation. Markets for other export crops like copra and cocoa have also faced market-related challenges since the 1970s that have led to reduced cultivation of these crops. As this chapter has shown, rural outmigration is also an important part of the story of agricultural decline in Saint Lucia, but its causal role remains less obvious. Evidence suggests that commodity market impacts were compounded by growing farm labour scarcity, the result of people departing the countryside to outmigrate or work in the booming domestic service/tourism and construction sectors. Might this movement of labour out of farming be simply an effect, however, rather than a cause of agricultural decline? The evidence suggests otherwise.

Research on human migration suggests that the decision to migrate may involve varied and re-enforcing "push" and "pull" factors. For example, Conway (1999/2000) has argued that significant outmigration occurred in the West Indies primarily as a result of the collapse of the sugar industry in the late 1800s and then mid-1900s. Yet scholars of the West Indies have tended to emphasize "pull" factors to explain post-war migrations. In short, people *usually* leave because of better opportunities elsewhere, not because of deteriorating conditions at home (Roberts 1958b; Peach 1965, 1967; Harris and Steer 1968; Welch 1968; Watson 1982; Kelly 1986; Thomas-Hope 1992; Abenaty 2000).

Labour scarcity has, in fact, been a recurring constraint on agricultural expansion and development in Saint Lucia since the onset of European settlement (Harmsen et al. 2014). For a time, bananas provided a uniquely attractive economic opportunity for both large and small farmers. Yet the first boom in bananas that emerged in the 1950s was still not enough to stem a mass exodus of young adults to the United Kingdom at this time. Likewise, near the peak of the second banana boom and before the deterioration of market conditions, officials identified the scarcity of farm labour resulting from its movement into the burgeoning tourism and construction sectors as a growing constraint to banana production (GOSL 1990, 6; GOSL 1991b). As severe market uncertainties then took hold, many farmers responded, not by downsizing or shifting production to other crops, but by departing farming altogether, exacerbating farm labour scarcity further. The influence of market and labour changes thus became positively re-enforcing, a causal synergy enabled by the coincidentally strong growth in alternative, domestic employment. Absent these alternatives, many more would have stayed in farming in spite of declining revenues, either shifting to other crops or to fair trade–certified banana production, which by the mid-2000s offered an attractive market (Moberg 2008).

The departure of people from agriculture (or in the case of youth, the *non-entry* into it) is not simply a matter of short-term, economic calculation. For most the move is permanent and so has lasting socio-economic and environmental consequences. The World Bank (1975) documented a region-wide trend in the Caribbean of people leaving farming and attributed this in part to its low social status. West Indian children are often discouraged to farm by their parents and from an early age are taught that migration is a more appealing option (Momsen 1986; Byron 1994). For example, Thomas-Hope (1992) found widespread antipathy to agricultural work among both farm labourers and independent smallholders in rural Jamaica, Barbados and Saint Vincent, as did Byron (1994) in her research on Nevis (see also Welch 1968, 235).

These findings help explain the relatively high *reserve price* (i.e., minimum acceptable payment) for agricultural labour in the West Indies and the apparent paradox that farm labour scarcity often coexists with high unemployment (Braithwaite 1968, 269; Dale 1977, 52; Axline 1986, 52; see also Harmsen et al. 2014, 243). In short, most people will simply not do local agricultural work for the wages or returns being offered because they perceive it as low status and assume there are – or will soon be – better alternatives available (e.g., occasional construction work, seasonal tourism employment, remittance income, overseas migration, etc.).

Return migrants were also found to have important, but contradictory, effects on land use and forests that have important spatial-geographic dimensions. On one hand, such returnees are largely responsible for the residential housing boom that has swept the island since the late 1980s, replacing extensive lowland agricultural and coastal dry forest. On the other hand, these migrants, whose earlier departure to the United Kingdom and North America contributed at the time to land abandonment and reforestation in the uplands, are once again influencing a similar outcome, but this time indirectly, by drawing significant labour out of farming to build and service their large, new homes or work in their various business enterprises. Return migrants thus embody a kind of boomerang urbanization which contributes substantially to a wider, island-wide trend in which landscape and environmental impacts have shifted from the mountainous interior to the lowlands and coast (Walters 2016a).

This trend appears to be common to other island states in the Caribbean and possibly elsewhere. The best-studied case of this is Puerto Rico, which experienced dramatic, widespread declines in farming and increased forests since the 1940s but which in recent decades has seen rapid urban and suburban expansion onto former farmlands and secondary forests (Lopez et al. 2001; Pares-Ramos et al. 2008; Alvarez-Berrios et al. 2013). These authors cite the importance of rural outmigration into wage labour as a key cause of these changes but do not mention the likely central role of remittance income and return migrants. Similarly, a study comparing land use in 1945 to 2000 found huge declines in agriculture and increases in forest cover on Saint Kitts, Nevis, Grenada and Barbados (Helmer et al. 2008). While not quantified, the extent of developed land on each island had also increased over this period. Similarly, the once heavily agricultural northern range in Trinidad is now mostly forested, due in part to the movement of labour from farming into oil and gas and service industries (Bekele 2004). On the south side of this range, vast lowland farms have been converted to commercial and residential development (personal observation). Changes like this have also been documented in parts of Cuba (Alvarez-Berrios et al. 2013), the Dominican Republic (Aide and Grau 2004) and Jamaica (Timms et al. 2013), and on island states outside the Caribbean (Tom Rudel, personal communication).

In all of the above cases, uplands have gained forest cover while development has substantially expanded on adjacent lowlands, especially near the coast. Yet, environmentalists and policymakers have been slow to acknowledge and respond to these trends. Their focus continues to be on improved protection of the uplands where, for pragmatic and historical reasons, they are best prepared to advance environmental objectives (Helmer et al. 2008; Walters and Hansen 2013). Meanwhile, the coast and lowlands are increasingly under siege by development that is for the most part little regulated. Tourism ranks among the most aggressive forms of this kind of development, although we shall see in the next chapter that its impacts are felt well beyond the coast.

CHAPTER SUMMARY

Human migration is a central feature of Caribbean societies and their history, yet its consequences for land use and forest change have been little studied. In Saint Lucia, outmigration to the United Kingdom and North America from the 1950s to 1970s contributed to reduced farming and increased upland reforestation. In the 1990s and early 2000s, a huge wave of farmland abandonment and ensuing reforestation swept across the island, triggered by the WTO rulings that sharply eroded export markets for bananas. These effects were compounded by growing shortages of agricultural labour as men and women departed the countryside to work in the fast-growing domestic construction, as well as tourism and related service sectors. Since the late 1980s, a kind of boomerang urbanization has occurred in which the return of earlier cohorts of outmigrants – who had departed rural areas to overseas urban centres in the 1950s, 1960s and 1970s – has fueled a residential home construction boom back home that is transforming extensive lowland agricultural lands and natural forests near the coast to peri-urban suburbs, while contributing to upland reforestation by drawing labour out of farming.

Understanding migration's specific causal role in land use and forest change is challenging, given it is linked in complex ways to changing labour and agricultural commodity markets. There is no straightforward way to parse-out the relative importance of these different influences, but it is nonetheless crucial that our causal story be at least clear about whether these different influences are generally contradictory or reinforcing in their effects. In this regard, the evidence is compelling that post-war outmigration significantly contributed to agricultural downsizing and reforestation, acting on its own in cases but more often in synergy with other causes by, for example, re-enforcing the causal effects of agricultural commodity price declines. This is an example of *conjunctural* causation or, more specifically, causal chains converging, the combined effect larger (but not strictly additive) than either one alone. Like the case of banana markets, the causal chains entailing migration may go far back and outward as, for example, when decisions to migrate from rural Saint Lucia are influenced by changes to UK or Canadian immigration policy, or when Saint

Lucians return home after four decades abroad. These are complicated stories, but causal-historical analysis can render them intelligible while revealing their explanatory significance.

CHAPTER 7

TROPICAL TOURISM
Blessing or Curse for Saint Lucia's Environment?

TOURISM HAS GRADUALLY OVERTAKEN AGRICULTURE AS THE PRIMARY economic sector throughout much of the Caribbean, and Saint Lucia is no exception. This has enormous consequences for the economies and environments of small islands (McElroy 2003). For some Caribbean islands, the agrarian landscapes that predominated for centuries have in only a few decades transformed into landscapes where tourism development now dominates (Weaver 1988, 1993a, 1993b; Koster and Seaborne 2003). Is Saint Lucia among this growing list of small island states now dominated by so-called tourism landscapes?

This chapter explores tourism's particular role in shaping Saint Lucia's rural landscape. Over the past three decades, farmland decline and upland reforestation have roughly correlated in time with the growth of tourism, yet tourism's influence on agriculture and landscape change is far from straightforward. It includes fairly direct, measurable effects like those associated with construction of infrastructure, but tourism's footprint on the landscape extends far beyond the immediate environment of its hotels and restaurants. These wider effects are mostly indirect, however, and cannot be readily separated from other causes already explored in this book. For example, farming has changed, not only because of export market challenges, but also because tourism has reshaped domestic farm produce and labour markets. Management of Crown and private estate lands has also shifted in response to tourism-related considerations.

TOURISM AND ENVIRONMENT IN THE CARIBBEAN

Tourism is the world's largest industry (McElroy 2003), and the Caribbean is among the most tourism-intensive regions (Weaver 1993a; Duval 2004a; Pattullo

2005). Modern mass tourism began in the 1950s with the advent of commercial jet flights, and growth in the sector surged in the 1960s as a number of Caribbean countries moving toward political independence actively encouraged tourism as a means to gain a degree of economic independence (Duval 2004b). Tourism visits to the region continued to grow strongly thereafter, driven by near continuous growth in the number and relative size of hotels built and cruise ships plying Caribbean waters (Bleasdale and Tapsell 2003; Wood 2004). By 2002 tourism was the single largest earner of foreign exchange for sixteen of thirty Caribbean countries (Meyer 2006).

The environmental impacts of tourism have become more apparent as the industry has grown, but surprisingly little research has been done on the subject (Buckley 2012). Impacts include the loss of productive farmland and destruction of natural habitats and species from built infrastructure and excessive visitor usage, plus degradation of coastal marine waters and habitats – like coral reefs – from sedimentation, excessive visitor usage, and hotel and cruise ship sewage (Wood 2004; Buckley 2011).

Since the late 1980s, support has grown for more sustainable ecotourism that seeks to minimize negative impacts on local communities and the environment, while better enabling benefits to accrue to local people and conservation initiatives (Butler 1991; Weaver 1993a; Stronza 2001; Conway 2004; Found 2004; Spencely 2008; Cousins et al. 2009; Buckley 2010, 2012). Ecotourism products range from physically demanding activities that target outdoor adventure enthusiasts (e.g., scuba diving, hiking) to softer experiences that facilitate access to places of interest for a wide audience (e.g., chartered bus and boat tours to unique natural or cultural-heritage sites) (Weaver 1993a, 2004).

Governments and the tourism industry in the Caribbean have increasingly embraced sustainable tourism, although often more in rhetoric than in practice (Weaver 1993a, 2004; Woodfield 1998; Bleasdale and Tapsell 2003, Wilkinson 2004). The Caribbean's environmental assets are its greatest appeal. Tourism development risks despoiling these assets, so it makes economic as well as environmental sense to protect them (Dixon et al. 2001; Duval and Wilkinson 2004; Buckley 2011). Nature and cultural heritage tourism also create opportunities to enhance and diversify tourism offerings (Weaver 1993a, 2004; Harrison 2007). Natural amenities like coral reefs, tropical forests, waterfalls and scenic vistas have great appeal, but tourists are also intrigued by the regions' agricultural history and are drawn to the unique aesthetic of its farmed landscapes (Found

2004; Meyer 2006). Saint Lucia has these tourism assets in abundance: first-class beaches, lush mountain valleys, waterfalls, hiking trails and several prime historical sites. In addition, the island possesses unique, marquee attractions, most notably the volcano and mineral baths at Sulphur Springs, as well as the nearby Pitons, a pair of stunning, cone-shaped mountains that rise up sharply more than 1,000 metres from the sea (France 1998; Nicholas and Thapa 2013).

LINKAGES BETWEEN TOURISM AND AGRICULTURE

Many Caribbean analysts, including Saint Lucia–born Nobel laureate and economist Arthur Lewis, have argued that development of non-agriculture industries like tourism should have spillover benefits for local farmers by creating new, more diversified markets for their products (Hope 1986a; Momsen 1998; Timms 2006). Yet tourism's expected boost for local agriculture has borne only modest fruit (Meyer 2006). In fact, tourism often simply outcompetes agriculture for scarce land and labour resources (Weaver 1988; Conway 2004).

Tourism infrastructure is commonly built on prime agricultural land, especially where these are found near the coast (Conway 2004), which inflates local land values, discouraging their use for agriculture, given its relatively low returns on capital (Meyer 2006). Tourism also draws labour out of agriculture by creating alternative employment that is relatively secure, well paid and higher in prestige compared to farming (Hope 1986b, 48; McElroy and de Albuquerque 1990; Stronza 2001; Torres and Momsen 2004; Harrison 2007). Finally, imports of food and beverage products to serve tourists may encourage a gradual shift in food preference by the local population, further undercutting local producers (Momsen 1998; Meyer 2006). These various effects are often magnified on smaller islands with heavy tourism development given their relatively scarce land and labour (Weaver 1988).

These trends have been countered by efforts to encourage sourcing of local farmed products by hotels and restaurants (Bleasdale and Tapsell 2003). Markets for street vendor food and locally processed food merchandise (rum, spices, hot sauce, etc.) are also lucrative and offer high value-added (Momsen 1998). Hotels have quality and supply requirements that are difficult for local producers to meet, and farmers often lack the financial capital, social network connections and management/business skills needed to upgrade their farm operations and engage effectively with hotel purchasers (Torres and Momsen 2004; Meyer 2006;

Timms 2006). Nonetheless, a combination of outreach to the tourism sector, farmer training and policy incentives (e.g., food import quotas) has increased local food sourcing in Saint Lucia and elsewhere (Momsen 1998; Conway 2004; Harrison 2007).

GROWTH AND GREENING OF TOURISM IN SAINT LUCIA

Modern tourism in Saint Lucia began in the 1960s with the advent of charter tours from the United Kingdom and construction of the first large hotels (Renard 2001). A significant boost came in 1970 with the onset of the Rodney Bay development, financed by the Caribbean Development Corporation. This major infrastructure project catalysed the transformation of the northern, Castries–Gros Islet corridor as Saint Lucia's primary tourism hub (Sahr 1998). By 1979 there were seven large hotels and a number of small ones on the island (World Bank 1979), making Saint Lucia a significant but still not leading Caribbean tourism destination (McElroy and de Albuquerque 1988; Koster and Seaborne 2003).

The Government of Saint Lucia had thus far taken a relatively hands-off approach to tourism development, dealing with individual proposals on a project-by-project basis (Wilkinson 2004). However, following a decade of only modest tourism growth in the 1980s and concern about the fate of the island's banana industry in light of unfolding WTO trade challenges, the government assumed a more direct and proactive role supporting growth of tourism. In 1994 the Saint Lucia Tourist Board – a statutory company tasked with tourism marketing – initiated a major international advertising campaign targeting niche markets, including honeymooners, nature tourism and business, and showcasing high-profile events like the annual Saint Lucia Jazz Festival (GOSL 1995; Meyer 2006). The Tourism Investment Act of 1996 provided tax holidays for investments and waived import duties on building materials, articles and equipment for tourism projects (GOSL 1996c; Mycoo 2005b). Major investments in tourism infrastructure were also made, including enhanced shopping amenities and upgrades to port docking facilities to enable access of more and bigger cruise ships to Castries Harbour. The centrepiece, La Place Carenage, opened in 1997, and a surge in cruise ship arrivals followed (figure 7.1).

An innovative component of Saint Lucia's tourism promotion is the Saint Lucia Heritage Tourism Programme, an attempt to promote eco-friendly tourism, one of the pillars of the country's tourism growth strategy (Renard

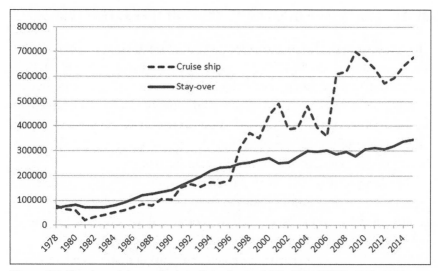

Figure 7.1. Tourism visitor arrivals in Saint Lucia, 1978–2015 (GOSL 1983, 1991c, 2002, 2011b, 2016)

2001; Duval and Wilkinson 2004). The programme was initiated in 1998 with financial support from Stabex, a fund of the European Commission created to facilitate the economic transition of Lomé countries affected negatively by liberalization of the EU banana market. Through this, the non-governmental Heritage Tourism Association of Saint Lucia was created with membership of owners of heritage site attractions and other agencies (National Trust, Saint Lucia Forestry Division, etc.). The association created a code of best practices, provided marketing support and coordinated the purchase of public liability insurance for its members, a key prerequisite for participation in the lucrative market for cruise ship visitors.

Until the 1990s, tourism development in Saint Lucia had mostly concentrated along the Castries–Gros Islet corridor, the north end of the island (Sahr 1988; figure 1.1). With its iconic Pitons and unique cultural-historical landscapes, the Soufrière area on the west coast had long been a tourist draw, but its development was constrained by rugged topography, limited port facilities and poor road access. This changed in the late 1980s with upgrading of the rugged west coast highway, which enabled easier vehicle access from Castries Harbour, a prerequisite for transport of day-trippers from visiting cruise ships. Soufrière thereafter became a premier destination for the rapidly growing cruise-ship tourist market and more attractive for hotel development (France 1988; GOSL 2002).

DIRECT LANDSCAPE IMPACTS OF TOURISM INFRASTRUCTURE

The construction of hotels and other tourism infrastructure (restaurants, gift shops, cruise ship facilities, etc.) in Saint Lucia has had a variety of environmental impacts, including destruction of natural habitats, loss of productive farmland, erosion of soils and coastlines, and pollution of coastal waters. With near-continuous growth in tourism since the late 1980s, the number of sites affected has multiplied, especially near the coast, where most development has occurred. In fact, managing the direct impacts of tourism is seen by many as the most pressing environmental challenge now facing the country. This represents a marked shift in priorities from less than two decades ago, when environmental concerns were fixated on agricultural activities and their mostly upland impacts (deforestation, soil erosion, pesticide pollution).

The Soufrière area, in particular, emerged as a major destination for tourism in Saint Lucia during the 1990s, following improvements in road access and the construction and refurbishment of several high-end resort hotels, including Anse Chastanet (1988), Jalousie (1992) and Ladera (1992), plus several smaller guesthouse villas. There are now five significant resort hotels and about a dozen small hotel villas, each located either adjacent to the shore or on nearby hillsides and ridgetops that possess unobstructed views of the Pitons. Some of these hotels were built on farmland, but others were built on rugged forested lands that had either never been farmed or were abandoned from farming long ago. Local habitat impacts have been significant, yet the cumulative direct footprint of these tourism developments in the Soufrière watershed is only a small fraction (app. 2 to 4 per cent) of the watershed landscape. The Mamiku watershed on the east coast has been even less directly impacted by tourism development, with only one small hotel and a botanical garden, with a combined area footprint of 1 to 2 per cent of the landscape.

That said, some of these developments have created significant environmental problems and controversies. Most notably, hotel and related developments within the UNESCO-designated Pitons Management Area, located adjacent to the Soufrière study watershed, have threatened the area's status as a World Heritage site (France 1998; Pattullo 2005; GOSL 2008b; Nicholas and Thapa 2013; UNESCO 2014). Also, erosion from building and road construction, plus pollution of nearby waters from inadequately treated hotel sewage, has contributed to the degradation of near-shore water quality and coral reefs (Begin et al. 2014). The extensive reefs in and around Soufrière Bay are environmentally significant and sustain significant dive-tourism (Conway and Lorah 1995).

TOURISM'S INFLUENCE ON FARM PRODUCTION

From the 1960s to 1990s Saint Lucian agriculture policy was preoccupied with those crops that formed the backbone of its exports: bananas especially, but also cocoa and copra. The promotion of farm diversification and so-called non-traditional crops were points of ongoing discussion, but this rarely commanded policy attention. In the 1980s there were modest attempts to diversify through initiatives like the Tree Crop Diversification Programme and Small Farmers Assistance Development Programme, but the intent of these was to promote crop diversification with export potential in mind (e.g., fruits and spices).

The potential to expand domestic agricultural markets by encouraging local sourcing from hotels and supermarkets had been discussed for some time by the government's officials and foreign economic advisers (e.g., World Bank 1983; 1988). Momsen (1986, cited in Conway 2004) found, from 1971 to 1985, modest increase in the amount of local food sourced by Saint Lucian hotels. Still, the issue did not garner serious policy attention until the early 1990s, when it became undeniable that the United Kingdom's protected market for bananas was coming undone. There followed a clear shift in focus towards more active promotion of tourism development and agricultural diversification and means by which to link the two (GOSL 1995).

The Ministry of Agriculture in collaboration with private sector and non-governmental organizations has applied a variety of strategies to address the challenge. It partnered with the Saint Lucia Hotel Association in 1994 to promote the "adopt a farmer" programme to facilitate direct marketing interactions between farmers and hotels (Momsen 1998; Meyer 2006). Beginning in 1998, it implemented the Rural Economic Diversification Project and Saint Lucia Rural Enterprise Initiative, which provided technical and capital assistance to farmers to enable their shift out of bananas to other crops (GOSL 1999; Timms 2006). A project of Oxfam International also provided support for production, marketing and sales arrangements through assistance to island farmer cooperatives, including the Belle Vue Coop, which serves members in the Soufrière area (Meyer 2006; GOSL 2007b).

Progress has been slow and plagued by ongoing challenges, notably inconsistencies of product quality and supply (GOSL 1999; Lowitt et al. 2015). None-theless, Timms (2006) identified a variety of marketing arrangements that had been established between local farmers and hotel purchasers in Saint Lucia. A significant, recent initiative entails the training and certification of farmers to strengthen links between them and local commercial buyers. Coordinated by the Saint Lucian grocery conglomerate Consolidated Foods Limited, with technical and training support of the Ministry of Agriculture, this programme has created a cadre of elite, smallholder farmers who serve as regular contracted suppliers to Consolidated Foods Limited stores and the hotel clients who buy through them. This initiative is at least partly responsible for the sizeable growth in sales of local vegetables to supermarkets and hotels since 2006 (GOSL 2014, app. tables 11–13).

The production of fresh vegetables is the most notable indicator of change here because these were not traditionally grown in abundance in Saint Lucia, yet tourists demand them. The national agricultural censuses reveal large increases from 1974 to 2007 in the percentage of farms growing vegetables (table 3.12; GOSL 1974, 1996a, 2007b; Saint Ville et al. 2016). My interviews of farmers confirm these trends for Soufrière and Mamiku and also reveal an increase in the cultivation of cut flowers for sale to the tourism market (table 3.9). In fact, improved local market opportunities for these products were among the few notable bright spots cited by some farmers in an otherwise dismal assessment of changes to agriculture in Saint Lucia.

Vegetable farming can be lucrative, but it is management intensive compared to most conventional crops and uses relatively less land. Vegetable farmers often employ irrigation and greenhouses to assist production, techniques rarely applied to conventional crops. Interviews suggest vegetable farming is concentrated on the largest and smallest farms. Specifically, eight of ten large farms (>10 acres, including five of the six estates) and eleven of fifteen small farms (<2 acres) grew mixed vegetables, but only four of seventeen mid-sized farms (2–10 acres) did so. On large farms, only a very small portion of total land was typically used for growing vegetables, but it often dominated land use on small farms. In the wider landscape, vegetables and ornamental plants occupy relatively little space compared to bananas, tree crops and even provisions. In fact, the cultivation of vegetables has in part contributed to a broader shift away from extensive hillside farming to more intensive farming on flatter, more accessible sites.

Interviews showed vegetable farming to be more commonly practised in

Soufrière (nineteen of twenty-nine) than Mamiku (four of fourteen), findings consistent with the 2007 National Agriculture Census (table 7.1). This difference appears to mainly reflect the relative proximity and tighter linkages between growers and local tourism and grocery store markets in Soufrière. For example, much of the fresh produce now grown on estates in Soufrière is consumed by tourists who eat in restaurants owned by those estates. In one notable case, a local hotelier acquired an underutilized agricultural estate and restored about half of its land to grow organic fruits, vegetables and ornamental plants for his two hotels. As of 2015, the estate employed twenty-five people and produced about 60 per cent of all fruits and vegetables, plus most of the ornamental plants consumed by the hotels. Similarly, long a prominent export crop of estates in Soufrière, cocoa beans are now often grown for local sale to tourists in the form of dry cocoa "sticks" (GOSL, 2002). Among smallholders in Soufrière, some were certified and sold produce to Consolidated Foods Limited (who, in turn, sell to hotels), but most sold their vegetables opportunistically to a variety of

Table 7.1. Percentage of farm holdings growing selected vegetables in Soufrière and Micoud Districts

	Soufrière District (n = 439)	Micoud District[a] (n = 1,968)	Saint Lucia (all districts) (n = 9,448)
Cucumbers	45.3	20.9	29.8
Peppers (sweet)	41.2	18.9	26.1
Tomatoes	46.9	15.3	23.4
Chives	33.5	19.4	20.2
Celery	46.0	10.2	19.3
Spinach	21.9	11.2	15.5
Parsley	43.3	5.2	14.4
Lettuce	28.5	7.5	13.5
Cabbages	37.6	5.5	11.1
Peppers (hot)	23.2	6.9	9.5
Carrots	28.2	2.4	7.0
Cut flowers	12.3	4.4	5.3

[a]Micoud District includes Mamiku watershed.

Source: National Agricultural Census (GOSL, 2007a, A41)

local venues, including hotels, supermarkets and weekend public markets in Soufrière and Castries.

ECOTOURISM AND THE "GREENING'" OF AGRICULTURAL ESTATES

"Tourism pays. There is no more money in agriculture."
—Anonymous estate owner, Soufrière (2007)

The agricultural estate sector in Saint Lucia has been in decline since the late 1800s when increasingly competitive export markets for their dominant export crop (sugar) drove many into bankruptcy while forcing others to radically diversify crop production. Coconuts (for copra), limes, cocoa and bananas have since figured prominently on the island's estates, but all of these have similarly struggled in the face of increasingly competitive markets in which the high costs of local production (especially labour) and limited economies of scale place Saint Lucian agriculture at great disadvantage (Welch 1993, 1996a, 1996b). Only a small fraction of the original estates have survived, and many today do so thanks largely to tourism.

No other region of the island has so many surviving estates as Soufrière, where almost half the land area still falls under ownership of a dozen estates. By contrast, Mamiku has one large active estate, which occupies about 30 per cent of the total area. Estate land use thus has a continued, dominant influence on the landscapes of both watersheds. Since the 1980s agriculture's footprint has been shrinking nationally, while tourism's has grown as more estates reconfigured themselves as tourism destinations. To do so, estates have pursued several, not necessarily mutually exclusive, strategies. One has been to capitalize on the large and growing number of day visitors, who mostly originate from cruise ships. For them, estates offer set-price package deals – brokered through tour operators who provide transport – that include a buffet lunch and usually some kind of natural or heritage tour on their property (table 7.2). Several estates have built restaurant facilities and gift shops for this purpose and made sizeable invest-ments in amenities that include botanical gardens, mineral baths, nature trails, outdoor adventure infrastructure and heritage restoration (e.g., refurbishing old sugar mills, plantation houses, etc.). Other estates, targeting the "stay-over" tourist market, have built hotels that range from modest to high-end/boutique accommodations, including bar-restaurants and other guest services, and are

Table 7.2. Tourism amenities/assets on agricultural estates in Soufriére and Mamiku with relative size ranked (+ = small; ++ = moderate; +++ = large)

Estate Name	Hotel	Restau- rant	Eco- tours	Botanic Garden	Heritage Tours	Food Gardens[a]	New Forest[b]
Mamiku		+	+	+++	+	+	+++
Ruby	+	++				++	++
Rabot	++	+++	+	++	++	++	+
Coubaril		++	+++	+	++	++	++
Soufriére		++	+	+++	++	++	+++
Emerald	+++	+++		++		+++	+
Fond Doux	+	++		+	++	++	++
La Haut	++	++		+	+	+	++
Stonefield	++	++		++	+	++	++

[a]"Food gardens" are where estate-farmed produce is consumed by tourists in estate-owned restaurant or hotel.

[b]"New forest" is where former agricultural lands on the estate have returned to forest because of farm abandonment or intentional reforestation.

Source: Based on interviews and field observations made by author in 2015.

typically situated within lush gardens or natural surroundings on the estate.

For many estates, tourism is a profitable alternative to conventional agriculture, given the weak export markets and given that tourist visits are relatively structured, predictable and entail better returns on both land and labour. As described in chapter 6, the relatively high cost of farm labour has contributed to agricultural decline in Saint Lucia, yet many estate workers who would otherwise have been let go have been kept on to perform the new tasks of landscaping, food gardening and hotel/restaurant service associated with tourism. In addition, estates save costs by growing much of the fresh produce consumed in their restaurants on their own lands.

These various tourism-related infrastructures and amenities are both often prominent in the landscape and the focal points of human activity, but in most cases they still occupy only a small fraction of an estate's total land area. In terms of the wider landscape, every estate examined has shown a net gain in the amount of land under forest since the 1980s (table 7.2). In fact, with few exceptions estate lands in both Soufrière and Mamiku are now dominated by natural forest, agroforest or some mixture of the two. Various factors have contributed to this, but every estate that has reconfigured as a tourism destination now promotes itself in terms of its natural beauty and eco-friendliness. As such, estates now have a strong incentive to protect the forested landscapes they have, regardless of their causal origins.

PROTECTING FORESTS ON PUBLIC LANDS FOR TOURISM

The more Saint Lucia embraces tourism, the stronger grows the dilemma that unbridled tourism growth threatens to undermine the natural resource base upon which the long-term viability of the industry depends. The most obvious effects are concentrated along the coast. The government's influence controlling land use and mitigating impacts there has been patchy but overall fairly weak. While political will is often lacking, well-intentioned efforts have been hamstrung by the prevalence of private landownership of most coastal lands and the long-felt absence of a comprehensive land use policy that could enable more rational planning and development.

The Government of Saint Lucia has played a more decisive role with environmental protection of uplands, where most of the country's public lands exist within a network of national forest reserves. The Forestry Division has played the lead role here and has supported tourism to further its goals of protecting forests and wildlife. Efforts to encourage public access through development of trails in and guided walks through the rain forest were begun in the late 1970s and expanded in the mid-1980s, as part of a national campaign to raise awareness and educate Saint Lucians about the value of the environment and critical conservation issues like deforestation and the status of the endangered Saint Lucian parrot (*Amazona versicolor*), the national bird (Christian et al. 1996). It was a logical step from this to supporting tourism by enhancing visitor amenities and services like improved trails, educational signage and guided hikes through the National Forest Reserves, thereby linking the health of the tourism sector to that of the forest reserves.

The Forestry Division established a second key link between tourism and forest health by helping to convince the wider Saint Lucia government that the island's fresh water supplies were dependent on protecting watersheds, especially in the rugged mountains. Shortages of fresh water during the dry season have posed a looming threat to normal operation of the tourism industry, a risk likely to increase as tourism continues to grow and weather anomalies associated with climate change increase. Concern about this has motivated the government to use its regulatory authority and financial resources to acquire private lands in strategic locations (e.g., steep slopes, proximate to water sources, etc.) to expand the land area under protected forest. For example, in the mid-1990s about 100 acres of steeply sloped uplands around Mount Tabac and a smaller property near the community of Fond Saint Jacques (both in Soufrière) were secured and protected in this way. The Crown has legal right to acquire private lands that have been abandoned and unclaimed for long periods. Where there is an identifiable owner, expropriation is permissible in the public interest, but the Crown is required by law to provide fair compensation in the form of agreed-upon purchase price or land swap. Acquisition efforts like this are made easier by recent declines in agriculture, because owners are less likely to be farming these lands (Walters and Hansen 2013). Still, soaring costs of real estate in Saint Lucia have limited the government's ambitions in this regard.

Public lands have also for the most part become better protected in recent years. Significant added investment and professionalization of the Forestry Division in the 1980s and early 1990s, aided by a grant from the Canadian International Development Agency, led to strengthened monitoring and enforcement of penalties for illegal farming and negotiated settlements to phase out use of the area by squatters. Both Forestry Division staff and local farmers agree that agricultural encroachment into reserves, once widespread, has been eliminated, with the exception of some ganja growing.

TOURISM EMPLOYMENT AND AGRICULTURAL DECLINE

Finally, the rise of tourism and fall of agriculture have profoundly changed Saint Lucia's labour market, which has, in turn, affected its landscapes. This issue was discussed in depth in chapter 6 (see also table 3.8). In summary, employment opportunities related to tourism are increasingly abundant and include a range of services in hospitality, transportation, landscaping, security, management, technology support, construction and maintenance. Work in tourism is typically viewed by educated and uneducated Saint Lucians alike as superior to work in agriculture because it is physically less demanding and wages are usually better or are at least more predictable. Agricultural labour is also widely perceived as being lower in status. Tourism employment has thus drawn many out of the agricultural labour force, contributing to labour shortages, farmland abandonment and reforestation.

IS SAINT LUCIA'S LANDSCAPE A "TOURISM LANDSCAPE"?

Weaver's (1988) seminal study of tourism's impact on the economy of Antigua shows an entire island transformed in three decades from a landscape dominated by plantation agriculture to one dominated by tourism:

> The growth of tourism in Antigua and many other destinations did not in itself cause the demise of agriculture. Rather, its decline may be attributed largely to the emergence of tourism as a viable alternative to a chronically unstable agricultural sector, prompting the lateral transfer of investment capital by local and expatriate plantation interests from agriculture to tourism. In this process, coastal plantations were often converted into estate housing developments, while their "great houses" were frequently renovated and reopened as hotels (Weaver 1988, 324).

Similar development trajectories have since been documented elsewhere in the Caribbean (McElroy and Albuquerque 1990; Weaver 1993b; Koster and Seaborne 2003). There are some clear parallels in Saint Lucia, notably the near-complete conversion of estate lands to tourism, commercial and residential infrastructure along the northern, Castries–Gros Islet corridor. Similar changes are at least partially underway on estate lands in Soufrière and Mamiku. Yet while tourism's significance to the economy of Saint Lucia is now enormous, isolating its specific influence on the landscape is difficult because effects are often indirect and are confounded by other factors.

This complexity is most evident as regards the diverse interactions between tourism, agriculture and land use change. Saint Lucia's upland landscape is more heavily forested today than it has been for at least seventy years (Walters and Hansen 2013). This profound change reflects to a large degree the moribund state of conventional, export-oriented agriculture, in particular the collapse of the export banana market in the late 1990s following a series of WTO rulings that eroded the West Indies' privileged market access to the United Kingdom. At first glance these developments seem unrelated to tourism, yet strong employment growth in tourism has without doubt accelerated agriculture's overall decline by contributing to farm labour scarcity. At the same time, tourism has stimulated growth in the markets for various niche farm products, including fresh fruits and vegetables, cocoa and cut flowers, and so contributes to that sector's ongoing viability. Following a lengthy period of downsizing, the agriculture sector appears overall to be stabilizing and even shows signs of renewed growth of some conventional crops like cocoa, copra and provisions, driven by demand growth in both export and domestic markets (figure 3.1; tables 3.9 and 3.11). While historically diminished, sizeable areas of the landscape continue to be shaped primarily by agriculture. Saint Lucia's landscape is thus not (or at least not yet) a fully transformed tourism landscape of the kind described by Weaver (1998; 1993b).

The causal relationship between tourism development and forest conservation is also difficult to untangle (cf., Buckley 2012). The literature makes frequent claims of there being a causal link between ecotourism and increased protected areas on both private and public lands (Buckley 2010, 2011), but many of the forests supposedly protected for tourism would likely still be conserved in its absence. For example, the collapse of cocoa farming and widespread reforestation in northern Trinidad long preceded its redevelopment as an ecotourism destination (Harrison 2007). That said, even if tourism does not explain why particular forests have been conserved, findings here suggest it can provide potent economic incentive and political justification for continuing to protect such forests into the future (Weaver 1993a, 2004).

CHAPTER SUMMARY

Saint Lucia's economy has transitioned since the late 1960s from predominantly agricultural to increasingly tourism-dominated. Five primary causal interactions were found between tourism development and landscape change. First, construction of tourism infrastructure has led to alteration and loss of forested and agricultural lands, especially near the coast. Second, growing demand for fresh produce from hotels and restaurants has encouraged smallholder and estate farmers to shift cultivation from conventional crops to more intensively farmed vegetables and ornamentals. Third, a number of surviving agricultural estates have transformed themselves into eco-friendly tourist attractions by restoring and protecting natural forests and cultural heritage assets on their properties. Fourth, government has enhanced forest lands acquisition and protection to support ecotourism and secure fresh water supplies to sustain ongoing tourism development. Finally, tourism-related employment has drawn labour out of farming, accelerating agricultural decline and reforestation. Tourism development and impacts are concentrated near the coast, yet it has contributed to net reforestation and protection of forests in the island's uplands.

The existence of such diverse causal interactions illustrates the complexity and challenge of doing explanatory, human-environment research in a fast-changing, developing society. For example, we can now see how what began as a fairly straightforward causal history linking local farmland abandonment to global trade policy is, in fact, a more complicated story, one entailing causal influences associated with human migration, changing domestic labour markets and the rise of tourism and related services industries. In short, our causal history has shifted from single causal chains, to multiple converging causal chains, to an increasingly complex, almost web-like causal story. Yet, amid this complexity, there remains considerable clarity and precision about the character and significance of these different causes. This is because the research investigation never lost sight of the primary object of explanation – changes in Saint Lucia's forests – and by using ACE it sought throughout to establish clear causal histories of these changes by following different causal chains backward and outward. It is doubtful that such clear, comprehensive explanations would have been attained using either a political ecology approach, which prioritizes structural-political causes, or a SES approach, which prioritizes systemic over contingent causes. In searching for causes, we need to be clear about what is to be explained, but otherwise cast our investigative net widely and always remain open to surprise and learning the unexpected.

THE GREENING OF SAINT LUCIA

In the Lesser Antilles, there is nothing that cannot be grown – but there is nothing that cannot be grown more cheaply somewhere else.
—Barbara Welch (1996b, 322); also cited in Wiley (2008).

THE LANDMARK PUBLICATION OUR COMMON FUTURE (WCED 1987) and the United Nations–Rio "Earth Summit" (UNSD 1992) established sustainable development as a core principle of international cooperation and development. Nation states around the world have since grappled with various strategies to reconcile economic growth with environmental conservation. This has for the most part proven to be a difficult task, and unqualified successes – particularly in the developing world – are seemingly few and far between. Saint Lucia's experience achieving major environmental gains during a period of significant economic development is thus important, not only for the country itself but also because it adds to our wider understanding of sustainable development and suggests potential pathways for countries to reach it. Largely overlooked or underappreciated by scholars, activists and policy makers, the widespread reforestation of the countryside – the greening of Saint Lucia – is arguably among the most significant events in the island's post-war history.

Nonetheless, Saint Lucia's greening requires additional scrutiny to assess its proper significance. First, we need to consider whether Saint Lucia's recent greening – its "forest transition" – is likely to last, given the island has experienced cycles of agricultural expansion and decline multiple times before. This discussion will link key findings emerging from chapters 2 and 4 on agriculture history with analysis of recent economic and social change (chapters 5, 6 and 7). Also, Saint Lucia's experience will be compared with other islands in the Caribbean, and an attempt will be made to draw generalizations about land use and forest change across the region. Second, we need to ask whether and in what ways the greening of Saint Lucia truly represents an environment and development success story. To do this, I will relate major findings from the watershed vegetation and land use analysis in chapter 3 to key threads of analysis that emerged in later chapters. Lastly, I revisit the issue of research methodology and review how this case study illustrates the advantages of using ACE as an alternative to other approaches commonly used in human-environment research. Before turning to these final three topics, however, it is worth recapping the study's main findings and relating these to the wider literature on forest transitions.

FOREST TRANSITIONS IN SAINT LUCIA AND ELSEWHERE

The most consequential change in recent decades to Saint Lucia's rural environment has been widespread reforestation of lands abandoned from farming. This change has occurred for the most part irrespective of the type of land tenure, but it is especially commonplace on lands with steeper slopes and further from roads. Marginal lands like these have been under abandonment since the 1960s (in some cases to be later reclaimed for farming), but an especially large wave of abandonment swept the island from the mid-1990s to early 2000s because of price uncertainties for exportable bananas, which were related to the erosion of preferential market access to the United Kingdom due to a series of WTO trade challenges. The effects on land abandonment of this and other commodity market–related challenges have been reinforced by wider demographic and economic changes. Specifically, many subsistence-focused farms in the countryside were abandoned in the 1960s/1970s (and probably earlier), in response to the gradual shift to smaller family sizes, plus large outmigrations of younger adults to the United Kingdom, United States and Canada. More recently, the movement of labour from farming to fast-growing construction, tourism and services sectors has sapped the agricultural sector of cheap labour, accelerating land abandonment. One major source of alternative employment for farmers has been an island-wide, residential construction boom caused by remittances from abroad and a protracted wave of return migrants, many themselves former farmers. The fast growth of tourism since the early 1990s has also drawn much labour out of farming and created economic incentive and political support for protecting more forests on both private estates and public lands to sustain ecotourism and freshwater supplies.

These findings are broadly consistent with studies of forest transitions elsewhere in the global south (Rudel et al. 2005). In particular, they support propositions about post-agrarian transitions being linked to societal modernization, notably the significance of rural-to-urban migration and globalization of agricultural commodity markets as causes of marginal farmland abandonment and reforestation (Mather and Needle 1998; Rudel 1998; Aide et al. 2013). While microeconomic considerations were clearly at play in the decisions of many individual land users to downsize cultivation and/or invest in the protection/restoration of forests on former agricultural land, it is difficult to argue that these decisions were motivated primarily as a response to the perceived scarcity of forest resources per se. Rather, for the most part land users were responding to challenging circumstances they faced as agriculturalists and to competing economic opportunities presented off farm. That many now extol the value of forests for watershed protection and ecotourism should not distract from the fact that most recovering and protected forests would still be there regardless of these considerations. That conservation and commodification of forests today coexist under a forest transition scenario is also unsurprising (Robbins and Fraser 2003).

In many respects, these findings are not surprising, given that West Indian economies have been inextricably linked to the international agricultural trade for several centuries and its people are among the world's most migratory (Richardson 1992). In fact, the Caribbean has the highest rate of net reforestation among the world's tropical regions in recent decades, and Saint Lucia's experience is not entirely unique (Atkinson and Marin-Spiotta 2015; Keenan et al. 2015; van Andel et al. 2016). The Caribbean island of Puerto Rico may well be the first tropical state to have ever experienced a forest transition. Widespread declines in farming and their replacement by forests began there in the 1940s, and these changes were linked to massive outmigration to the United States (Rudel et al. 2000; Lopez et al. 2001; Grau et al. 2003). Like Saint Lucia, urbanization and suburban expansion have in recent years slowed and in places reversed this reforestation trend (Pares-Ramos et al. 2008; Alvarez-Berrios et al. 2013).

Little is known about the causal dynamics of Caribbean forest transitions outside of Puerto Rico and Saint Lucia, but there are parallels elsewhere. Specifically, a study comparing land use in 1945 to 2000 found huge declines in agriculture and increases in forest cover on Saint Kitts, Nevis, Grenada and Barbados (Helmer et al. 2008). The extent of developed (built) land on each island had also increased dramatically over this period. Likewise, the once heavily agricultural northern range in Trinidad is now mostly forested in part due to the movement of labour from farming into oil and gas and service industries (Bekele 2004). On the south side of this range, extensive lowland farms have also been converted into vast residential and commercial developments (personal observation). Changes like this have also been documented in Antigua (Weaver 1988) and parts of Cuba (Alvarez-Berrios et al. 2013), the Dominican Republic (Aide and Grau 2004) and Jamaica (Timms et al. 2013; Newman et al. 2014, 2018).

One challenge comparing islands across the Caribbean is that data are patchy and inconsistent and analyses rarely integrate biophysical assessments of forest change with social scientific analysis of its causes (Alvarez-Berrios et al. 2013). In this regard, only Puerto Rico and Saint Lucia have been studied in depth and on a time frame spanning the entire post-war period. Other detailed analysis, like Newman et al. (2014, 2018), are limited to subnational districts and so are of limited value for generalizing about entire countries/islands. Likewise, Helmer et al.'s (2008) study is among the few that have examined post-war land cover change on small island states in the Lesser Antilles (Grenada, Barbados, Saint Kitts and Nevis), but their focus was mapping land cover change, not understanding its causes.

A second challenge reflects the uniqueness of each island's geography and history. For example, given Puerto Rico's close proximity and distinct political-economic relationship to the United States, is that island's forest transition likely to be comparable to other Caribbean islands? Neighboring islands of similar size – for example, Saint Lucia, Barbados and Martinique – have vastly different economies and terrain, not to mention cultural and political histories. As this study showed, even two watersheds on the same small island (about 10 km apart) differed in their particular trajectories of land use and forest cover change: Soufrière experienced a fairly steady downward trend in farming and increase in forest cover, whereas Mamiku had bouts of agricultural expansion and contraction (of bananas) that delayed its eventual reforestation.

Over the longer term, however, there has been a clear convergence in the trajectories of land use and forests across watersheds within Saint Lucia and across islands throughout much of the Caribbean. Agriculture, long the dominant economic sector and land use across the region, has collapsed or is waning on almost every island for which published data are available. Forests are usually returning in its place, although residential and urban development are displacing both, especially along the coasts and where lands are relatively flat (Grau et al. 2003; Helmer et al. 2008; Alvarez-Berrios et al. 2013; Atkinson and Marin-Spiotta 2015). The notable exception to these trends is Haiti, where high population growth, chronic underdevelopment and forest loss continue (Keenan et al. 2015).

Haiti's exceptionalism provides a sharp contrast to those aspects of the island Caribbean that are widely shared and no doubt key to understanding the region's widespread forest resurgence. Most notable among these is the region's high rates of outmigration that in part reflect its deep colonial history and connectedness to the wider world in terms of the region's economic mainstays: export-oriented agriculture and (more recently) tourism. In fact, the first published account of what appears (in hindsight) to constitute the Lesser Antilles earliest forest transition was by Lowenthal and Comitas (1962), who documented widespread agricultural decline and reforestation on the island of Montserrat during the 1950s, the direct result of an especially massive (in relative terms) outmigration event to the United Kingdom. As noted, massive, post-war outmigration was central to explaining Puerto Rico's early forest transition (Rudel et al. 2000). Significant outmigrations also occurred during the early post-war period from many other Caribbean islands, including Saint Lucia, but these were smaller as a proportion of overall population, so their effects on the landscape were not so dramatic. Substantial outmigration from many Caribbean islands continued through the 1970s and 1980s to foreign destinations and also (and increasingly) from rural to urban destinations within the Caribbean as the region developed and diversified into construction, manufacturing and service sectors, especially tourism.

The geography of forest transitions in the Caribbean is thus profoundly tied to the region's relatively deep integration in the global economy of trade in agricultural commodities and movement of people. Local geographic characteristics of island size and topography are also key to understanding how forest transitions have unfolded on particular islands. The limited "economies of scale" in Caribbean agriculture have essentially condemned it to marginal status as agro-industries relentlessly consolidate and commodity markets continuously expand their global trade reach. Relatively large islands (Jamaica, Hispaniola, Cuba) and topographically varied islands (Grenada, Saint Lucia, Saint Vincent, etc.) have had more diverse agricultural economies and patterns of landownership, so forest transitions have tended to unfold more gradually and patchily in the landscape, with marginal farmlands (on steep slopes, far from roads, etc.) the first to be abandoned and reforested (Rudel et al. 2000; Helmer et al. 2008; Newman et al. 2014).

Newman et al. (2018) also make an important observation regarding the persistence of small farms in Jamaican Cockpit country that is probably relevant to other Caribbean islands. Specifically, they note that many farmers practise a "dual commuter existence", whereby farming is done part-time or seasonally in concert with other, often urban-based employment. Caribbean labour is well known for its occupational multiplicity (Carnegie 1982; Momsen 1986), but the key point here is that the small size of most islands enables people who own land to commute comfortably as needed between town and rural farm. Where town-based employment is unpredictable or seasonal, as it is in tourism for example, such farming may be practical and persist despite wider economic forces that discourage it. It also suggests there exists a reserve pool of labour that could, given the right conditions, return to farming in a more serious way and, by doing so, slow or even reverse larger trends of reforestation.

In fact, it is notable that Saint Lucia's forest transition probably began over fifty years ago but was interrupted – not once, but twice – as bananas took hold and spread widely under the unique circumstances of a highly protected export market, an estate farm sector in decline and a smallholder sector in ascendency. Agriculture in Saint Lucia has been characterized over three centuries by recurring bouts of agricultural expansion and associated deforestation followed by agricultural decline and subsequent reforestation. What then is the likelihood that Saint Lucia's recent forest transition will last? To shed light on this, we need to clarify the causes of past agricultural expansions and declines and compare these with recent experience.

WILL SAINT LUCIA'S FOREST TRANSITION LAST?

The Caribbean islands of the Lesser Antilles, including Saint Lucia, are in key respects blessed from an agricultural standpoint. Geologically young, fertile soils and varied geography and microclimates combine with a typically stable, warm and wet climate to provide near-ideal growing conditions for a rich variety of crops, the most valuable of which (sugar cane, cocoa, coffee, nutmeg, limes, coconuts, bananas) cannot be grown outside the tropics. While geo-strategic considerations had a decisive influence on European behavior towards these islands, their social and economic development over three centuries was driven largely by agricultural interests founded on the production of commodities destined for export back to imperial states of Europe. This trade depended on advances in maritime shipping and developed in tandem with colonial interests and loyalties. Thus, produce of French-owned colonies was mostly destined to markets in France; produce from the British West Indies to England, etc. As such, development of key agricultural industries in Saint Lucia and elsewhere in the British West Indies usually occurred with direct support of the British Crown and, most importantly, under the guise of protected export market arrangements with the United Kingdom.

The problem is that these various supports and protections were often costly to Britain and fostered agricultural industries in the West Indies that were fragile in the face of external shocks and growing external competition. This competition grew increasingly intense as industries for tropical agricultural commodities expanded and consolidated on the larger Caribbean islands (Trinidad, Hispaniola, Cuba) and then into continental territories of Latin America, Africa and Southeast Asia. Challenges were especially acute for small-island nations like Saint Lucia, where agricultural development is typically constrained by limited productive land, extreme weather events, geographic isolation from markets and scarcity of labour, capital and technology (McElroy and de Albuquerque 1990; Briguglio 1995).

Nonetheless, constraints facing small islands are not necessarily fixed. For example, human toil and technology enable biophysical constraints to be stretched or exceeded for periods under favourable market and policy conditions. The extraordinary production of bananas in the 1960s and late 1980s/ early 1990s strikingly illustrates this. Yet agriculture at the margins rarely persists: low productivity, high production costs and environmental degradation increase its vulnerability to the effects of events like severe storms, disease outbreaks or downturns in market price. At such times, the unsustainability of marginal farm operations is laid bare: no longer profitable and possibly facing bankruptcy, they must downsize or abandon farming altogether.

There is little governments or other actors can do to forestall agricultural decline in cases like this where external shocks are severe and lasting in their effects. However, where shocks are short lived (e.g., a severe weather event, short-term market shock, manageable pest outbreak), strategic investments in industry recovery or adaptation may play a decisive role restoring it to viability. For example, UK aid funding and active intervention from governments and banana growers' associations were key to restoring the Windward Island banana industry following its decline in the late 1960s (Romalis 1975; Grossman 1994). Yet such external investments can be costly and run the risk of further sowing the seeds of inevitable decline by, for example, institutionalizing support for otherwise unsustainable farm operations. This is arguably what happened during the respective banana booms of the mid-1960s and late 1980s, when banana growers' associations established costly financial and infrastructure supports that encouraged farmers to clear and cultivate lands that were recognized at the time as exceedingly marginal (Welch 1993; Grossman 2003; Moberg 2008). In this regard, geographer Barbara Welch's (1968, 234) observations forty-five years ago of the banana industry on neighboring Dominica were prescient:

> Given the manifold physical disabilities of the Dominican terrain, the area of land that could be termed "cultivable" may fluctuate widely and rapidly. Ten years ago, with high banana prices, peasant farmers would fairly readily exploit holdings up to seven miles from a road, and even in some cases, ten miles or more. Now, holdings more than two or three miles from the road are rather marginal. If the preferential tariff accorded by Britain to Commonwealth bananas were removed it is likely that the area of economically cultivable land would be drastically reduced – possibly to an extent where the organization of the industry collapsed and export ceased to be worthwhile.

Drawing from chapters 2 and 4, I have summarized major agricultural declines in Saint Lucia and their causes through history in table 8.1. Notably, early agricultural declines were usually caused by geopolitical or weather-related events. These events were often devastating to the predominant plantation economies of the day and had seismic social and demographic consequences for the overall country (Harmsen et al. 2014). While detailed observations are unavailable, the effects on the rural landscape were surely dramatic in terms of alternating bouts of land clearing, followed by widespread abandonment, reforestation and then land clearing again.

By contrast, since the late 1880s agricultural declines were most often caused by commodity market changes reflecting reduced market protections, increased competition from other sources or declining demand (table 8.1). For example, the relative importance of different causes of the late 1800s sugar crisis – reduced

Table 8.1. Major agricultural declines in Saint Lucia and their causes

Dates	Key Features of Decline	Primary Causes of Decline
1600s	Amerindian gardens abandoned	Indigenous populations decimated by disease and conflict with Europeans
1780	Widespread damage and abandonment of plantations (cocoa, coffee, cotton, sugar)	Struck by severe hurricane
1792–1798	Exodus of French planters and abandonment of many estates	Slave revolts and "Brigands Wars" inspired by the French Revolution; colonial-military conflict
1831–1840s	Widespread downsizing, sale and abandonment of estates	Struck by hurricane (1831); post-emancipation labour shortages
1880s–1890s	Marginal sugar estates reduce production, are abandoned outright, or sold off to smallholders	Collapse of sugar export prices caused by surge in cane and beet sugar production elsewhere
1930s	Production of sugar ceased by marginal estates, many of which are abandoned; sugar production reduced in remaining estates	Depression-driven decline in sugar export prices; labour strife among sugar workers
1957–1963	Collapse of remaining sugar industry	Weak export prices; labour strife
1950s–1970s	Widespread decline in subsistence cultivation ("provisions" gardens)	Declining birth rates plus increased outmigration of young adults to United Kingdom, North America, etc.
1968–1970	Sharp drop in banana production from estates and smallholders	Cost of farm inputs raised by weakening currency, causing declines in quality and production; growing market competition from producers elsewhere
1996–2000	Collapse of dominant, smallholder banana industry; widespread farm abandonment in uplands	Protected UK market for banana exports eroded by WTO ruling; decline exacerbated by farm labour migration to services sector

market protection, increased production of cane from competitors, subsidies to European beet sugar, etc. – was vigorously debated at the time (see Cox 1897; "Jamaica's Sugar Industry: Threatened with Ruin by the Bounty System", *New York Times*, 17 January 1897; WIRC 1897; Brassey 1898). Cox (1897) is especially convincing in having argued that, absent politically and economically acceptable levels of colonial intervention, the decline of sugar on the islands of the West Indies was inevitable, given competitive disadvantages related to their small size, high labour costs and geographical constraints on production and distribution. The parallels here with the recent banana collapse are striking. Agricultural sectors less prominent than sugar or bananas have also struggled with high-cost domestic production in the face of external market competition. For example, Saint Lucia's coconut industry generated significant exports of copra and coconut oil for nearly a century before entering a period of chronic decline. This decline appears to have begun with damages caused by Hurricane Allen in 1980, but it has since continued because of low export market prices compounded by domestic competition for land and labour from the more lucrative banana, construction and tourism sectors.

As described in chapter 5, researchers and policymakers have for over a century lamented the stagnation of agriculture and underutilization of land across the West Indies (Cox 1897; WIRC 1897; Beckford 1966, 1969; Welch 1968, 1996a; Lowenthal 1972; Romalis 1975; Rubenstein 1975; Rojas 1984; Brierley 1985a, 1987, 1992; Besson and Momsen 1987; Walters 2012b; Harmsen et al. 2014). For example, early twentieth century studies of the cocoa and coconut industries in Trinidad document how dramatic expansion into increasingly marginal lands occurred under favourable market conditions, only to be followed by rapid contraction back onto only the most optimal lands when market conditions turned sour (James 1926; Shepard 1927).

History thus shows that Saint Lucian agriculture has been down before but always came back. Is the current agricultural downturn likely to be any different? Prediction is fraught with difficulty, yet there are good reasons to believe that this time is indeed different. In a nutshell, this is because earlier agricultural declines always left in their wake conditions that created potential for a return to growth, notably an abundance of underutilized land and a sizeable labour force with few alternatives for employment outside of agriculture. By contrast, commodity market challenges that caused the most recent collapse occurred alongside demographic, cultural and structural-economic changes that are all inimical to future agriculture expansion. The fall of bananas is indicative of not just another agricultural downturn but rather constitutes a broader, post-agrarian transition with accompanying shifts from farms to forests and other land uses.

This transition reflects, first, a long-term downward trend in birth rates and family size that has substantially reduced the need for subsistence-oriented farming. Hobby gardening is common, and the cultivation of vegetables, fruit and provisions for cash sale remains important. Unlike the past, when it was commonplace for adults to devote sizeable effort to growing food for their families, few do so today. Second, broad structural shifts in employment towards a services-dominated economy (especially in tourism and construction) have since the early 1990s sapped the farming sector of labour, a trend that reinforces a shift in cultural attitudes that discourages farming as an occupation. Finally, the availability of potentially farmable land has been shrinking even as agriculture has declined because of widespread conversion of prime agricultural lands to residential subdivisions and increased protection of lands for conservation purposes by both government and the private sector to support ecotourism, watershed protection and to satisfy international commitments on climate change and biodiversity preservation (Walters and Hansen 2013).

Circumstances could, however, change in ways that favour reinvestment in Saint Lucian agriculture. For example, export prices for cocoa, coconut oil or bananas could surge or tourism might collapse in response to natural, economic or geopolitical events, thereby encouraging a return of labour to farming. One such scenario is that the United Kingdom exiting from the European Union under Brexit might lead to restructuring of trade policies in a way that benefits West Indian agricultural producers. It seems unlikely, however, that Brexit would prompt a return to preferential trade arrangements between the United Kingdom and its former colonies. By leaving the European Union, the United Kingdom may free itself of certain legal requirements involving liberalized trade under the European Common Market, but the WTO already ruled that such policies run afoul of the GATT, and it seems unlikely that the United Kingdom would spoil for yet another trade fight on this front, given all the trade-related troubles likely to unfold with Brexit.

Data nonetheless suggest that the decades-long trend of agricultural decline and reforestation has stalled and may even show signs of limited recovery with increasing production of cocoa, fresh fruits, vegetables and cut flowers (figure 3.1). Agricultural sectors that are showing signs of recovery currently serve mostly niche markets and so, compared to crops like sugar or bananas that so dominated the country's economy and rural landscape, are relatively small in scale of production. The upward mobility and changing expectations of Saint Lucians also suggests they are more likely to respond to an employment crisis in the services sector by out-migrating or increasing their dependence on remittance income than by going back to farming.

Still, any predictions about the future are tentative, and arguments to the effect of "this time it really *is* different", will remain suspect until further evidence (and more time) confirms them. The notion of a "forest transition" is appealing to many because it conveys a sense that modernization and economic development are not only not at odds with environmental conservation but may be beneficial to it (Robbins and Fraser 2003). Central to this conception of the forest transition is the assumption that the turnaround in forest cover (from net loss to gain) is relatively permanent. Saint Lucia's history of recurring bouts of deforestation and reforestation suggests that such an assumption may be unwarranted.

IS THE GREENING OF SAINT LUCIA AN ENVIRONMENTAL SUCCESS STORY?

Assuming it does last, the significance of Saint Lucia's forest transition still needs to be assessed in light of associated wider changes in land use both within and outside Saint Lucia. For one, the infrastructure and activities associated with tourism is concentrated and increasingly impacts terrestrial and marine environments near the coast. Equally important is the fast-growing footprint of residential sprawl, which is also concentrated in the lowlands and near the coast (Walters 2016a, 2016b). These developments have had some indirect benefit for upland forests by drawing labour out of farming and incentivizing their protection for ecotourism and water supply, but as the following examples illustrate, environmental impacts near the coast are growing and increasingly serious.

The Pitons Management Area on the west coast near Soufrière is renowned for its stunning beauty and geologic uniqueness. The iconic landscape created by the breathtaking twin pillars of the two pitons is profiled in most visual advertising for the island. Despite its acknowledged importance, the management area is currently at risk of losing its World Heritage status designation because of continued tourism development and residential construction in and around the site (Nicholas and Thapa 2013; UNESCO 2014).

The marine environment adjacent and nearby the Piton Management Area is also at risk. Waters here include some of the finest coral reefs in Saint Lucia, and their proximity to shore have made this area the premier dive site on the island. These reefs have been significantly degraded in recent years, however, from the combined impacts of water pollution from inadequately treated sewage; coral bleaching and algal infestations due to ocean warming events; and sedimentation associated with nearby road building for residential and tourism expansion (Begin et al. 2014).

On Saint Lucia's east coast, several endangered animal species are at growing risk of extinction because of coastal development. Among these are the endangered white-breasted thrasher (*Ramphocinclus brachyurus*) and Saint Lucia iguana (*Iguana iguana*) which are threatened by ongoing and proposed tourism developments in remaining stands of coastal dry forest (Young et al. 2010). The world's rarest snake, the Saint Lucia racer (*Liophis ornatus*), and the endangered Saint Lucia whiptail lizard (*Cnemidophorus vanzoi*), both found only on the southeast coast's tiny Maria Islands, are also threatened by a major proposed tourism development nearby (Wrathall 2017).

It is impossible to ignore the mounting evidence of impacts growing along the coast, yet decision-makers have for the most part been slow to acknowledge and respond to these concerns. For many, the focus continues to be on improved protection of the uplands where, for pragmatic and historical reasons, government is best prepared to advance environmental objectives (Helmer et al. 2008; Walters and Hansen 2013). Meanwhile, the coast and lowlands are increasingly under siege by development that is actively encouraged, yet little regulated.

The issue of agricultural displacement also needs to be factored into assessments of Saint Lucia's greening (Meyfroidt et al. 2010; Kozak and Szwagrzyk 2016). Banana farming collapsed in Saint Lucia, and this has indeed benefited the local forest and upland environment. Banana cultivation has not ceased altogether; rather, a roughly equivalent amount of bananas once grown in Saint Lucia are now cultivated elsewhere in Latin America. Is Saint Lucia's gain simply offset by another country's loss? To some extent, yes, but not entirely. This is because declines in banana cultivation in Saint Lucia occurred predominantly on marginal hillside lands that were estimated to have production levels 50 to 75 per cent lower than those attained on better-quality lands elsewhere (Welch

1996a; Moberg 2008). This means the shift from Saint Lucia to sites in Latin America that are more optimal for growing bananas almost certainly resulted in significant net land-sparing and a reduction in the sorts of impacts (soil erosion, leaching of agrochemicals) typically associated with steep-hillside farming of bananas. In fact, this scenario is increasingly common across Latin America and elsewhere, as industrialization of food production and liberalization of trade drives production from marginal to more optimal farmlands (Mather and Needle 1998; Rudel et al. 2005; Gau and Aide 2008; Meyfroidt et al. 2010; Aide et al. 2013).

Finally, one needs to appreciate the downsides of Saint Lucia's reforestation story: thousands of farmers and dozens of rural communities endured much hardship as a result of the collapse of the banana industry. While beyond the scope of this book, these social and economic impacts have been examined in detail by other scholars (e.g., Reynolds 2008; Moberg 2008; Harmsen et al. 2014). The preceding analysis nonetheless suggests a certain inevitability to the decline of Saint Lucian agriculture as a major export industry given wider changes to the Saint Lucian economy and international agribusiness and trade. As has been shown, Saint Lucia's newfound prosperity, attained through developments in tourism, real estate and other services, is inextricably linked to declines in its export agricultural sectors.

Concerns over domestic food security remain: with less land under cultivation, how can Saint Lucia expect to feed itself in the future? In fact, Saint Lucia has long been both a major exporter *and* importer of food, and its agricultural sector remains vibrant in fruit and vegetable production, in particular. Still, the loss of farmland is a legitimate, long-term concern. The replacement of upland farms with forest is arguably a less serious matter than the loss of lowlands to hard development. This is because the uplands are less productive and could in theory be brought back under cultivation if needed, whereas infrastructure development (homes, hotels, roads, etc.) alienates farmland permanently.

These various considerations suggest that Saint Lucia's greening is significant but by no means an unqualified success story. The widespread reforestation of Saint Lucia's uplands is for the most part an unintended outcome of forces largely beyond government control, but this fact should not diminish its importance. The country's watersheds, soils and water supply are now far more secure; its tropical forest biodiversity is better protected, and its extraordinary natural heritage value is growing. These all bode well for a country increasingly based on a tourism- and services-centred economy, all the more so given the sorts of challenges now emerging with climate change (Courchamp et al. 2014; Moore et al. 2017).

As long as the country's lowlands and coastal environments continue to deteriorate, not only will the environment suffer, but so too will core pillars of the new economy be put at long-term risk. To avert this, Saint Lucia must strengthen its land use planning and empower its regulatory capacities to ensure that species at risk and key natural heritage sites are protected and critical coastal and marine habitats are not damaged beyond repair. While reduced in scale, agriculture will always be part of the Saint Lucian economy, so it would also be wise to prioritize the securing of remaining prime agricultural lands as permanent farmland reserve. At the same time, widespread abandonment of farming from marginal lands creates tremendous opportunity for government and private actors to secure these lands for long-term conservation. Such actions stand to benefit biodiversity and watershed health, but they also entail significant carbon storage, which may enable Saint Lucia to secure significant external funding to support conservation land acquisition. Otherwise, the growing of diverse tree crops will hopefully remain a significant feature of Saint Lucia's upland landscapes. These crops are the best suited for marginal land farming, and they provide many of the benefits associated with natural forests (Walters and Hansen 2013). It is no accident that the farming of these tree crops has long outlasted the booms and busts in cotton, sugar and bananas.

REFLECTIONS ON RESEARCH METHODOLOGY

A central aim of this book has been to demonstrate the applicability of a novel research methodology, ACE, for doing research on such things as land use and forest change. In this regard, the proof should be in the pudding: if readers are persuaded by the evidence and analyses presented in this book, then the case for ACE has been made successfully. Having now presented the study in full, however, it is worth making a few final points about research methodology, comparing ACE with the three alternative approaches – LCS, SES and political ecology – that were described in chapter 1. What insights can be drawn from the Saint Lucia case study regarding these different approaches to human-environment research?

First, LCS and ACE are alike (but different from SES and political ecology) in their insistence on being clear in the beginning about the "explanandum" event – that is, the environmental change(s) for which an explanation is being sought (Meyfroidt 2015; Efroymson et al. 2016). The two approaches are likely to diverge on the next steps. In LCS, researchers typically proceed (using causes-to-effects reasoning) to compile large data sets and build models to test for statistical associations between variables, which may suggest possible causation. Explanations that may be derived from this work still depend on qualitative reasoning and are, ultimately, only as credible as established theory and empirical knowledge of the cases at hand permit. For this reason, LCS tends to be at its best when quantitative-statistical work is well integrated with in-depth, qualitative research of the cases under study (e.g., Shaver et al. 2015; Turner et al. 2016; see also Meyfroidt 2015).

With ACE, having identified the explanandum event, research then proceeds to build causal explanations using abductive (effects-to-causes) reasoning as a guide to inquiry, drawing on diverse sources of evidence and selecting methods appropriately suited for evaluating alternative causal hypothesis as these emerge through the course of subsequent investigations (Walters and Vayda 2009). In the research presented here, quantitative data were also compiled and subject to statistical analysis, but this was done in a more targeted manner to evaluate specific causal hypotheses that had been conjectured as plausible on the basis of general knowledge of the situation and qualitative observations and investigations already made on the ground. This approach enabled a precise, efficient use of statistical tools that generated reliable results. For example, statistical tests confirmed an already suspected causal relationship between topographical conditions (slope, elevation, road access) and reforestation (chapter 3), but refuted – rather unexpectedly – land tenure as a decisive cause (chapter 5). At the same time, bioecological and socio-economic information were gathered and analysed in tandem, not treated as separate study components with attempts at integration made after the fact. Rather, with an eye kept on the guiding research questions, different sources of evidence were integrated and causal hypotheses formulated and evaluated in an iterative, stepwise manner through the course of the research.

That said, some LCS researchers have proposed using "integrated land history" as a way to incorporate longer time frames and deeper engagement with historical events and processes (Klepeis and Turner 2001). This is a positive development, but its advocates continue to treat historical and scientific research components as qualitatively distinct endeavors, the former focused on creating qualitative narratives and the latter focused on compiling and modelling quantitative data. History thus provides contextual information, but ultimately science delivers the hard explanations. In contrast, a causal-historical perspective – which guides ACE – views such distinctions as inaccurate and ultimately counterproductive, because qualitative evidence may be equally or even more compelling than quantitative evidence for assessing causal claims.

Second, it is not easy relating the case study findings writ large to SES concepts of resilience and the adaptive cycle because these ideas are so conceptually and ontologically ill-defined (Walters 2012a). This poses a serious problem for explanation-oriented research because clarity and precision are core criteria for evaluating the success of explanations (McCullagh 1998; Gaddis 2002; Hedstrom and Ylikoski 2010; Ylikoski and Kuorikoski 2010; Priest 2017; see also Walters and Vayda 2009; Vayda and Walters 2011; Meyfroidt 2015, 12–13; Efroymson et al. 2016).

For many of its advocates, SES concepts and frameworks serve primarily as analytical heuristics (Folke 2006; Walker et al. 2006; Carter et al. 2014; Burns and Rudel 2015). Heuristics have value as guides to intellectual inquiry, but they do not explain phenomena, and so are of little concrete interest here. It is also not apparent what insights are gained in the Saint Lucia case by granting theoretical-explanatory weight to SES concepts and schema because these simply do not readily incorporate the decisive causal influence of such disparate and historically contingent phenomena as the rise of tourism, out- and return migration and fluctuating international commodity markets (see also Bunce et al. 2009). As such, it is hard to conceive how concepts like "resilience", "stable states" and "adaptive cycles" could in any but the most facile theoretical way impart real understanding of a society and environment that has for so long been in such dramatic, open-ended flux (Harmsen et al. 2014; Walters 2017).

That said, there are sub-elements of the Saint Lucia case that showed evidence of tight couplings and genuinely system-like behavior. Specifically, banana farming and its gradual development in Saint Lucia reveal a clear trend in increased complexity (and, arguably, "rigidity") as farmers were required over time to adhere to ever-more elaborate on-farm management and off-farm marketing protocols intended to boost productivity (fertilizers, pest management) and deliver optimum product quality (e.g., field packing, harvest scheduling) (Romalis 1975; Fingal 2008; Moberg 2008). In fact, Grossman's (1994, 1998,

2003) research on the banana industry in neighboring Saint Vincent, which he characterizes as a "contract-farming system", elucidates important insights of a systemic nature about its evolution and response to internal pressures and externally imposed shocks.

In Saint Lucia, an argument could be made that the first banana bust in the late 1960s was reflective of systemic "collapse" brought on by a combination of external shocks and internal management breakdown, which was then followed by a "reorganization" phase and return to "growth" of the system (i.e., an adaptive cycle). A similar argument cannot be made about the recent banana collapse, which was caused largely by events and trends that lay well beyond and often had nothing to do with the farming system per se. In short, this recent decline reflected not a collapse of the banana farming system per se but rather a gradual, voluntary abandonment of farming from less productive sites in response to wider socio-economic changes. In fact, banana farming persists today in Saint Lucia, but in much reduced form and on the most productive sites only (personal observation). What production has been lost from Saint Lucia has only been transferred to other, likely even more management-intensive farming "systems" elsewhere. Concepts of resilience and adaptive cycle are just not helpful for understanding, yet alone explaining, these recent changes.

Finally, political ecology has sought to incorporate history and historical analysis in a variety of ways, some heavily theoretical (Watts 2003; Watts and Peet 2004) and others more empirical, based on the application of historical methods and case-by-case construction of historical narratives (Peluso 1992; Leach and Mearns 1996; Batterebury and Bebbington 1999; Shaver et al. 2015). As with historical research more generally, so-called historical political ecology is often not explicit about analytical methodology and, where it is, may approach research and analysis differently than ACE. A notable example of this is Blaikie and Brookfield's (1987) "chains of explanation" approach, which has commonalities with ACE but differs in placing emphasis on social structures (rather than events) and in insisting that lower-level phenomena (e.g., land users) are causally nested and thereby determined by higher-level phenomena (e.g., government policies). But this rigid prescription is simply not consistent with the indeterminate nature of historical causation.

Either way, this study should put to rest concerns raised by some political ecologists that the methodological approach used with ACE fails to account for politics and structural factors in explanations (e.g., Robbins 2004, 208; Watts and Peet 2004, 18; Perramond 2007, 503; Penna-Firme 2012, 200). As illustrated here, the influence of both structural factors (e.g., land tenure) and political events (e.g., changes in trade policy and international banana markets) were rigorously evaluated as possible causes of rural reforestation, in each case with attention to the actual evidence of causation and being as clear and precise as possible about the causal chains involved. By doing this abductively, reasoning from effects to causes rather than from causes to effects, existing theories and hypotheses about the political economy of environmental degradation were considered but not prioritized. In fact, two major study findings – that reforestation was caused in part by increased trade liberalization and was equally widespread on large estates and on small farms – contradict widely held assumptions in political ecology about inequality and trade liberalization being dominant causes of environmental degradation in the global south. Much social and environmental damage across the Caribbean can be causally linked to the region's long history of colonial and capitalist exploitation, but the specific socio-economic and environmental changes captured in this study do not conform to this general narrative.

APPENDIX 1

Summary of Tree Species (by Habitat Type) Identified in Vegetation Surveys of Soufrière and Mamiku Watersheds in 2006

Botanical Name	Local/Common Names	Ag	AF	SF	MF	Status
Acacia retusa (Jacq.) Howard, Fabaceae. Mimosoideae (sub fam)	Bwa bondé/ Zamouwet			X	X	Indigenous, very common
Acnistus arborescens (L.) Schlechtendal, Solanaceae	Bwa mou limou/ Casia latta		X			Indigenous, locally common
Acrocomia aculeata (Jacq.) Lodd. ex Mart., Palmae	Gwi-gwi		X		X	Endemic to Lesser Antilles, rare, endangered
Anacardium occidentale L., Anacardiaceae	Pom akajou/ Cashew Nut		X			Cultivated, naturalized
Annona muricata L., Annonaceae	Kòsòl/Soursop		X			Introduced, cultivated
Aniba bracteata (Nees) Mez, Laureacea	Lowyé jonn			X	X	Indigenous, common
Artocarpus altilis (Parkinson), Moraceae	Bwapen/ Breadfruit		X			Introduced, cultivated, very common
Beilschmiedia pendula (Sw.) Hemsley, Laureaceae	Lowyé wouj			X		
Bourreria succulenta Jacq., Boraginaceae	Pis a cheval			X		Indigenous, very common
Bursera simaruba L. Sarg, Burseraceae	Gomyé wouj/ Turpentine tree			X	X	Indigenous, common
Byrsonima spicata (Cav.) DC., Malpighiaceae	Bwa tan			X		Indigenous, very common
Byrsonima trinitatis A. Juss, Malpighiaceae	Bwa tan wouj			X	X	Indigenous, common
Capparis indica (L.) Druce, Capparaceae	Bwa puant				X	Indigenous, common
Carica papaya L., Caricaceae	Pawpaw/Papaya		X			Introduced, cultivated, very common

Botanical Name	Local/Common Names	Ag	AF	SF	MF	Status
Casearia decandra Jacq., Salicaceae	Bwa koko kawèt			X	X	Indigenous, very common
Cecropia schreberiana Miq, Urticaceae	Bwa Kannon		X	X		Indigenous, very common
Cedrela odorata L., Meliaceae	Acajou/Red cedar		X		X	Indigenous, locally common
Ceiba pentandra (L.) Gaertner, Malvaceae	Fonmajé/Silk cotton		X		X	Indigenous, quite common
Charianthus alpinus (Sw.) R.A. Howard, Melastomataceae	Bwa sen			X		Indigenous, locally common
Chimarrhis cymosa Jacq., Rubiaceae	Bwa wivyé			X		Indigenous, common
Chrysophyllum argenteum Jacq., Sapotaceae	Bwi-bwi			X	X	Indigenous, very common
Cinnamomum verum Bercht. & Presl., Lauraceae	Kannèl/ Cinammon		X			Introduced, cultivated, common
Citharexylum spinosum L., Verbenaceae	Bwa koklet		X		X	Indigenous, very common
Citrus medica L., Rutaceae	Lemon		X			Introduced, cultivated, common
Citrus x paradisi Macf., Rutaceae	Grapefruit	X	X			Introduced, cultivated, very common
Citrus reticulata Blanco, Rutaceae	Madawin/ Tangerine mandarine		X			Introduced, cultivated, common
Clusia major L., Clusiaceae	Awalie			X		Indigenous, common
Clusia plukenetii Urban, Clusiaceae	Awalie			X		Indigenous, very common
Coccoloba pubescens L., Polygonaceae	Bwa gwan fey			X		Indigenous, common
Coccoloba swartzii Meisssner, Polygonaceae	Bwa lanmowi			X		Indigenous, very common
Cocos nucifera L., Palmae	Koko/Coconut	X	X	X		Introduced, cultivated, naturalized, very common
Cordia collococca L., Boraginaceae	Bwa flo/Sip		X	X		Indigenous, quite common

Botanical Name	Local/Common Names	Ag	AF	SF	MF	Status
Cordia martinicensis (Jacq.) Roemer & Schultes, Boraginaceae	Maho nwé/ Black sage		X			Indigenous, very common
Cordia reticulata Vahl., Boraginaceae	Sip nwé/maho noir			X	X	Indigenous, quite common
Cordia sulcata DC., Boraginaceae	Bwa sip, maho gwan fey			X		Indigenous, common
Cornutia pyramidata L., Lamiaceae	Bwa Kasav			X		Indigenous, common
Croton bixoides Geiseler, Euphorbiaceae	Gwo bonm			X		Indigenous, very common
Croton niveus Jacq., Euphorbiaceae	Ti bam				X	Indigenous, very rare
Cyathea sp.	Giant tree fern		X	X		Common
Dacryodes excelsa Vahl., Burseraceae	Gonmyé			X	X	Indigenous, common
Daphnopsis americana (Miller) J. Johnston, Thymelaeaceae	Maho piman	X	X	X	X	Indigenous, very common
Delonix regia (Bojer) Raf., Fabaceae, Caesalpinoideae (sub fam)	Flamboyant		X			Introduced, culti- vated, naturalized
Endlicheria sericea Nees, Lauraceae	Lowyé fè			X	X	Indigenous, quite common
Erythrina fusca (Lour.), Fabaceae	Bwa mowtel/ Immortal	X	X			Cultivated, natural- ized, common
Erythroxylum squamatum Sw., Erythroxylaceae	Bwa gwiv				X	Indigenous, common
Eugenia confusa DC., Myrtaceae	Bwa etti			X		Indigenous, common
Eugenia duchassaingiana O. Berg, Myrtaceae	Bwa dibas				X	Indigenous, rare
Eugenia monticola (Sw.) DC., Myrtaceae	Bwa (di bas) ti fey			X	X	Indigenous, very common
Eugenia pseudopsidium Jacq., Myrtaceae				X		Indigenous, rare
Eugenia tapacumensis Berg., Myrtaceae				X		Indigenous, very rare, endangered

Botanical Name	Local/Common Names	Habitat Type				Status
		Ag	AF	SF	MF	
Exostema sanctae-luciae (Kentish) Britten, Rubiaceae	China tree			X	X	Indigenous, not common
Faramea occidentalis (L.) A. Richard, Rubiaceae	Ti café				X	Indigenous, quite common
Gliricidia sepium (Jacq.) Kunth ex Walp., Fabaceae	Glory cedar		X	X		Cultivated, naturalized
Gonzalagunia hirsuta (Jacq.) Schum., Rubiaceae	Bwa Kilibwe		X			Indigenous, common
Guatteria caribaea Urb, Annonaceae	Kòsòl mawon				X	Indigenous, quite common
Guettarda scabra (L.) Vent, Rubiaceae	Bwa madam			X		Indigenous, very common
Haematoxylon campe-chianum L., Fabaceae, Caesalpinioidea (sub fam)	Kanmpèch/ Logwood			X		Indigenous, very common
Hibiscus elatus Sw., Malvaceae	Blue maho		X			Planted (forestry), common
Hibiscus rosa-sinensis L., Malvaceae	Hibiscus		X			Cultivated (orna-mental), common
Hirtella pendula Solander ex Lam., Chrysobalanaceae	Zikak fwans, pan zòwéy				X	Indigenous, uncommon
Hyeronima laxiflora (Tul.) Muell.-Arg, Euphorbiaceae	Bwa damand			X	X	Indigenous, common
Ilex sideroxyloides (Sw.) Griseb., Aquifoliaceae	Ti citon bleu			X		Indigenous, very common
Inga ingoides (Rich.) Willd., Fabaceae, Mimisoideae	Kakoli		X	X	X	Indigenous, very common
Laureacea sp.	Laurier mabre		X	X	X	
Licania ternatensis Hooker f. ex Duss, Chrysobalanaceae	Bwa dimas			X	X	Indigenous, very common

Botanical Name	Local/Common Names	Habitat Type Ag	AF	SF	MF	Status
Lonchocarpus heptaphyllus (Poir.) DC., Fabaceae	Savonnèt gwan fey		X	X		
Lonchocarpus punctatus Kunth., Fabaceae	Savonnèt ti fey		X	X	X	
Mammea americana L., Calophyllaceae	Zabwiko/Apricot		X			Cultivated, quite common
Mangifera indica L., Anacardiaceae	Mango		X		X	Introduced, naturalized, cultivated, very common
Manilkara bidentata (A.D.C.) A. Chev., Sapotaceae	Balata	X				Indigenous, uncommon
Margaritaria nobilis L.fil., Phyllanthaceae	Bwa mil bwanch				X	Indigenous, common
Miconia cornifolia (Desr.) Naudin, Melastomataceae	Bwa kot, bwa savan			X		Indigenous, very common
Miconia furfuracea (M. Vahl) Griseb., Melastomataceae	Bwa sen, Bwa cot			X		Indigenous, common
Miconia luciana H.A.Gleason, Melastomataceae	Bwa sen		X			Common, endemic to Saint Lucia
Miconia sp. Melastomataceae	Bwa kot			X	X	
Micropholis guyanensis (A.D.C.) Pierre, Sapotaceae	Fey dowé, be pwel			X		Indigenous, very common
Myrcia deflexa (Poiret) DC., Myrtaceae	Bwa kwéyòl			X		Indigenous, very common
Myrtaceae sp.	Bwa gwi				X	
Ocotea cernua (Nees) Mez, Lauraceae	Laurel			X	X	Indigenous, quite common
Ocotea leucoxylon (Sw.) De Laness, Lauraceae	Lowyé mabwé			X	X	Indigenous, common
Ocotea membranaceae (Sw.) R. Howard, Lauraceae	Lowyé sann				X	Indigenous, common
Ormosia monosperma (Sw.) Urban, Fabaceae	Didi fudit/ bouwik			X		Indigenous, very common

Botanical Name	Local/Common Names	Habitat Type				Status
		Ag	**AF**	**SF**	**MF**	
Persea americana Miller, Lauraceae	Zaboka/Avocado		X			Introduced, cultivated, common
Phyllanthus acidus (L.) Skeels, Phyllanthaceae	Siwet/Gooseberry		X			Introduced, cultivated, uncommon
Pilosocereus royenii L. Byles & G. Rowley, Cactaceae	Syéj/Candelabra cactus				X	Indigenous, common
Pimenta rac-emosa (Miller) J. Moore, Myrtaceae	Bwa den/Bay rum tree			X		Indigenous, cultivated, common
Pisonia fragrans Dum.-Cours., Nyctaginaceae	Mapou/Black loblolly		X	X	X	Indigenous, very common
Pisonia suborbiculata Hemsley ex Duss, Nyctaginaceae	Mapou ti fey			X		Indigenous, rare
Pithocellobium jupunba (Willd.) Urban, Fabaceae, Mimosaceae (sub fam)	Dalmawi			X	X	Indigenous, common
Pouteria multiflora (A.D.C.) Eyma., Sapotaceae	Pennepis				X	Indigenous, very common
Pouteria pallida (Gaertner f.) Baehni, Sapotaceae	Balata chen				X	Indigenous, very common
Pouteria semecarpi-folia (Pierre) Pierre, Sapotaceae	Bwa contweven				X	Indigenous, common
Prestoea acuminata (Willd.) H. E. Moore, Palmae	Palmiste			X	X	Indigenous, common
Protium attenu-atum (Rose) Urban, Burseraceae	Inscence/ Frankinscence			X	X	Indigenous, very common
Psidium guajava L., Myrtaceae	Gwijav/Guava		X			Introduced, cultivated, naturalized, common
Psychotria mapourioides DC., Rubiaceae	Lowre glo				X	Very common
Randia aculeata L., Rubiaceae	Bwa lans			X		Indigenous, very common
Rhizophora mangle, L., Rhizophoraceae	Mang wouj/Red mangrove				X	Indigenous, common

Botanical Name	Local/Common Names	Habitat Type				Status
		Ag	AF	SF	MF	
Rondeletia parviflora Poir., Rubiaceae	Mayan			X	X	Indigenous, common
Rudgea citrifolia (Sw.) K. Schum, Rubiaceae	Bwa lay			X	X	Indigenous, very common
Rubiaceae sp.	Café marron			X	X	
Sapium caribaeum Urban, Euphorbiaceae	La gli			X		Indigenous, very common
Sapindaceae sp.					X	
Simaruba amara Aublet, Simarouobaceae	Bwa blanc			X	X	Indigenous, common
Solanum racemosum Jacq., Solanaceae	Savonette ti fey				X	Common
Solanum torvum Sw., Solanaceae	Belanjen Djab/ Wild aubergine (eggplant)		X			Very common
Spondias cytherea Sonnerat, Anacardiaceae	Pom site/Golden apple		X			Introduced, cultivated, uncommon
Spondias mombin L., Anacardiaceae	Mouben/Hog plum		X			Introduced, cultivated, naturalized, common
Sterculia caribaea R. Br., Malvaceae	Maho kochon			X	X	Indigenous, very common
Styrax glaber Sw., Styracaceae	Sip jowanj			X		
Swartzia caribaea Griseb., Fabaceae, Caesalpinoideae (sub fam)	Mawon/Kas				X	Indigenous, common
Swietenia macrophylla King, Meliaceae	Honduras mahogany		X			Introduced, cultivated (timber), naturalized, common
Symplocos martinicensis Jacq., Symplocaceae	Bwa blé			X		Indigenous, very common
Syzgium jambos (L.) Alston, Myrtaceae	Pomme weez		X			Introduced, naturalized, common
Tabebuia hetero- phylla (DC.) Britton, Bignoniaceae	Bwa powyé/ White cedar			X		Indigenous, very common
Tabernaemontana citrifo- lia L., Apocynaceae	Bwa let	X	X	X		Indigenous, very common

Botanical Name	Local/Common Names	Habitat Type				Status
		Ag	AF	SF	MF	
Tapura latifolia Benth., Dichapetalaceae	Bwa cot wouj			X	X	Endemic, Lesser Antilles, common
Ternstroemia elliptica Sw., Theaceae	Lowyé glo			X		
Theobroma cacao L., Malvaceae	Kako/Cocoa		X			Introduced, culti-vated, very common
Tovomita plumieri Griseb., Clusiaceae	Palitivyé (jonn)			X	X	Indigenous, common
Trichilia pallida Sw., Meliaceae	Chatoneye			X		
Turpinia occidentalis (Sw.) Don., Staphyleaceae	Bwa lat			X		Indigenous, rare
Vangueria madagas-cariensis J.F. Gmelin, Rubiaceae	Tamawin dezenn		X			Introduced, culti-vated, naturalized
Vitex divaricata Sw., Lamiaceae	Bwa leza			X		Indigenous, common
Zanthoxylum sp., Rutaceae	Lepinee			X		
Total species counts	125	5	44	72	57	

Notes: Familial nomenclature follows the APGIII System of Plant Taxonomy, and spe-cies names were verified using Howard (1974). Conservation status is from the Saint Lucia Herbarium's plant data base (Graveson 2005).

Habitat types: Ag = agriculture; AF = agroforest; SF = secondary forest; MF = mature forest.

NOTES

CHAPTER 1

1. Inductive reasoning is the drawing of generalizations or probabilities from empirical observations (including experiments); for example, "Every farmer surveyed in this village had planted tree crops; therefore, all farmers plant tree crops in this village". Deductive reasoning uses existing generalizations or theories to account for empirical observations; for example, "All farmers plant tree crops; this is a farmer; therefore, she plants tree crops".

2. *Post-positivism* views science as the search for general causal relationships, accomplished by way of isolating and measuring variables (usually quantitatively) and then evaluating their relation to one another using experimental, modelling or statistical treatments. *Structuralism* situates understanding of human-environment interactions in the context of relations of power, social differentiation and inequality. *Constructivist* explanations focus on human-environment interactions, as these are understood in thought, communicated in language and established as shared theories or "narratives" (Turner and Robbins 2008; Mann 2009).

CHAPTER 2

1. One carre is equal to 3.33 acres or about 1.5 hectares.

2. Watershed and property boundaries are not always clear on the map, so figures here are estimates. The uppermost part of Mamiku is undefined, and so presumably is Crown land.

3. Saint Lucia switched between British and French control fourteen times before finally being ceded to Britain in 1814 under the Treaty of Paris at the end of the Napoleonic Wars (Thomas 2006; Moberg 2008). Merchants and sugar planters, who were usually welcomed by respective English and French colonial administrators, were to a large degree unaffected by changes in territorial control. "When a West Indian territory exchanged one European master for another, its planters and slaves, merchants, and even officials, often carried on regardless" (Lowenthal 1972, 29).

CHAPTER 3

1.   A full list of tree species, identified by habitat, is presented in appendix 1.

CHAPTER 4

1.   Modern edible bananas originated from two seeded species, both originating from SE Asia: *Musa acuminata Colla*, the source of sweeter varieties like Gros Michel and Cavendish, and *M. balbisiana Colla*, the source of starchier plantains (Robinson 1996). As bananas and plantains ripen, their starch converts to sugar, a process that occurs more slowly in cooking varieties (plantains). But unripened sweet bananas are also frequently cooked in the Caribbean. The modern banana trade was founded on the Gros Michel variety, a sweet banana introduced to Jamaica from Martinique (McFarlane 1964). Panama disease led to its replacement by the Cavendish-variety bananas and, in some cases, Lacatan variety.

2.   The UFC was founded in 1899 by the merger of the Boston Fruit Company and various other banana companies. Its name was changed to Chiquita in 1986 (Myers 2004). The early history of the commercial banana industry and UFC's dominant role in it is an intriguing story. UFC and its various subsidiary companies practised vertical integration and established near total control over the industry through ownership of vast plantations, networks of distribution and a large fleet of transport ships (Clegg 2002a; Myers 2004). By 1930 UFC was controlling 3.4 million acres of tropical landholdings and a fleet of a hundred cargo ships (Wiley 2008). West Indian producers were unusual, in that ownership of banana plantations remained largely in local hands.

3.   This tonnage figure is extrapolated from a total count of 11 million (i.e., "bunches") exported. Based on statistics where both weight and stem counts are provided (e.g., Analyst 1957, 33; McFarlane 1964, 90), it is estimated that 80 stems = 1 tonne of bananas for the Gros Michel variety. Post–World War II yields of Cavendish variety bananas would have been about double the weight per stem (Moberg 2008).

4.   In response to these concerns, in 1928 the UK government supported establishment of the Jamaica Banana Producers Association, which included independent shipping and marketing service to bring Jamaican bananas to the United Kingdom. The association struck an agreement with UFC and Standard Fruit, enabling it to sell all its produce in the UK market, with the understanding that it no longer sell bananas in the North American market (Myers 2004).

5.   In fact, there is some disagreement as to whether these early exports (1923–

1927) were destined to markets in the United Kingdom (e.g., McFarlane 1964; Mathurin 2012) or to markets in North America (e.g., Welch 1994; Harmsen et al. 2014).

6. Authors differ on whether the name of the second exporting firm was Canada Banana Co. (McFarlane 1964; Moberg 2008; Torgerson 2010) or Canadian Buying Company (Romalis 1975; Welch 1994; Mathurin 2012).

7. Practical policy discussions on these matters unfolded as well through the Banana Advisory Committee, a negotiating body created in 1973 with representatives from the UK government, banana importing companies and the two main West Indian banana trade associations, the Windward Island Banana Growers Association and the Jamaica Banana Producers Association (Clegg 2002a).

8. The guiding principle of the Lomé Banana Protocol, Article I, states, "As regards to exports of bananas to markets of the Community, no ACP state will be placed, as regards to access to its traditional markets and its advantages in those markets, in a less favourable situation than in the past or at the present" (Clegg 2002a, 123).

9. Geest's Cul de Sac estate lands were also sold off in the late 1970s and some of these lands used for additional smallholder settlement. In 1995 Geest sold the remainder of its Windward Island banana business to a consortium of Fyffes Limited and WIBDECO (Windward Island Banana Development and Export Company), a newly formed company that was jointly owned by the grower associations and governments of the four Windward Islands (Myers 2004). WIBDECO is responsible for buying, shipping and marketing bananas, while Fyffes manages ripening and distribution (Fairtrade Foundation 2003).

10. For example, in November 1984 heavy rainfall triggered a 10-acre landslide in Forestière which was attributed to banana cultivation on steep slopes.

11. ECU stands for the "European Currency Unit", the precursor to the euro (€).

12. EC member banana producers included the French Caribbean departments of Martinique and Guadeloupe and (after Spain's entry into the European Economic Community in 1986) the Canary Islands (Myers 2004).

13. The WTO was founded during the Uruguay Round of GATT negotiations, creating a powerful trade dispute body. This challenge was led by the United States but included Mexico, Ecuador, Honduras and Guatemala as plaintiffs (Myers 2004). US involvement was controversial. On the one hand, the United States had a range of concerns about the European Union's protectionist agricultural policies and was eager to flex the WTO's new muscles by instigating a trade challenge. The banana case was, in fact, the first transatlantic trade dispute to be adjudicated under the newly created WTO (Alter and Meunirer 2006).

Yet its choice of the banana issue was strange, given that the country was not itself a producer of bananas, even if Chiquita was a US-based corporation. A convincing case has been made that the United States acted at the behest of Chiquita, the president of which (Carl Lindner) was a close friend and financial contributor to several influential Washington politicians (Clegg 2002a; Myers 2004).

14.   The original 1993 Banana Protocol included individual quotas for ACP countries that added up to 857,000 tonnes. Revisions replaced this with one global ACP quota of 857,000 tonnes, thus opening up competition between ACP members (Clegg 2002a; Myers 2004). This did not bode well for the Windward Islands, although it benefited other ACP member producers in West Africa, Belize and the Dominican Republic, as they were able to subsequently expand production through corporate investment in industrial plantations (Myers 2004). Other revisions to the Banana Protocol pertained to the allocation of quota licences to banana importers (Wiley 2008).

15.   The origins of the fair-trade movement can be traced back decades to the work of faith-based groups in Europe and the United States and wider discussions advocating "trade, not aid" as a solution for Third World Development (Fridell 2004; Moberg 2005). The first independent fair-trade label was founded in 1988, the Dutch Max Havelaar. By 2001 the Fair Trade Labelling Organization had established international standards for seven agricultural commodities: coffee, cocoa, honey, cane sugar, tea, bananas, and oranges.

16.   The fair-trade movement in the United Kingdom included a network of over four hundred fair-trade towns and five thousand fair-trade–registered faith groups (Fairtrade Foundation 2009a). Fair-trade bananas first entered the European market in 1996 (Raynolds 2003), and early market development began in the Netherlands, Denmark, Belgium, Germany and Switzerland, targeting producers in Ghana, Ecuador, Dominican Republic and Costa Rica (Murray and Raynolds 2000). But once established, UK markets for fair-trade bananas grew rapidly and surpassed in size those on the Continent (Smith 2010).

17.   The Windward Islands Farmers Association is a non-governmental organization, made up of farmers, that was founded in 1982 to promote and protect the interests of Windward Island farmers. It is headquartered in Saint Vincent (Torgerson 2010).

18.   The guaranteed, fair-trade minimum price for bananas is calculated by the Fair Trade Labelling Organization for each country, based on estimates of how much it costs to produce in a sustainable way in that environment, taking into account labour costs, geographical considerations and so forth. Importers must pay this minimum price even when the going market price falls below it, and

they must likewise pay more should the going market price rise above it. As a result, fair-trade producers should always be paid a relatively higher price than the going rate for conventional bananas (Lamb 2008).

19.   Of the US$1.75 per-box social premium, US$0.75 goes to cover administrative costs incurred by the Saint Lucia National Fair Trade Organization and Windward Islands Farmers Association, and US$1.00 is returned to the local fair-trade producer group for investment in community projects and collective business development. In Saint Lucia, such projects have included health insurance coverage for member families, scholarships and local school equipment purchases, charity support for the elderly, road maintenance, post–Hurricane Dean (2007) recovery and purchase of group-owned, mechanical weed eaters (Fingal 2008; Moberg 2008; Fairtrade Foundation 2009b). According to Fingal (2008), the social premium on Saint Lucia bananas was reduced from US$1.75 per box to $1.00 per box because of competitive considerations.

20.   The social premium of US$1.75 per 18-kilogram box is constant, and the guaranteed minimum farm-gate price was set at US$7.60 per 18-kilogram box (or more, should the market rise). However, the critical issue is how much more farmers typically make by selling fair trade versus conventional, that is, the "price premium" of fair trade. This value varies with changing market conditions, but it showed a trend upward after inception (Fingal 2008). Specifically, the following price premiums were cited: US$1.00 per box in 2003 (Fairtrade Foundation 2003), US$3.00 per box in 2004 (Moberg 2008) and US$7.00 per box in 2008 (Fairtrade Foundation 2009b), although it is unclear if this last figure is in fact the farm-gate price or the price paid to the banana company.

CHAPTER 5

1.   See Barrow (1992, 3–10) for a particularly good summary of what she views as a negative stereotyping of family land and the justifications behind it.

CHAPTER 6

1.   Opportunities for Saint Lucians in seasonal farm work in North America vary year to year. While I do not have recent statistics for this, the number averaged about 390 Saint Lucians per year (range of 100–741) from 1988 to 1993 (GOSL 1994, 152).

2.   When interviews were conducted, minimum daily wages for farm labour were EC$30 and for construction EC$40 (more for skilled trades).

REFERENCES

Abdulah, N. 1977. *The Labour Force in the Commonwealth Caribbean: A Statistical Analysis*. St Augustine, Trinidad: Institute of Social and Economic Research, University of the West Indies.

Abenaty, F.K. 2000. "Saint Lucians and Migration: Migrant Returnees, Their Families and Saint Lucian Society". PhD diss., South Bank University, London.

Abend, G. 2008. "The Meaning of 'Theory' ". *Sociological Theory* 26:173–99.

Acheson, J.A., and J. McCloskey. 2008. "Causes of Deforestation: The Maine Case". *Human Ecology* 36:909–22.

ACP (African, Caribbean and Pacific Group of States). 2005. "The ACP Group". The Secretariat of the African, Caribbean and Pacific Group of States. www.aspsec.org, accessed 18 June 2009.

ACP-EU (African, Caribbean and Pacific Group of States–European Union). 2009. "Report of the ACP-EU Joint Parliamentary Assembly Delegation Fact-Finding Mission to Suriname, Saint Vincent and Saint Lucia, May 29–June 3, 2008". ACP–EU Joint Parliamentary Assembly Bureau. CR\772490EN.doc; AP/100.574. 21pp.

Adamo, S., and H. Izazola. 2010. "Human Migration and the Environment". *Population and Environment* 32:105–8.

Adams, N. 1969. "Internal Migration in Jamaica: An Economic Analysis". *Social and Economic Studies* 18 (2): 137–51.

Adger, W.N. 2000. "Social and Ecological Resilience: Are They Related?" *Progress in Human Geography* 24:347–64.

Agnoletti, M., and S. Anderson, eds. 2000. *Forest History: International Studies on Socio-economic and Forest Ecosystem Change*. New York: CAB International.

Agnoletti, M., and I.D. Rotherham. 2015. "Landscape and Biocultural Diversity". *Biodiversity and Conservation* 24:3155–65.

Agrawal, A., and C.C. Gibson. 1999. "Enchantment and Disenchantment: The Role of Community in Natural Resource Conservation". *World Development* 27 (4): 629–49.

Agrawal, A., and C.S. Benson. 2011. "Common Property Theory and Resource Governance Institutions: Strengthening Explanations of Multiple Outcomes". *Environmental Conservation* 38 (2): 199–210.

Aide, T.M., and H.R. Grau. 2004. "Globalization, Migration, and Latin American Ecosystems". *Science* 305:1915–16.

Aide, T.M., M.L. Clark, H.R. Grau, D. Lopez-Carr, M.A. Levy, D. Redo, M. Bonilla-Moheno, G. Riner, M.J. Andrade-Nunez and M. Muniz. 2013. "Deforestation and Reforestation of Latin America and the Caribbean (2001–2010)". *Biotropica* 45:262–71.

Aldrich, S., R. Walker, C. Simmons, M. Caldas and S. Perz. 2012. "Contentious Land Change in the Amazon's Arc of Deforestation". *Annals of the Association for American Geographers* 102:103–28.

Alleyne, F.W., ed. 1994. *Land Tenure and Development in the Eastern Caribbean: Proceedings of a Symposium*. Bridgetown, Barbados: Carib Research and Publications.

Alter, K.J., and S. Meunirer. 2006. "Nested and Overlapping Regimes in the Transatlantic Banana Trade Dispute". *Journal of European Public Policy* 13 (3): 362–82.

Alvarez-Berrios, N.L., D.J. Redo, M.T. Aide, M.L. Clark and R. Grau. 2013. "Land Change in the Greater Antilles between 2001 and 2010". *Land* 2:81–107.

Analyst. 1957. "Expansion of British Caribbean Trade with Europe". *Social and Economic Studies* 6 (1): 29–58.

Angelsen, A., and D. Kaimowitz. 2004. "Is Agroforestry Likely to Reduce Deforestation?" In *Agroforestry and Biodiversity Conservation in Tropical Landscapes*, edited by G. Schroth, G.A.B. da Fonseca, C.A. Harvey, C. Gascon, H.L. Vasconcelos, and A.N. Izac, 87–106. Washington, DC: Island Press.

Armitage, D., and D. Johnson. 2006. "Can Resilience Be Reconciled with Globalization and the Increasingly Complex Conditions of Resource Degradation in Asian Coastal Regions?" *Ecology and Society* 11 (1): 19p.

Asase, A., and D.A. Tetteh. 2010. "The Role of Complex Agroforestry Systems in the Conservation of Forest Tree Diversity and Structure in Southeastern Ghana". *Agroforestry Systems* 79:355–68.

Atkinson, E.E., and E. Marin-Spiotta. 2015. "Land Use Legacy Effects on the Structure and Composition of Subtropical Dry Forests in St Croix, U.S. Virgin Islands". *Forest Ecology and Management* 335:270–80.

Axline, W.A. 1986. *Agricultural Policy and Collective Self-Reliance in the Caribbean*. Boulder, CO: Westview.

Baggio, J.A., K. Brown and D. Hellebrandt. 2015. "Boundary Object or Bridging Concept? A Citation Network Analysis of Resilience". *Ecology and Society* 20 (2): 2, doi:10/5751/ES-07484-200202.

Balee, W., ed. 1998. *Advances in Historical Ecology*. New York: Columbia University Press.

Baptista, S. 2008. "Metropolitanization and Forest Recovery in Southern Brazil: A

Multiscale Analysis of the Florianopolis City-Region, Santa Catarina State, 1970 to 2005". *Ecology and Society* 13 (2): 21p.

Barbier, E.B., P. Delacote and J. Wolfersberger. 2017. "The Economic Analysis of the Forest Transition: A Review". *Journal of Forest Economics* 27:10–17.

Barbier, E.B., J.C. Burgess and A. Grainger. 2010. "The Forest Transition: Towards a More Comprehensive Theoretical Framework". *Land Use Policy* 27:98–107.

Barkham, P. 1999. "The Banana Wars Explained". *Guardian*, 5 March, www.guardian .co.uk/world/1999/mar/05/eu.wto3.

Barrow, C. 1992. *Family Land and Development in St Lucia*. Monograph Series No. 1. Cave Hill, Barbados: Institute of Social and Economic Research, University of the West Indies.

Basken, P. 2013. "That Elastic Term". *Chronicle of Higher Education*, 6 May.

Batterbury, S., and A. Bebbington. 1999. "Environmental Histories, Access to Resources and Landscape Change: An Introduction". *Land Degradation and Development* 10:279–90.

BBC. 2000. "U.K. Gets 'Fair Trade' Bananas". BBC News, 17 January. www.bbc.co.uk /1/hi/business/605642.stm.

Beckford, G.L.F. 1966. "Agricultural Development in 'Traditional' and 'Peasant' Economies". *Social and Economic Studies* 15 (2): 151–61.

———. 1969. "The Economics of Agricultural Resource Use and Development in Plantation Economies". *Social and Economic Studies* 18 (4): 321–47.

Begin, C., G. Brooks, R.A. Larson, S. Dragicevic, C. Ramos Scharron and I. Cote. 2014. "Increased Sediment Loads over Coral Reefs in Saint Lucia in Relation to Land Use Change in Contributing Watersheds". *Ocean and Coastal Management* 95:35–45.

Behnke, R., and M. Mortimore. 2016. "Introduction: The End of Desertification?" In *The End of Desertification? Disputing Environmental Change in the Drylands*, edited by R.H. Behnke and M. Moritmore, 1–34. New York: Springer Earth Systems Science, doi:10.1007/978-3-642-16014-1_1.

Bekele, F. 2004. "The History of Cocoa Production in Trinidad and Tobago". In *Revitalization of the Trinidad and Tobago Cocoa Industry*, edited by L. Wilson, 4–12. Proceedings of the APASTT Seminar-Exhibition, St Augustine, Trinidad, 20 September 2003. Trinidad and Tobago: Association of Professional Agricultural Scientists of Trinidad and Tobago.

Benayas, J., A. Martins, J. Nicolau and J. Schulz. 2007. "Abandonment of Agricultural Land: An Overview of Drivers and Consequences". *Perspectives in Agriculture, Veterinary Science, Nutrition and Natural Resources* 2, no. 057:1–14.

Berkes, F., and C. Folke, eds. 1998. *Linking Social and Ecological Systems: Manage-*

ment Practices and Social Mechanisms for Building Resilience. Cambridge: Cambridge University Press.

Besson, J. 1987. "A Paradox in Caribbean Attitudes to Land". In *Land and Development in the Caribbean*, edited by J. Besson and J. Momsen, 13–45. London: Macmillan.

Besson, J., and J. Momsen, eds. 1987. *Land and Development in the Caribbean.* London: Macmillan.

Bhagwat, S.A., S. Willis, H. Birks and R. Whittaker. 2008. "Agroforestry: A Refuge for Tropical Biodiversity?" *Trends in Ecology and Evolution* 23(5): 261–67.

Binder, C.R., J. Hinkel, P. Bots and C. Pahl-Wostl. 2013. "Comparison of Frameworks for Analyzing Social-Ecological Systems". *Ecology and Society* 18 (4): 26p, http://dx.doi.org/10.5751/ES-05551-180426.

Blaikie, P. 1999. "A Review of Political Ecology: Issues, Epistemology and Analytical Narratives". *Zeitschrift fur Wirtschaftsgeographie* 43:131–47.

Blaikie, P., and H. Brookfield. 1987. *Land Degradation and Society.* New York: Methuen.

Blaut, J.M., R.P. Blaut, N. Harman and M. Moerman. 1959. "A Study of Cultural Determinants of Soil Erosion and Conservation in the Blue Mountains of Jamaica". *Social and Economic Studies* 8 (4): 403–20.

Bleasdale, S., and S. Tapsell. 2003. "Matching Sustainable Tourism with Socialist Goals: Can Cuba Have It All?" In *Resources, Planning, and Environmental Management in a Changing Caribbean*, edited by D. Barker and D. McGregor, 173–95. Kingston, Jamaica: University of West Indies Press.

Bloch, P.C., S. Lastarria-Cornhiel, C. Griffith-Charles, C. Baptiste and R. Baptiste. 2005. *Property Rights and Land Markets in St Lucia.* Madison, WI: USAID/Development Alternatives/Land Tenure Center.

Bonell, M., and L.A. Bruijnzeel, eds. 2004. *Forests, Water and People in the Humid Tropics: Past, Present, and Future Hydrological Research for Integrated Land and Water Management.* Cambridge: Cambridge University Press.

Bonilla-Moheno, M., D.J. Redo, T.M. Aide, M.L. Clark and H.R. Grau. 2013. "Vegetation Change and Land Tenure in Mexico: A Country-Wide Analysis". *Land Use Policy* 30:355–64.

Bottazzi, P., and H. Dao. 2013. "On the Road through the Bolivian Amazon: a Multilevel Governance Analysis of Deforestation". *Land Use Policy* 30:137–46.

Braithwaite, L. 1968. "Social and Political Aspects of Rural Development in the West Indies". *Social and Economic Studies* 17 (3): 264–75.

Brand, F.S., and K. Jax. 2007. "Focusing the Meaning (s) of Resilience: Resilience as a Descriptive Concept and a Boundary Object". *Ecology and Society* 12 (1): 23p.

Brassey, T.A. 1898. "Sugar Bounties in the West Indies". In *Problems of Empire: Papers and Addresses by the Rt. Hon. T.A. Brassey*, 131–33. N.p.

Breen, H.H. 1844. *St Lucia: Historical, Statistical and Descriptive*. London: Longman, Brown, Green and Longman's.

Brierley, J.S. 1985a. "Idle Land in Grenada: A Review of Its Causes and the PRG's Approach to Reducing the Problem". *Canadian Geographer* 29 (4): 298–309.

——. 1985b. "A Review of Development Strategies and Programs of the Peoples' Revolutionary Government in Grenada, 1979–83". *Geographical Journal* 151:40–52.

——. 1987. "Agricultural Policies and Their Impact in the West Indies". *Rural Systems* 5 (1): 8–72.

——. 1992. "A Study of Land Redistribution and the Demise of Grenada's Estate Farming System 1940–1988". *Journal of Rural Studies* 8 (1): 67–84.

Briguglio, L. 1995. "Small Island Developing States and Their Economic Vulnerabilities". *World Development* 23:1615–32.

Brown, S., and A.E. Lugo. 1990. "Tropical Secondary Forests". *Journal of Tropical Ecology* 6:1–32.

Bruce, J.W. 1983. "Family Land Tenure and Agricultural Development in St Lucia". *Research Paper No. 79*. Madison, WI: Land Tenure Centre.

Bruijnzeel, L.A. 1991. "Hydrological Impacts of Tropical Forest Conversion". *Nature and Resources* 27:36–46.

Bruneau-Latouche, E.R., ed. 1989. *Saint-Lucie Fille de la Martinique*, Published by author.

Bryant, R.L., and S. Bailey. 1997. *Third World Political Ecology*. London: Routledge.

Buckley, R. 2010. *Conservation Tourism*. Oxfordshire: CABI International.

——. 2011. "Tourism and Environment". *Annual Review of Environment and Resources* 36, doi:10.1146/annurev-environ-041210-132637E.

——. 2012. "Sustainable Tourism: Research and Reality". *Annals of Tourism Research* 39 (2): 528–46.

Bunce, M., L. Mee, L.D. Rodwell and R. Gibb. 2009. "Collapse and Recovery in a Remote Small Island: A Tale of Adaptive Cycles or Downward Spirals?" *Global Environmental Change* 19:213–26.

Burns, T.J., and T.K. Rudel. 2015. "Metatheorizing Structural Human Ecology at the Dawn of the Third Millennium". *Human Ecology Review* 22:13–33.

Butler, R. 1991. "Tourism, Environment and Sustainable Development". *Environmental Conservation* 18 (3): 201–9.

Butler, S. 2006. "Supermarkets Switch to Fairtrade Bananas". *Times* (London), 13 December.

Byrne, J. 1969. "Population Growth in St Vincent". *Social and Economic Studies* 18 (2): 152–88.

Byron, M. 1994. *Post-War Caribbean Migration to Britain: The Unfinished Cycle*. Avebury, UK: Ashgate Publishing.

———. 2000. "Return Migration to the Eastern Caribbean: Comparative Experiences and Policy Implications". *Social and Economic Studies* 49 (4): 155–88.

———. 2007. "Collateral and Achievement: Land and Caribbean Migration". In *Caribbean Land and Development Revisited*, edited by J. Besson and J. Momsen, 243–53. New York: Palgrave Macmillan.

Byron, M., and S. Condon. 1996. "A Comparative Study of Caribbean Return Migration from Britain and France: Towards a Context-Dependent Explanation". *Transactions of the Institute for British Geographers NS* 21:91–104.

———. 2008. *Migration in Comparative Perspective: Caribbean Communities in Britain and France*. London: Routledge.

Campbell, B., A. Mandondo, N. Nemarundwe, B. Sithole, W. De Jong, M. Luckbert and F. Matose. 2001. "Challenges to Proponents of Common Property Resource Systems: Despairing Voices from the Social Forests of Zimbabwe". *World Development* 29 (4): 589–600.

Campbell, L.M. 2007. "Local Conservation Practice and Global Discourse: A Political Ecology of Sea Turtle Conservation". *Annals of the Association of American Geographers* 97 (2): 313–34.

Campos, D.G. 2011. "On the Distinction between Peirce's Abduction and Lipton's Inference to the Best Explanation". *Synthese* 180:419–42.

Carnegie, C. 1982. "Strategic Flexibility in the West Indies: A Social Psychology of Caribbean Migration". *Caribbean Review* 11 (1): 10–13.

Carr, D. 2009. "Population and Deforestation: Why Rural Migration Matters". *Progress in Human Geography* 33 (3): 355–78.

Carter, N.H., A. Vina, V. Hull, W.J. McConnell, W. Axinn, D. Ghimire and J. Liu. 2014. "Coupled Human and Natural Systems Approach to Wildlife Research and Conservation". *Ecology and Society* 19 (3): 43p. http://dx.doi.org/10.5751/ES-06881-190343.

Casse, T., and A. Milhoj. 2011. "Community Forestry and Forest Conservation: Friends or Strangers?" *Environmental Policy and Governance* 21:83–98.

Castellani, F. 2007. "International Skilled Migration: The Caribbean Experience in Perspective". *Social and Economic Studies* 56 (4): 165–206.

Castro, A.P. 1991. "Indigenous Kikuyu Agroforestry: A Case Study of Kirinyaga, Kenya". *Human Ecology* 19 (1): 1–18.

Chamberlin, T.C. 1965. "The Method of Multiple Working Hypotheses". *Science* 148:754–59. Republished (2011) in *Causal Explanation for Social Scientists: A Reader*, edited by A.P. Vayda and B.B. Walters, 168–78. Lanham, MD: AltaMira Press.

Chazdon, R.L. 2003. "Tropical Forest Recovery: Legacies of Human Impact and Natural Disturbances". *Perspectives in Plant Ecology, Evolution and Systematics* 6:51–71.

Chowdhury, R.R., and B.L. Turner II. 2005. "Reconciling Agency and Structure in Empirical Analysis: Smallholder Land Use in the Southern Yucatan, Mexico". *Annals of the Association of American Geographers* 96:302–22.

Christian, C.S., T.D. Potts, G.W. Burnett and T.E. Lacher Jr. 1996. "Parrot Conservation and Ecotourism in the Windward Islands". *Journal of Biogeography* 23:387–93.

Clarke, C. 1974. "Urbanization in the Caribbean". *Geography* 59:223–32.

Clarke, E. 1953. "Land Tenure and the Family in Four Selected Communities in Jamaica". *Social and Economic Studies* 1 (4): 81–118.

Clegg, P. 2002a. *The Caribbean Banana Trade: From Colonialism to Globalization.* New York: Palgrave Macmillan.

———. 2002b. "The Establishment of the Windward Islands Banana Industry: Commercial Opportunity and Colonial Necessity". *Social and Economic Studies* 51 (2): 155–74.

Clemens, M., C. Ozden and H. Rapoport. 2014. "Migration and Development Is Moving Far beyond Remittances". *World Development* 64:121–24.

Clement, F. 2012. "For Critical Socio-ecological Systems Studies: Integrating Power and Discourses to Move Beyond the Right Institutional Fit". *Environmental Conservation* 40:1–4.

Cole, J. 1994. "Socio-political Problems of the Tenurial System in St Lucia". In *Land Tenure and Development in the Eastern Caribbean: Proceedings of a Symposium*, edited by F.W. Alleyne, 32–44. Bridgetown, Barbados: Carib Research and Publications.

Conway, D. 1999/2000. "The Importance of Migration for Caribbean Development". *Global Development Studies* 2 (1–2): 73–105.

———. 1993. "Rethinking the Consequences of Remittances for Eastern Caribbean Development". *Caribbean Geography* 4 (2): 116–30.

———. 2004. "Tourism, Environmental Conservation and Management and Local Agriculture in the Eastern Caribbean: Is There an Appropriate, Sustainable Future for Them?" In *Tourism in the Caribbean: Trends, Development, Prospects*, edited by D.T. Duval, 187–204. London: Routledge.

Conway, D., and P. Lorah. 1995. "Environmental Protection Policies in Caribbean Small Islands: Some St Lucian Examples". *Caribbean Geography* 6 (1): 16–27.

Corlett, R.T. 1995. "Tropical Secondary Forests". *Progress in Physical Geography* 19 (2): 159–72.

Costa, R.L., J.A. Prevedello, B. de Souza and D.C. Cabral. 2017. "Forest Transitions in

Tropical Landscapes: A Test in the Atlantic Forest Biodiversity Hotspot". *Applied Geography* 82:93–100.

Cote, M., and A.J. Nightingale. 2012. "Resilience Thinking Meets Social Theory: Situating Social Change in Socio-ecological Systems (SES) Research". *Progress in Human Geography* 36:1–15.

Courchamp, F., B. Hoffmann, J. Russell, C. Leclerc and C. Bellard. 2014. "Climate Change, Sea-Level Rise, and Conservation: Keeping Island Biodiversity Afloat". *Trends in Ecology and Evolution* 29:127–30.

Cousins, J.A., J. Evans and J. Sadler. 2009. "Selling Conservation? Scientific Legitimacy and the Commodification of Conservation Tourism". *Ecology and Society* 14 (1): 32.

Cox, H. 1897. "West Indian Sugar". *Economic Journal* 7 (28): 599–605.

Crichlow, M.A. 1994. "An Alternative Approach to Family Land Tenure in the Anglophone Caribbean: The Case of St Lucia". *New West Indian Guide* 68 (1): 77–99.

Cronon, W. 1983. *Changes in the Land: Indians, Colonists and the Ecology of New England*. New York: Hill and Wang.

Dale, E.H. 1977. "Spotlight on the Caribbean, a Microcosm of the Third World". Regina Geographical Studies No. 2, University of Regina, Saskatchewan.

Dalla-Nora, E.L., A.P.D. Aguiar, D.M. Lapola and G. Woltjer. 2014. "Why Have Land Use Change Models for the Amazon Failed to Capture the Amount of Deforestation over the Last Decade?" *Land Use Policy* 39:403–11.

da Silva Moco, M.K., E. da Gama-Rodrigues, A. da Gama-Rodrigues, R. Machado and V. Baligar. 2009. "Soil and Litter Fauna of Cacao Agroforestry Systems in Bahia, Brazil". *Agroforestry Systems* 76:127–38.

Davidson, D.J. 2010. "The Applicability of the Concept of Resilience to Social Systems: Some Sources of Optimism and Nagging Doubts". *Society and Natural Resources* 32:1135–49.

Davis, B., G. Carletto and P. Winters. 2010. "Migration, Transfers and Economic Decision Making among Agricultural Households: An introduction". *Journal of Development Studies* 46 (1): 1–13.

Davis-Morrison, V. 1998. "The Sustainability of Small-Scale Agricultural Systems in the Millbank Area of the Rio Grande Valley, Portland, Jamaica". In *Resource Sustainability and Caribbean Development*, edited by D. McGregor, D. Barker and S.L. Evans, 296–316. Kingston: University of the West Indies Press.

Degrande, A., K. Schreckenberg, C. Mbosso, P. Anegbeh, V. Okafor and J. Kanmegne. 2006. "Farmers' Fruit Tree-Growing Strategies in the Humid Forest Zone of Cameroon and Nigeria". *Agroforestry Systems* 67:159–75.

de Jong, W., U. Chokkalingam and J. Smith. 2001. "Tropical Secondary Forests in Asia: Introduction and Synthesis". *Journal of Tropical Forest Science* 13 (4): 563–76.

de Latour, L. 1883. *Map of Saint Lucia, 1787: Together with a General Description of the Island*. Colonial Office West Indian Report No. 44, London. In *Saint-Lucie Fille de la Martinique*, edited (1989) by E.R. Bruneau-Latouche. Paris: Published by author.

Denevan, W.M., and C. Padoch, eds. 1987. *Swidden-Fallow Agroforestry in the Peruvian Amazon*. Advances in Economic Botany, vol. 5. New York: New York Botanical Garden.

Dewees, P.A., and N.C. Saxena. 1997. "Wood Product Markets as Incentive for Farmer Tree Growing". In *Farms, Trees and Farmers: Responses to Agricultural Intensification*, edited by J.E.M. Arnold and P.A. Dewees, 198–241. London: Earthscan.

Dixon, J., K. Hamilton, S. Pagiola and L. Segnestan. 2001. "Tourism and the Environment in the Caribbean: An Economic Framework". Environment Department Papers No. 80. Washington, DC: World Bank.

Dolisca, F., J.M. McDaniel, L.D. Teeter and C.M. Jolly. 2007. "Land Tenure, Population Pressure, and Deforestation in Haiti: The Case of Foret des Pins Reserve". *Journal of Forest Economics* 13:277–89.

Downes, B.J., F. Miller, J. Barnett, A. Glaister and H. Ellemor. 2013. "How Do We Know about Resilience? An Analysis of Empirical Research on Resilience, and Implications for Interdisciplinary Praxis". *Environmental Research Letters* 8:8p, doi:10.1088/1748-9326/8/1/014041.

Dray, W.H. 1957. *Laws and Explanation in History*. Oxford: Oxford University Press.

——. 1964. *Philosophy of History*. Englewood Cliffs, NJ: Prentice-Hall.

Dujon, V. 1997. "Communal Property and Land Markets: Agricultural Development Policy in St Lucia". *World Development* 25 (9): 1529–40.

——. 2000. "Caribbean Peasants in the Global Economy: Popular Resistance to the Privatization of Communal Land in the Twentieth Century and Beyond". *Global Development Studies* 2 (1–2): 199–221.

Duval, D.T., ed. 2004a. *Tourism in the Caribbean: Trends, Development, Prospects*. London: Routledge.

——. 2004b. "Trends and Circumstances in Caribbean Tourism". In *Tourism in the Caribbean: Trends, Development, Prospects*, edited by D.T. Duval, 3–22. London: Routledge.

Duval, D.T., and P.F. Wilkinson. 2004. "Tourism Development in the Caribbean: Meaning and Influences". In *Tourism in the Caribbean: Trends, Development, Prospects*, edited by D.T. Duval, 59–80. London: Routledge.

Ebach, M.C., M.S. Michael, W.S. Shaw, J. Goff, D.J. Murphy and S. Matthews. 2016. "Big Data and the Historical Sciences: A Critique". *Geoforum* 71:1–4.

Ebanks, G., P. George and C. Nobbe. 1979. "Emigration from Barbados, 1951–1970". *Social and Economic Studies* 28 (2): 431–49.

Efroymson, R.A., K. Kline, A. Angelsen, P.H. Verburg, V. Dale, J. Langeveld and A. McBride. 2016. "A Causal Analysis Framework for Land-Use Change and the Potential Role of Bioenergy Policy". *Land Use Policy* 59:516–27.

European Commission. 2009a. "The Lomé Convention", 18 June 2009. www.ec .europa.eu.

———. 2009b. "The Cotonou Agreement", 18 June 2009. www.ec.europa.eu.

Fairtrade Foundation. 2003. "WINFA Fairtrade Unit". London: Fairtrade Foundation. www.fairtrade.org.uk, accessed 18 June 2009.

———. 2009a. *Fairtrade Foundation Annual Review 2008/2009*. London: Fairtrade Foundation. www.fairtrade.org.uk, accessed 18 June 2009.

———. 2009b. *Fairtrade Bananas Case Study; Windward Islands: Dominica, Saint Lucia, and St Vincent*. London: Fairtrade Foundation. www.fairtrade.org.uk, accessed 18 June 2009.

FAO (Food and Agriculture Organization). 1998. "Banana Exports from Latin America and the Caribbean: The Market, the Evolving Policy Framework and Development Options". Paper presented at the seminar, *Latin American and the Caribbean in Face of the Furthering Process of Multilateral Agricultural Reform*, 23–24 November. Rome: FAO/IICA/World Bank. Food and Agriculture Organization of the United Nations.

Fearnside, P. 2008. "Will Urbanization Cause Deforested Areas to Be Abandoned in Brazilian Amazonia?" *Environmental Conservation* 35 (3): 197–99.

Feeny, D., F. Berkes, B.J. McCay and J.M. Acheson. 1990. "The Tragedy of the Commons: Twenty-Two Years Later". *Human Ecology* 18:1–19.

Finegan, B. 1996. "Pattern and Process in Neotropical Secondary Forests: The First 100 Years of Succession". *Trends in Ecology and Evolution* 11:119–24.

Fingal, C. 2008. "Fair 'Trade not Aid': Globalization, Fair Trade and the Saint Lucia Banana Industry". *Caribbean Geography* 15 (2): 118–29.

Finkel, H.J. 1964. "Patterns of Land Tenure in the Leeward and Windward Islands and Their Relevance to Problems of Agricultural Development in the West Indies". *Economic Geography* 40 (2): 163–72.

———. 1971. "Patterns of Land Tenure in the Leeward and Windward Islands". In *Peoples and Cultures of the Caribbean: An Anthropological Reader*, edited by M. Horrowitz. Garden City, New York: Natural History Press.

Folke, C. 2006. "Resilience: The Emergence of a Perspective for Socio-ecological Systems Analysis". *Global Environmental Change* 16:253–67.

Forsyth, T. 2008. "Political Ecology and the Epistemology of Social Justice". *Geoforum* 39:756–64.

Fortmann, L. 1985. "The Tree Tenure Factor in Agroforestry with Particular Reference to Africa". *Agroforestry Systems* 2:229–51.

Foster, A., and M. Rosenzwig. 2003. "Economic Growth and Rise of Forests". *Quarterly Journal of Economics* 118:601–37.

Foster, D.R. 1992. "Land-Use History (1730–1990) and Vegetation Dynamics in Central New England, USA". *Journal of Ecology* 80:753–72.

Found, W.C. 2004. "Historic Sites, Material Culture and Tourism in the Caribbean Islands". In *Tourism in the Caribbean: Trends, Development, Prospects*, edited by D.T. Duval, 136–51. London: Routledge.

France, L. 1998. "Sustainability and Development of Tourism on the Islands of Barbados, St Lucia and Dominica". In *Resource Sustainability and Caribbean Development*, edited by D.F.M. McGregor, D. Barker and S.L. Evans, 109–25. Kingston: University of the West Indies Press.

Fraser, E.D.G., and L.C. Stringer. 2009. "Explaining Agricultural Collapse: Macro-Forces, Micro-Crises and the Emergence of Land Use Vulnerability in Southern Romania". *Global Environmental Change* 19:45–53.

Freedman, D.A. 1991. "Statistical Models and Shoe Leather". In *Sociological Methodology*, vol. 21, edited by P.V. Marsden, 291–313. Oxford: Basil Blackwell for the American Sociological Association. Reprinted (2011) in *Causal Explanation for Social Scientists: A Reader*, edited by A.P. Vayda and B.B. Walters, 151–67. Lanham, MD: AltaMira Press.

Fridell, G. 2004. "The Fair Trade Network in Historical Perspective". *Canadian Journal of Development Studies* 25 (3): 411–28.

———. 2011. "The Case against Cheap Bananas: Lessons from the EU-Caribbean Banana Agreement". *Critical Sociology* 37 (3): 285–307.

Friis, C., and J.O. Nielsen. 2017. "Land Use Change in a Telecoupled World: The Relevance and Applicability of the Telecoupling Framework in the Case of Banana Plantation Expansion in Laos". *Ecology and Society* 22 (4): 30.

Frundt, H.J. 2009. *Fair Bananas! Farmers, Workers and Consumers Strive to Change an Industry.* Tucson: University of Arizona Press.

Gaddis, J.L. 2002. *The Landscape of History: How Historians Map the Past.* Oxford: Oxford University Press.

Galaty, J.G. 2013. "Comment on 'Response Diversity and Resilience Socio-Ecological Systems'". *Current Anthropology* 54 (2): 130–31.

Geist, H., W. McConnell, E.F. Lambin, E. Moran, D. Alves and T. Rudel. 2006. "Causes and Trajectories of Land-Use/Cover Change". In *Land-Use and Land-Cover Change: Local Processes and Global Impacts*, edited by E.F. Lambin and H. Geist, 41–70. Berlin: Springer-Verlag.

Gellrich, M., and N. Zimmermann. 2007. "Investigating the Regional-Scale Pattern of Agricultural Land Abandonment in the Swiss Mountains: A Spatial Statistical Modeling Approach". *Landscape and Urban Planning* 79:65–76.

Giordano, M. 2003. "The Geography of the Commons: the Role of Scale and Space". *Annals of the Association of American Geographers* 93 (2): 365–75.

GLP (Global Land Project). 2005. *Science Plan and Implementation Strategy.* IGBP Report No. 53/IHDP Report No. 19. Stockholm: IGBP Secretariat.

Gmelch, G. 1980. "Return Migration". *Annual Review of Anthropology* 9:135–59.

——. 1992. *Double Passage: The Lives of Caribbean Migrants Abroad and Back Home.* Ann Arbor: University of Michigan Press.

Goba, G. 2008. "Re-conceptualizing Generalization: Old Issues in a New Frame". In *The Sage Handbook of Social Research Methods*, 193–213. New York: Sage.

Godoy, R.A. 1992. "Determinants of Smallholder Commercial Tree Cultivation". *World Development* 20 (5): 713–25.

Gonzalez-Insuasti, M.S., C. Martorell and J. Caballero. 2008. "Factors that Influence the Intensity of Non-Agricultural Management of Plant Resources". *Agroforestry Systems* 74:1–15.

GOSL (Government of Saint Lucia). 1974. *The Agricultural Census Data of St Lucia, 1973/74.* Castries: Ministry of Agriculture, Government of Saint Lucia.

——. 1983. *Saint Lucia Economic Review, 1982.* Castries: Ministry of Finance, Planning and Statistics, Government of Saint Lucia.

——. 1984. *Saint Lucia Economic Review, 1983.* Castries: Ministry of Finance, Planning and Statistics, Government of Saint Lucia.

——. 1985. *Saint Lucia Economic Review, 1984.* Castries: Ministry of Finance, Statistics and Negotiating, Government of Saint Lucia.

——. 1986. *Saint Lucia Economic Review, 1985.* Castries: Ministry of Finance, Statistics and Negotiating, Government of Saint Lucia.

——. 1987a. *Final Report on the 1986 Census of Agriculture in Saint Lucia.* Castries: Ministry of Agriculture, Lands, Fisheries and Co-operatives, Government of Saint Lucia.

——. 1987b. *Saint Lucia Economic and Social Review, 1986.* Castries: Ministry of Finance, Statistics and Negotiating, Government of Saint Lucia.

——. 1989. *Saint Lucia Economic and Social Review, 1988.* Castries: Ministry of Finance, Statistics and Negotiating, Government of Saint Lucia.

——. 1990. *Saint Lucia Economic and Social Review, 1989.* Castries: Ministry of Finance, Statistics and Negotiating, Government of Saint Lucia.

——. 1991a. *St Lucia Country Environmental Profile.* Saint Michael, Barbados: Caribbean Conservation Association, and Castries: Government of Saint Lucia.

——. 1991b. *Saint Lucia Economic and Social Review, 1990*, Castries: Ministry of Finance, Planning and Statistics, Government of Saint Lucia.

——. 1991c. *Saint Lucia Economic Review: January–March, 1991.* Castries: Ministry of Finance, Statistics and Negotiating, Government of Saint Lucia.

——. 1993. *Saint Lucia Economic and Social Review, 1992.* Castries: Ministry of Finance, Statistics and Negotiating, Government of Saint Lucia.

——. 1994. *Saint Lucia Economic and Social Review, 1993.* Castries: Ministry of Finance, Statistics and Negotiating, Government of Saint Lucia.

——. 1995. *Saint Lucia Economic and Social Review, 1994.* Castries: Ministry of Finance, Planning and Statistics, Government of Saint Lucia.

——. 1996a. *1996 St Lucia Census of Agriculture, Final Report.* Castries: Ministry of Agriculture, Lands, Fisheries and Forestry, Government of Saint Lucia.

——. 1996b. *Saint Lucia Economic and Social Review, 1995.* Castries: Ministry of Finance, Statistics and Negotiating, Government of Saint Lucia.

——. 1996c. *Tourism Incentives Act.* Laws of the Government of Saint Lucia, No. 7, 21–36. Castries: Government of Saint Lucia.

——. 1997. *Saint Lucia Economic and Social Review, 1996.* Castries: Ministry of Finance, Statistics and Negotiating, Government of Saint Lucia.

——. 1998a. *Economic and Social Review, 1997.* Castries: Ministry of Finance and Planning, Government of Saint Lucia.

——. 1998b. *Biodiversity Country Study Report of Saint Lucia.* Castries: Ministry of Agriculture, Forestry, Fisheries and the Environment, Government of Saint Lucia and UNEP.

——. 1999. *Economic and Social Review, 1998.* Castries: Ministry of Finance and Planning, Government of Saint Lucia.

——. 2000. *Economic and Social Review, 1999.* Castries: Ministry of Finance and Economic Affairs, Government of Saint Lucia.

——. 2002. *Economic and Social Review, 2001.* Castries: Ministry of Finance, International Financial Services and Economic Affairs, Government of Saint Lucia.

——. 2006a. *Economic and Social Review, 2005.* Castries: Ministry of Finance, Economic Affairs and National Development, Government of Saint Lucia.

——. 2006b. *Annual Statistical Digest, 2006.* Castries: Central Statistics Office, Government of Saint Lucia.

——. 2007a. *2007 St Lucia Census of Agriculture, Final Report.* Castries: Ministry of Agriculture, Forestry and Fisheries, Government of Saint Lucia.

——. 2007b. *Economic and Social Review, 2006.* Castries: Ministry of Finance, Economic Affairs and National Development, Government of Saint Lucia.

——. 2008a. *Economic and Social Review, 2007.* Castries: Ministry of Finance, Economic Affairs and National Development, Government of Saint Lucia.

——. 2008b. *Pitons Management Area and Soufrière Region Integrated Development Plan.* Castries: Ministry of Physical Development, Housing, Urban Renewal and Local Government, Government of Saint Lucia.

——. 2011a. *2010 Population and Housing Census, Preliminary Report.* Castries: Government of Saint Lucia.

——. 2011b. *Economic and Social Review, 2010.* Castries: Ministry of Finance, Economic Affairs and National Development, Government of St. Lucia.

——. 2012a. *Economic and Social Review, 2011.* Castries: Ministry of Finance, Economic Affairs and National Development, Government of Saint Lucia.

——. 2012b. *Annual Statistical Digest, 2012.* Castries: Central Statistics Office, Government of Saint Lucia.

——. 2014. *Economic and Social Review, 2013.* Castries: Ministry of Finance, Economic Affairs and National Development, Government of Saint Lucia.

——. 2015. *Review of the Economy, 2014.* Castries: Ministry of Finance, Economic Affairs, Planning and Social Security, Government of Saint Lucia.

——. 2016. *Review of the Economy, 2015.* Castries: Ministry of Finance, Economic Affairs, Planning and Social Security, Government of Saint Lucia.

Gould, S.J. 1989. *Wonderful Life: The Burgess Shale and the Nature of History.* New York: W.W. Norton.

Grau, H., T. Aide, J. Zimmerman, J. Thomlinson, E. Helmer and X. Zou. 2003. "The Ecological Consequences of Socio-economic Land-Use Changes in Postagriculture Puerto Rico". *BioScience* 53 (12): 1159–68.

Grau, H.R., and M. Aide. 2008. "Globalization and Land-Use Transitions in Latin America". *Ecology and Society* 13 (2): 16.

Graveson, R. 2005. "Plants of Saint Lucia". Unpublished electronic data base. http://saintlucianplants.com.

Gray, C., and R. Bilsborrow. 2014. "Consequences of Out-Migration for Land Use in Rural Ecuador". *Land Use Policy* 36:182–91.

Griffith-Charles, C. 2011. "The Application of the Social Tenure Domain Model (STDM) to Family Land in Trinidad and Tobago". *Land Use Policy* 28:514–22.

Grimm, V., and C. Wissel. 1997. "Babel, or the Ecological Stability Discussions: An Inventory and Analysis of Terminology and a Guide for Avoiding Confusion". *Oecologia* 109:323–34.

Grossman, L.S. 1993. "The Political Ecology of Banana Exports and Local Food Production in St Vincent, Eastern Caribbean". *Annals of the Association of American Geographers* 83 (2): 347–67.

——. 1994. "British Aid and Windwards Bananas: The Case of St Vincent and the Grenadines". *Social and Economic Studies* 43 (1): 151–79.

——. 1997. "Soil Conservation, Political Ecology, and Technological Change on Saint Vincent". *Geographical Review* 87 (3): 353–74.

——. 1998. *The Political Ecology of Bananas.* Chapel Hill: University of North Carolina.

——. 2003. "The St Vincent Banana Growers' Association, Contract Farming, and the Peasantry". In *Banana Wars: Power, Production and History in the Americas,* edited by S. Striffler and M. Moberg, 286–315. Durham, NC: Duke University Press.

Guariguata, M.R., and R. Ostertag. 2001. "Neotropical Secondary Forest Succession: Changes in Structural and Functional Characteristics". *Forest Ecology and Management* 148:185–206.

Gunderson, L., and C.S. Holling, eds. 2002. *Panarchy: Understanding Transformations in Human and Natural Systems*. Washington, DC: Island Press.

Harmsen, J., G. Ellis and R. Devaux. 2014. *A History of Saint Lucia*. Vieux Fort, Saint Lucia: Lighthouse Road Publications.

Harrington, D.E. 1987. "St Lucia Land Registration and Titling Project". In *Proceedings of a Symposium on Land Registration, Tenure Reform and Land Information Systems in the Caribbean (October 6–8, 1986, Castries, Saint Lucia)*, 125–27. Castries: Government of Saint Lucia, and Washington, DC: Organization of American States.

Harris, R., and E. Steer. 1968. "Demographic-Resource Push in Rural Migration: A Jamaican Case Study". *Social and Economic Studies* 17 (4): 398–406.

Harrison, D. 2007. "Cocoa, Conservation and Tourism, Grande Reviere, Trinidad". *Annals of Tourism Research* 34 (4): 919–42.

Hawthorn. G. 1991. *Plausible Worlds: Possibility and Understanding in History and the Social Sciences*. Cambridge, MA: Cambridge University Press.

Hazell, P., C. Poulton, S. Wiggins and A. Dorward. 2010. "The Future of Small Farms: Trajectories and Policy Priorities". *World Development* 38 (10): 1349–61.

Hecht, S. 2010. "The New Rurality: Globalization, Peasants and The Paradoxes of Landscapes". *Land Use Policy* 27:161–69.

Hecht, S.B., S. Kandal, I. Gomes, N. Cuellar and H. Rosa. 2005. "Globalization, Forest Resurgence, and Environmental Politics in El Salvador". *World Development* 34 (2): 308–23.

Hedstrom, P., and P. Ylikoski. 2010. "Causal Mechanisms in the Social Sciences". *Annual Review of Sociology* 36:49–67.

Helmer, E., T. Kennaway, D. Pedreros, M. Clark, H. Marcano, L. Tieszen, T. Ruzycki, S. Schill and S. Carrington. 2008. "Land Cover and Forest Formation Distributions for St Kitts, Nevis, St Eustatius, Grenada and Barbados from Decision Tree Classification of Cloud-Cleared Satellite Imagery". *Caribbean Journal of Science* 44 (2): 175–98.

Hills, T.L., and S. Iton. 2000. "A Re-assessment of the 'Traditional' in Caribbean Small-Scale Agriculture". 1983. Reprint, *Caribbean Geography* 11 (2): 108–17.

Hintikka, J. 1998. "What Is Abduction? The Fundamental Problem of Contemporary Epistemology". *Transactions of the Charles Saunders Peirce Society* 34 (3): 503–33.

Holling, C.S. 1996. "Engineering Resilience versus Ecological Resilience". In *Engi-

neering within Ecological Constraints, 31–43. Washington, DC: National Academy of Sciences.

Holm, P., M.E. Goodsite, S. Cloetingh, M. Agnoletti, B. Moldan, R.D. Lang, R. Leemans, J.O. Moeller, M.P. Buendia, W. Pohl, R.W. Scholz, A. Sors, B. Vanheusden, K. Yusoff and R. Zondervan. 2013. "Collaboration between the Natural, Social and Human Sciences in Global Change Research". *Environmental Science and Policy* 28:25–35.

Homewood, K. 2013. "Comment on 'Response Diversity and Resilience Socio-ecological Systems'". *Current Anthropology* 54:131–32.

Hope, K.R. 1986a. *Economic Development in the Caribbean*. New York: Praeger.

——. 1986b. *Urbanization in the Commonwealth Caribbean*. Boulder, CO: Westview.

Hornborg, A. 2009. "Zero-Sum World: Challenges in Conceptualizing Environmental Load Displacement and Ecologically Unequal Exchange in the World-System". *International Journal of Comparative Sociology* 50 (3–4): 237–62.

Howard, R. 1974. *Flora of the Lesser Antilles: Leeward and Windward Islands*. 6 vols. Jamaica Plains, MA: Arnold Arboretum.

Hoy, D.R. 1962. "The Banana Industry of Guadeloupe, French West Indies". *Social and Economic Studies* 11 (3): 260–66.

IGBP (International Geosphere-Biosphere Program). 2006. *Science Plan and Implementation Strategy*. IGBP Report No. 55. Stockholm: IGBP Secretariat.

Innes, D.Q. 1961. "The efficiency of Jamaican peasant land use". *Canadian Geographer* 5 (2): 19–23.

James, P.E. 1926. "Geographic factors in the Trinidad coconut industry". *Economic Geography* 2 (1): 108–25.

Jennings, T.L. 2011. "Transcending the Adaptation/Mitigation Climate Change Science Policy Debate: Unmasking Assumptions about Adaptation and Resilience". *Weather, Climate Society* 3:238–48.

Johnson, C. 2004. "Uncommon Ground: The 'Poverty of History' in Common Property Discourse". *Development and Change* 35 (3): 407–33.

Jones, P.J.S. 2012. "Governing Protected Areas to Fulfill Biodiversity Conservation Obligations: From Habermasian Ideals to a More Instrumental Reality". *Environment, Development and Sustainability*, doi:10.1007/s10668-012-9375-3.

Jose, S. 2009. "Agroforestry for Ecosystem Services and Environmental Benefits: An Overview". *Agroforestry Systems* 76:1–10.

Joseph, M. 2004. "The Windward Island Banana Industry: Its Preferences, Challenges and Uncertainties". Presentation to the Castries Chapter of the KIWANIS Club, Castries, Saint Lucia, 12 August.

Junqueira, A.B., G. Shepard and C. Clement. 2010. "Secondary Forests on Anthropogenic Soils in Brazilian Amazonia Conserve Agrobiodiversity". *Biodiversity and Conservation* 19:1933–61.

Kearney, M. 1986. "From the Invisible Hand to Visible Feet: Anthropological Studies of Migration and Development". *Annual Review of Anthropology* 15:331–61.

Keenan, R.J., G. Reams, F. Achard, J.V. de Freitas, A. Grainger and E. Lindquist. 2015. "Dynamics of Global Forest Area: Results from the FAO Global Forest Resources Assessment 2015". *Forest Ecology and Management* 352:9–20.

Kelly, A.M. 2016. *The Discovery of Chance: The Life and Thought of Alexander Herzen*. Cambridge, MA: Harvard University Press.

Kelly, D. 1986. "St Lucia's Female Electronics Factory Workers: Key Components of an Export-Oriented Industrialization Strategy". *World Development* 14 (7): 823–38.

Kimber, C.T. 1988. *Martinique Revisited: The Changing Plant Geographies of a West Indian Island*. College Station: Texas A & M University Press.

Kirby, K.J., and C. Watkins, eds. 1998. *The Ecological History of European Forests*. New York: CAB International.

Kirchhoff, T., F.S. Brand, D. Hoheisel and V. Grimm. 2010. "The One-Sidedness and Cultural Bias of the Resilience Approach". *GAIA: Ecological Perspectives on Science and Society* 19 (1): 25–32.

Klepeis, P., and B.L. Turner II. 2001. "Integrated Land History and Global Change Science: The Example of the Southern Yucatan Peninsular Region Project". *Land Use Policy* 18:27–39.

Klooster, D. 2003. "Forest Transitions in Mexico: Institutions and Forests in a Globalized Countryside". *Professional Geographer* 55 (2): 227–37.

Koster, R.L., and A.A. Seaborne. 2003. "Resort Evolution in a Narrowly Based Economy of the Pleasure Periphery: A Case Study of Montego Bay, Jamaica". In *Resources, Planning, and Environmental Management in a Changing Caribbean*, edited by D. Barker and D. McGregor, 197–223. Kingston: University of West Indies Press.

Kozak, J., and M. Szwagrzyk. 2016. "Have There Been Forest Transitions? Forest Transition Theory Revisited in the Context of the Modifiable Areal Unit Problem". *Area* 48 (4): 504–12.

Kueffer, C., and K. Kinney. 2017. "What Is the Importance of Islands to Environmental Conservation?" *Environmental Conservation* 44:311–22.

Kull, C.A., C.K. Ibrahim and T.C. Meredith. 2007. "Tropical Forest Transitions and Globalization: Neo-Liberalism, Migration, Tourism, and International Conservation Agendas". *Society and Natural Resources* 20:723–37.

Kummer, D., and B.L Turner II. 1994. "The Human Causes of Deforestation in Southeast Asia". *BioScience* 44 (5): 323–28.

Kummer, D.M. 1992. *Deforestation in the Post-War Philippines.* Chicago: University of Chicago Press.

Lamb, H. 2008. *Fighting the Banana Wars and Other Fair Trade Battles.* London: Fairtrade Foundation.

Lambin, E.F., and P. Meyfroidt. 2010. "Land Use Transitions: Socio-Ecological Feedback Versus Socio-Economic Change". *Land Use Policy* 27:108–18.

Lambin, E.F., X. Baulies, N. Bockstael, G. Fischer, T. Krug, R. Leemans, E.F. Moran, R.R. Rindfuss, Y. Sato, D. Skole, B.L. Turner II and C. Vogel. 1999. "Land-Use and Land-Cover Change (LUCC) Implementation Strategy". International Geosphere-Biosphere Programme and International Human Dimensions Programme on Global Environmental Change. *IGBP Report 48/IHDP Report 10.* www.geo.ucl.ac.be/LUCC/implstrategy, accessed 21 June 2009.

Lambin, E.F., B.L. Turner, H. Geist, S. Agbola, A. Angelsen, J. Bruce, O. Coomes, R. Dirzo, G. Fischer, C. Folke, P. George, L. Homewood, J. Imbernon, R. Leemans, X. Li, E. Moran, M. Mortimore, P. Ramakrishnan, J. Richards, H. Skanes, W. Steffan, G. Stone, U. Svedin, T. Veldkamp, C. Vogel and J. Xu. 2001. "The Causes of Land-Use and Land-Cover Change: Moving beyond Myths". *Global Environmental Change* 11:261–69.

Lambin, E.F., H. Geist and R.R. Rindfuss. 2006. "Introduction: Local Processes with Global Impacts". In *Land-Use and Land-Cover Change: Local Processes and Global Impacts,* edited by E.F. Lambin and H. Geist, 1–8. Berlin: Springer-Verlag.

Larson, A.M., D. Barry and G.R. Dahal. 2010. "New Rights for Forest-Based Communities? Understanding Processes of Forest Tenure Reform". *International Forestry Review* 12:78–96.

Laurence, K. 1971. *Immigration into the West Indies in the 19th Century.* Bridgetown, Barbados: Caribbean Universities Press and University of West Indies.

Leach, M., and R. Mearns, eds. 1996. *The Lie of the Land: Challenging Received Wisdom on the African Environment.* Oxford: International African Institute in association with James Curry.

Le Franc, E.R-M. 1979. *Rural Land Tenure Systems in St Lucia and Their Relevance to Agricultural Development.* Kingston: Institute of Social and Economic Research, University of the West Indies.

——. 1994. "Discussion". In *Land Tenure and Development in the Eastern Caribbean: Proceedings of a Symposium,* edited by F.W. Alleyne, 57–60. Bridgetown, Barbados: Carib Research and Publications Inc.

Leslie, P., and J.T. McCabe. 2013. "Response Diversity and Resilience Socio-Ecological Systems". *Current Anthropology* 54:114–43.

Lewis, D. 1986. *Philosophical Papers,* vol. 2. Oxford: Oxford University Press.

Reprinted (2011) in *Causal Explanation for Social Scientists: A Reader*, edited by A.P. Vayda and B.B. Walters, 25–39. Lanham, MD: Altamira Press.

Liu, J., T. Dietz, S. Carpenter, C. Folke, M. Alberti, C. Redman, S. Schneider, E. Ostrom, A. Pell, J. Lubchenco, W. Taylor, Z. Ouyang, P. Deadman, T. Kratz and W. Provencher. 2007. "Coupled Human and Natural Systems". *Ambio* 36 (8): 639–49.

Liverpool, N. 1994. "Land Laws and Their Relationship to Farmer Incentives and Productivity". In *Land Tenure and Development in the Eastern Caribbean: Proceedings of a Symposium*, edited by F.W. Alleyne, 7–28. Bridgetown, Barbados: Carib Research and Publications.

Lombard, L.B. 1991. "Events". In *Handbook of Metaphysics and Ontology*, vol. 1, edited by H. Burkhardt and B. Smith, 256–59. Munich: Philosophia Verlag.

Lopez, E., G. Bocco, M. Mendoza, A. Velazquez and J. Aguirre-Rivera. 2006. "Peasant Emigration and Land Use Change at the Watershed Level: A GIS-based Approach in Central Mexico". *Agricultural Systems* 90:62–78.

Lopez, T., T. Aide, and J. Thomlinson. 2001. "Urban Expansion and the Loss of Prime Agricultural Land in Puerto Rico". *Ambio* 30 (1): 49–54.

Lowenthal, D. 1961. "Caribbean Views of Caribbean Land". *Canadian Geographer* 5 (2): 1–9.

——. 1972. *West Indian Societies*. London: Oxford University Press.

Lowenthal, D., and L. Comitas. 1962. "Emigration and Depopulation: Some Neglected Aspects of Population Geography". *Geographical Review* 52 (2): 195–210.

Lowitt, K., G.M. Hickey, A. Saint Ville, K. Raeburn, T. Thompson-Colon, S. Laszlo and L.E. Phillip. 2015. "Factors Affecting the Innovation Potential of Smallholder Farmers in the Caribbean Community". *Regional Environmental Change* 15:1367–77.

Ludeke, M.K.B., G. Petschel-Held and H.-J. Schellnhuber. 2004. "Syndromes of Global Change: the First Panoramic View". *GAIA* 13 (1): 42–9.

Ludewigs, T., A. D'Antona, E. Brondizio and S. Hetrick. 2009. "Agrarian Structure and Land-Cover Change along the Lifespan of Three Colonization Areas in the Brazilian Amazon". *World Development* 37:1348–59.

Lugo, A.E., R. Schmidt, and S. Brown. 1981. "Tropical Forests in the Caribbean". *Ambio* 10 (6): 318–24.

Lukas, M.C. 2014. "Eroding Battlefields: Land Degradation in Java Reconsidered". *Geoforum* 56:87–100.

Mann, G. 2009. "Should Political Ecology Be Marxist? A Case for Gramsci's Historical Materialism". *Geoforum* 40:335–44.

Mansfield, B. 2004. "Neoliberalism in the Oceans: 'Rationalization', Property Rights, and the Commons Question". *Geoforum* 35:313–26.

Marshall, D. 1982. "Migration as an Agent of Change in Caribbean Island Ecosystems". *International Social Science Journal* (UNESCO) 34 (3): 451–67.

Marshall, O.R. 1971. "West Indian Land Law: Conspectus and Reform". *Social and Economic Studies* 20 (1): 1–14.

Marshall, W.K. 1968. "Notes on Peasant Development in the West Indies since 1838". *Social and Economic Studies* 17 (3): 252–63.

Massey, D., J. Arango, G. Hugo, A. Kouaouci, A. Pellegrino and J. Taylor. 1993. "Theories of International Migration: A Review and Appraisal". *Population and Development Review* 19 (3): 431–66.

Mather, A.S. 1992. "The Forest Transition". *Area* 24:367–79.

Mather, A.S., and C.L. Needle. 1998. "The Forest Transition: A Theoretical Basis". *Area* 30:117–24.

Mathurin, D.C.E. 1967. "An Unfavourable System of Land Tenure: The Case of St Lucia". In *Proceedings of the Second West Indian Agricultural Economics Conference*, 139–52. St Augustine, Trinidad: University of the West Indies.

Mathurin, L. 2012. "Short Shipped: The Saint Lucia Banana Industry 1920–1945". Paper presented at the Saint Lucia Country Conference, University of the West Indies, Castries, Saint Lucia, May.

McCay, B.J., and J.A. Acheson, eds. 1987. *The Question of the Commons: The Culture and Ecology of Communal Resources*. Tucson: University of Arizona Press.

McCay, B.J., and S. Jentoft. 1998. "Market or Community Failure? Critical Perspectives on Common Property Research". *Human Organization* 57 (1): 21–29.

McConnell, W.J., J. Millington, N. Reo, M. Alberti, H. Asbjornsen, L. Baker, N. Brozovic, L. Drinkwater, S. Drzyzga, J. Fragaso, D. Holland, C. Jantz, T. Kohler, H. Maschner, M. Monticino, G. Podesta, R. Pontius Jr., C. Redman, D. Sailor, G. Urquhart and J. Liu. 2011. "Research on Coupled Human and Natural Systems (CHANS): Approach, Challenges and Strategies". *Bulletin of the Ecological Society of America* 92:218–28.

McCullagh, C.B. 1984. *Justifying Historical Descriptions*. Cambridge: Cambridge University Press.

——. 1998. *The Truth of History*. London: Routledge.

McElroy, J., and K. de Albuquerque. 1988. "Migration Transition in Small Northern and Eastern Caribbean States". *International Migration Review* 22 (3): 30–58.

——. "Sustainable Small-Scale Agriculture in Small Caribbean Islands". 1990. *Society and Natural Resources* 3:109–29.

McElroy, J.L. 2003. "Tourism Development in Small Islands across the World". *Geografiska Annaler* 85B: 231–42.

McFarlane, D. 1964. "The Future of the Banana Industry in the West Indies". *Social and Economic Studies* 13 (1): 38–93.

McGuire, T. 1997. "The Last Northern Cod". *Journal of Political Ecology* 4:41–54.

McQueen, M., C. Philips, D. Hallman and A. Swinbank. 1997. "Chapter 8: The Lomé Banana Protocol". In *ACP-EU Trade and Aid Co-operation Post Lomé IV*. www .acpsec.org, accessed 18 July 2009.

Mena, C.F., A.F. Barbieri, S.J. Walsh, C.M. Erlien, F.L. Holt and R. Bilsborrow. 2006. "Pressure on the Cuyabeno Wildlife Reserve: Development and Land Use/Cover Change in the Northern Ecuadorian Amazon". *World Development* 34:1831–49.

Mendoza, M.E., E.L. Grandos, D. Geneletti, D.R. Perez-Salicrup and V. Salinas. 2011. "Analyzing Land Cover and Land Use Change Processes at Watershed Level: A Multitemporal Study in the Lake Cuitzeo Watershed, Mexico (1975–2003)". *Applied Geography* 31:237–50.

Meyer, D. 2006. *Caribbean Tourism, Local Sourcing, and Enterprise Development: Review of the Literature*. PPT Working Paper No. 18. London: Centre for Responsible Tourism, International Institute for Environment and Development and Overseas Development Institute.

Meyfroidt, P. 2015. "Approaches and Terminology for Causal Analysis in Land Systems Science". *Journal of Land Use Science* 11:501–22, doi:10.1080/1747423X .2015.1117530.

Meyfroidt, P., T.K. Rudel and E.F. Lambin. 2010. "Forest Transitions, Trade and the Global Displacement of Land Use". *Proceedings of the National Academy of Sciences* 107 (49): 20917–22.

Midgett, D. 1977. "West Indian Migration and Adaptation in St Lucia and London". PhD diss., University of Illinois at Urbana-Champaign.

Mills, B. 2007. "'Leave to Come Back': The Importance of Family Land in a Transnational Caribbean Community". In *Caribbean Land and Development Revisited*, edited by J. Besson and J. Momsen, 233–41. New York: Palgrave Macmillan.

Mintz, S.W. 1974. *Caribbean Transformations*. Chicago: Aldine.

——. 1985. "From Plantations to Peasantries in the Caribbean". In *Caribbean Contours*, edited by S.W. Mintz and S. Price, 127–53. Baltimore: Johns Hopkins University Press.

Moberg, M. 2005. "Fair Trade and Eastern Caribbean Banana Farmers: Rhetoric and Reality in the Anti-globalization Movement". *Human Organization* 64 (1): 4–15.

——. 2008. *Slipping Away: Banana Politics and Fair Trade in the Eastern Caribbean*. New York: Berghan Books.

Momsen, J.D. 1986. "Migration and Rural Development in the Caribbean". *Tijdschrift voor Economic En Social Geografie* 77 (1): 50–58.

Momsen, J.H. 1998. "Caribbean Tourism and Agriculture: New Linkages in the Global Era?" In *Globalization and Neoliberalism: The Caribbean Context*, edited by T. Klak, 115–34. Lanham, MD: Rowman and Littlefield.

Moore, W., W. Elliott and T. Lorde. 2017. "Climate Change, Atlantic Storm Activity and the Regional Socio-Economic Impacts on the Caribbean". *Environment, Development and Sustainability* 19:707–26.

Moran, E.F. 1993. "Deforestation and Land Use in the Brazilian Amazon". *Human Ecology* 21:1–21.

Moran-Taylor, M., and M. Taylor. 2010. "Land and Lena: Linking Transnational Migration, Natural Resources, and the Environment in Guatemala". *Population and Environment* 32:198–215.

Murray, D.L., and L.T. Raynolds. 2000. "Alternative Trade in Bananas: Obstacles and Opportunities for Progressive Social Change in the Global Economy". *Agriculture and Human Values* 17:65–74.

Mycoo, M. 2005a. "Minimising Foreign Control of Land in an Era of Globalization: Prospects for St Lucia". *Land Use Policy* 22:345–57.

——. 2005b. "Poverty Alleviation through Sustainable Tourism: Livelihood Strategies in Anse La Raye, St Lucia". *Caribbean Geography* 14:1–14.

Myers, G. 2004. *Banana Wars: The Price of Free Trade*. London: Zed Books.

Nadasdy, P. 2007. "Adaptive Co-management and the Gospel of Resilience". In *Adaptive Co-management: Collaboration, Learning and Multi-Level Governance*, edited by D. Armitage, F. Berkes and N. Doubleday, 208–26. Vancouver: University of British Columbia Press.

Nagendra, H. 2007. "Drivers of Reforestation in Human-Dominated forests". *Proceedings of the National Academy of Sciences* 104 (39): 15218–23.

Naughton-Teves, L. 2002. "Wild Animals in the Garden: Conserving Wildlife in Amazonian agroecosystems". *Annals of the Association of American Geographers* 92 (3): 488–506.

Neocleous, M. 2013. "Resisting Resilience". *Radical Philosophy* 178:2–7.

Newell, B., C. Crumley, N. Hassan, E.F. Lambin, C. Pahl-Wostle, A. Underdal and R. Wasson. 2005. "A Conceptual Template for Integrative Human-Environment Research". *Global Environmental Change* 15:299–307.

Newman, M.K., K.P. McLaren and B.S. Wilson. 2014. "Long-Term Socio-economic and Spatial Pattern Drivers of Land Cover Change in a Caribbean Tropical Moist Forest". *Agriculture, Ecosystems and Environment* 186:185–200.

——. 2018. "Using the Forest Transition Model and a Proximate Cause of Deforestation to Explain Long-Term Forest Cover Trends in a Caribbean Forest". *Land Use Policy* 71:395–408.

Nicholas, L., and B. Thapa. 2013. "The Politics of World Heritage: A Case Study of the Pitons Management Area, St Lucia". *Journal of Heritage Tourism* 8:37–48.

Nickerson, R.S. 1998. "Confirmation Bias: A Ubiquitous Phenomenon in Many Guises". *Reviews in General Psychology* 2:175–220.

Norris, K. 2008. "Agriculture and Biodiversity Conservation: Opportunity Knocks". *Conservation Letters* 1:2–11.

Nyerges, A.E. 2008. "Orthodoxy and Revision in West African Guinea Savanna Ecology". In *Against the Grain: The Vayda Tradition in Human Ecology and Ecological Anthropology*, edited by B.B. Walters, B.J. McCay, P. West and S. Lees, 81–98. Lanham, MD: AltaMira Press.

Nygren, A., and S. Rikoon. 2008. "Political Ecology Revisited: Integration of Politics and Ecology Does Matter". *Society and Natural Resources* 21:767–82.

OAS (Organization of American States). 1986. "Saint Lucia Natural Resources and Agricultural Development Project: Studies and Proposals for the Implementation of a Land Registration Programme 1981". Washington, DC: Department of Regional Development, Executive Secretariat for Economic and Social Affairs, Organization of American States.

——. 1991. *Integrated Land Development: The Case of the Mabouya Valley in Saint Lucia*. Washington, DC: Department of Regional Development, Executive Secretariat for Economic and Social Affairs, Organization of American States.

Ogden, L., N. Heynen, U. Oslender, P. West, K-A. Kassam and P. Robbins. 2013. "Global Assemblages, Resilience, and Earth Stewardship in the Anthropocene". *Frontiers in Ecology and the Environment* 11 (7): 341–47.

Oliveira, J.A.P. 2008. "Property Rights, Land Conflicts and Deforestation in the Eastern Amazon". *Forest Policy and Economics* 10:303–15.

O'Loughlin, C. 1968. *Economic and Political Change in the Leeward and Windward Islands*. New Haven, CT: Yale University Press.

O'Neil, H.W. 1964. "The Economy of Saint Lucia". *Social and Economic Studies* 13:440–70.

Ostrom, E. 1990. *Governing the Commons: The Evolution of Institutions for Collective Action*. Cambridge: Cambridge University Press.

——. 2009. "A General Framework for Analyzing Sustainability of Social-Ecological Systems". *Science* 325:419–22.

Palmer, R. 1974. "A Decade of West Indian Migration to the United States, 1962–1972: An Economic Analysis". *Social and Economic Studies* 23 (4): 571–87.

Palsson, G., B. Szerszynski, S. Sorlin, J. Marks, B. Avrisl, C. Crumley, H. Hackmann, P. Holm, J. Ingram, A. Kriman, M.P. Buendia and R. Weehuizen. 2013. "Reconceptualizing the 'Anthropos' in the Anthropocene: Integrating the Social Sciences and Humanities in Global Environmental Change Research". *Environmental Science and Policy* 28:3–13.

Pares-Ramos, I., W. Gould and T. Aide. 2008. "Agricultural Abandonment, Suburban Growth, and Forest Expansion in Puerto Rico between 1991–2000". *Ecology and Society* 13 (2): 15p.

Pattanayak, S.K. 2004. "Valuing Watershed Services: Concepts and Empirics from Southeast Asia". *Agriculture, Ecosystems and Environment* 104:171–84.

Pattanayak, S.K., D.E. Mercer, E. Sills and J-C. Yang. 2003. "Taking Stock of Agroforestry Adoption Studies". *Agroforestry Systems* 57:173–86.

Pattullo, P. 2005. *Last Resorts: The Cost of Tourism in the Caribbean*. 2nd ed. New York: Monthly Review Press.

Peach, C. 1965. "West Indian Migration to Britain: The Economic Factors". *Race and Class* 7:31–46.

———. 1967. "West Indian Migration to Britain". *International Migration Review* 1 (2): 34–45.

Peirce, C.S. 1932. *Collected Papers of Charles Saunders Peirce*, edited by C. Hartshorne and P. Weiss. Vol. 1. Cambridge, MA: Harvard University Press.

Peluso, N. 1992. *Rich Forests, Poor People: Resource Control and Resistance in Java*. Berkeley: University of California Press.

Penna-Firme, R. 2012. "Political and Event Ecology: Critiques and Opportunities for Collaboration". *Journal of Political Ecology* 20:199–216.

Perfecto, I., R.A. Rice, R. Greenberg and M.E. Van der Voort. 1996. "Shade Coffee: A Disappearing Refuge for Biodiversity". *BioScience* 46 (8): 598–608.

Perramond, E.P. 2007. "Tactics and Strategies in Political Ecology Research". *Area* 39:499–507.

Perz, S.G. 2007. "Grand Theory and Context-Specificity in the Study of Forest Dynamics: Forest Transition Theory and Other Directions". *Professional Geographer* 59:105–14.

Piguet, E. 2013. "From 'Primitive Migration' to 'Climate Refugees': The Curious Fate of the Natural Environment in Migration Studies". *Annals of the Association of American Geographers* 103:148–62.

Place, F. 2009. "Land Tenure and Agricultural Productivity in Africa: A Comparative Analysis of the Economic Literature and Recent Policy Strategies and Reforms". *World Development* 37 (8): 1326–36.

Plieninger, T., H. Draux, N. Fagerholm, C. Bieling, M. Burgi, T. Kizos, T. Kuemmerle, J. Primdahl and P.H. Verburg. 2016. "The Driving Forces of Landscape Change in Europe: A Systematic Review of the Evidence". *Land Use Policy* 57:2014–214.

Pollini, J. 2010. "Environmental Degradation Narratives in Madagascar: From Colonial Hegemonies to Humanist Revisionism". *Geoforum* 41:711–22.

Pooley, S.P., J.A. Mendelsohn and E.J. Milner-Gulland. 2013. "Hunting Down the Chimera of Multiple Disciplinarity in Conservation Science". *Conservation Biology* 28:22–32.

Porter, E. 2009. "Banana Wars". *New York Times*, 29 December. www.nytimes.com/2009/12/29/opinion/29tue4.html.

Potter, R. 1993. "Urbanization in the Caribbean and Trends in Global Convergence-Divergence". *Geographical Journal* 159 (1): 1–21.

——. 1995. "Urbanization and Development in the Caribbean". *Geography* 80 (4): 334–41.

Preston, D. 1998. "Post-peasant Capitalist Graziers: The 21st Century in Southern Bolivia". *Mountain Research and Development* 18 (2): 151–58.

Priest, G. 2017. "Framing Causal Questions about the Past: The Cambrian Explosion as Case Study". *Studies in the History and Philosophy of Biology and Biomedical Sciences* 63:55–63.

Radel, C., B. Schmook and S. McCandless. 2010. "Environment, Transnational Labor Migration, and Gender: Case Studies from Southern Yucatan, Mexico and Vermont, USA". *Population and Environment* 32:177–97.

Ragin, C.S. 1987. *The Comparative Method*. Berkeley: University of California Press.

Raintree, J.B., ed. 1987. *Land, Trees and Tenure*. Nairobi: International Center for Research on Agroforestry, and Madison, WI: Land Tenure Center.

Rangan, H., and C.A. Kull. 2009. "What Makes Ecology 'Political'? Rethinking 'Scale' in Political Ecology". *Progress in Human Geography* 33:28–45.

Raynolds, L.T. 2000. "Re-embedding Global Agriculture: The International Organic and Fair Trade Movements". *Agriculture and Human Values* 17:297–309.

——. 2003. "The Global Banana Trade". In *Banana Wars: Power, Production and History in the Americas*, edited by S. Striffler and M. Moberg, 23–47. Durham, NC: Duke University Press.

Read, R. 1994. "The EC Internal Banana Market: The Issues and the Dilemma". *World Economy* 17 (2): 219–35.

Redo, D.J., T.M. Aide and M.L. Clark. 2012. "The Relative Importance of Socioeconomic and Environmental Variables in Explaining Land Change in Bolivia, 2001–2010". *Annals of the Association of American Geographers* 102:778–807.

Reenberg, A. 2001. "Agricultural Land Use Pattern Dynamics in the Sudan-Sahel – Towards an Event-Driven Framework". *Land Use Policy* 18:309–19.

Renard, Y. 2001. *Practical Strategies for Pro-Poor Tourism: A Case Study of the St Lucia Heritage Tourism Programme*. PPT Working Paper No. 7. London: Centre for Responsible Tourism, International Institute for Environment and Development and Overseas Development Institute.

Reynolds, A. 2006. *The Struggle for Survival: An Historical, Political, and Socioeconomic Perspective of Saint Lucia*. Vieux Fort, Saint Lucia: Jako Books.

Reynolds, T. 2008. "Ties That Bind: Families, Social Capital and Caribbean Second-Generation Return Migration". London: Families and Social Capital Research Group, South Bank University.

Richardson, B. 1983. *Caribbean Migrants: Environment and Human Survival on St Kitts and Nevis*. Knoxville: University of Tennessee Press.

———. 1992. *The Caribbean in the Wider World, 1492–1992: A Regional Geography*. Cambridge: Cambridge University Press.

———. 2004. "The Migration Experience". In *General History of the Caribbean*. Vol. 5: *The Caribbean in the Twentieth Century*, edited by B. Brereton, 434–64. Paris: UNESCO.

———. 2007. "The Importance of the 1897 British Royal Commission". In *Caribbean Land and Development Revisited*, edited by J. Besson and J. Momsen, 17–28. New York: Palgrave Macmillan.

Robbins, P. 2004. *Political Ecology: A Critical Introduction*. London: Blackwell.

Robbins, P., and K.M. Bishop. 2008. "There and Back Again: Epiphany, Disillusionment, and Rediscovery in Political Ecology". *Geoforum* 39:747–55.

Robbins, P., and A. Fraser. 2003. "A Forest of Contradictions: Producing the Landscapes of the Scottish Highlands". *Antipode* 35:95–118.

Roberts, C. 1996. *The Logic of Historical Explanation*. University Park: The Pennsylvania State University Press.

Roberts, G. 1955. "Emigration from the Island of Barbados". *Social and Economic Studies* 4 (3): 245–88.

———. 1958a. "Note on Population and Growth". *Social and Economic Studies* 7 (3): 24–32.

———. 1958b. "Study of External Migration Affecting Jamaica, 1953–55". *Social and Economic Studies* 7 (2, Supplement): 1–126.

Roberts, G., and J. Byrne. 1966. "Summary Statistics for Indenture and Associated Migration Affecting the West Indies, 1834–1918". *Population Studies* 20 (1): 125–34.

Robinson, J.C. 1996. *Bananas and Plantains*. Wallingford, UK: CAB International.

Robinson, B.E., M.E. Holland and L. Naughton-Tevis. 2014. "Does secure land tenure save forests? A meta-analysis of the relationship between land tenure and tropical deforestation". *Global Environmental Change* 29:281–93.

Robson, J., and F. Berkes. 2011. "Exploring Some of the Myths of Land Use Change: Can Rural to Urban Migration Drive Declines in Biodiversity?" *Global Environmental Change* 21:844–54.

Rojas, E. 1984. "Agriculture Land in the Eastern Caribbean". *Land Use Policy* 1 (1): 39–54.

Rojas, E., and R.A. Meganck. 1987. "Land Distribution and Land Development in the Eastern Caribbean". *Land Use Policy* (April): 157–67.

Romalis, R. 1975. "Economic Change and Peasant Political Consciousness in the Commonwealth Caribbean". *Journal of Commonwealth and Comparative Politics* 13:219–41.

Rubenstein, H. 1975. "The Utilization of Arable Land in an Eastern Caribbean Valley". *Canadian Journal of Sociology* 1 (2): 157–67.

———. 1977. "Economic History and Population Movements in an Eastern Caribbean Valley". *Ethnohistory* 24:19–45.

———. 1983a. "Migration and Underdevelopment: The Caribbean". *Cultural Survival Quarterly* 7 (4): 30–32.

———. 1983b. "Remittances and Rural Underdevelopment in the English-Speaking Caribbean". *Human Organization* 42 (4): 295–306.

———. 1987. "Folk and Mainstream Systems of Land Tenure in St Vincent". In *Land and Development in the Caribbean*, edited by J. Besson and J. Momsen, 70–87. London: Macmillan.

Rudel, T.K. 1993. *Tropical Deforestation: Small Farmers and Land Clearing in the Ecuadorian Amazon*. New York: Columbia University Press.

———. 1995. "When Do Property Rights Matter? Open Access, Informal Social Controls, and Deforestation in the Ecuadorian Amazon". *Human Organization* 54 (2): 187–94.

———. 1998. "Is There a Forest Transition? Deforestation, Reforestation, and Development". *Rural Sociology* 63:533–52.

———. 2005. *Tropical Forests: Regional Paths of Destruction and Regeneration in the Late Twentieth Century*. New York: Columbia University Press.

———. 2008. "Meta-analysis of Case Studies: A Method for Studying Regional and Global Environmental Change". *Global Environmental Change* 18:18–25.

Rudel, T., D. Bates and R. Machinguiashi. 2002. "A Tropical Forest Transition? Agriculture Change, Out-Migration, and Secondary Forests in the Ecuadorian Amazon". *Annals of the Association of American Geographers* 92 (1): 87–102.

Rudel, T.K., M. Perez-Lugo and H. Zichal. 2000. "When Fields Revert to Forest: Development and Spontaneous Reforestation in Post-War Puerto Rico". *Professional Geographer* 52:386–97.

Rudel, T.K., O.T. Coomes, E. Moran, F. Achard, A. Angelsen, J.C. Xu and E. Lambin. 2005. "Forest Transitions: Towards a Global Understanding of Land Use Change". *Global Environmental Change* 15:23–31.

Rudel, T.K., L. Schneider and M. Uriarte. 2010. "Forest Transitions: An Introduction". *Land Use Policy* 27:95–97.

Sagoff, M. 2016. "Are There General Causal Forces in Ecology?" *Synthese* 193:3003–24.

Sahr, W.-D. 1998. "Micro-metropolis in the Eastern Caribbean: the Example of St Lucia". In *Resource Sustainability and Caribbean Development*, edited by D.F.M. McGregor, D. Barker and S.L. Evans, 69–86. Kingston: University of the West Indies Press.

Sainsbury's. 2007. "Sainsbury's Converts All of Its Bananas to Fairtrade". Press release, Sainsbury's, April 2007. www.sainsburys.co.uk, accessed 21 May 2009.

Saint Ville, A., G. Hickey, U. Locher and L. Phillip. 2016. "Exploring the Role of Social Capital in Influencing Knowledge Flows and Innovation in Smallholder Farming Communities in the Caribbean". *Food Security* 8:535–49.

Sambuichi, R.H.R., and M. Maridasan. 2007. "Recovery of Species Richness and Conservation of Native Atlantic Forest Trees in the Cacao Plantations of Southern Bahia in Brazil". *Biodiversity and Conservation* 16:3681–701.

Schmook, B., and C. Radel. 2008. "International Labor Migration from a Tropical Development Frontier: Globalizing Households and an Incipient Forest Transition". *Human Ecology* 36:891–908.

Schroth, G., G. da Fonseca, C. Harvey, C. Gascon, H. Vasconcelos and A.N. Izac, eds. 2004 *Agroforestry and Biodiversity Conservation in Tropical Landscapes*. Washington, DC: Island Press.

Scriven, M. 1966. "Causes, Connections and Conditions in History". In *Philosophical Analysis in History*, edited by W.H. Dray, 238–64. New York: Harper and Row.

———. 2008. "A Summative Evaluation of RTC Methodology: And an Alternative Approach to Causal Research". *Journal of MultiDisciplinary Evaluation* 5 (9): 11–24.

Shaver, I., A. Chain-Guadarrama, K. Cleary, A. Sanfiorenzo, R. Santiago-Garcia, B. Finegan, L. Hormel, N. Sibelet, L. Vierling, N. Bosque-Perez, F. DeClerck, M. Fagan and L. Waits. 2015. "Coupled Social and Ecological Outcomes of Agricultural Intensification in Costa Rica and the Future of Biodiversity Conservation in Tropical Agricultural Regions". *Global Environmental Change* 32:74–86.

Shearer, E.B., S. Lastarria-Cornhiel and D. Mesbah. 1991. "The Reform of Rural Land Markets in Latin America and the Caribbean: Research, Theory, and Policy Implications". *LTC Paper* 141. Madison: Land Tenure Center, University of Wisconsin.

Shepard, C.Y. 1927. "Economic Survey of the Cacao Industry of Trinidad, British West Indies". *Economic Geography* 3 (2): 239–58.

Shi, M., R. Yin, L. Zulu, J. Qi, M. Freudenberger and M. Sommerville. 2016. "Empirical Linkages between Devolved Tenure Systems and Forest Conditions: Selected Case Studies and Country Experiences". *Forest Policy and Economics* 73:286–93.

Silva, R.F.B., M. Batistella and E. Moran. 2016. "Drivers of Land Change: Human-Environment Interactions and the Atlantic Forest Transition in the Paraiba Valley, Brazil". *Land Use Policy* 58:133–44.

Simmons, C.S., R.T. Walker and C.H. Wood. 2002. "Tree Planting by Small Producers in the Tropics: A Comparative Study of Brazil and Panama". *Agroforestry Systems* 56:89–105.

Sloan, S. 2007. "Fewer People May Not Mean More Forest For Latin American Forest Frontiers". *Biotropica* 39 (4): 443–6.

Smith, M.G. 1956. "The Transformation of Land Rights by Transmission in Carriacou". *Social and Economic Studies* 5 (2): 103–38.

Smith, R.T. 1955. "Land Tenure in Three Negro Villages in British Guiana". *Social and Economic Studies* 4 (1): 64–81.

Smith, S. 2010. *Fairtrade Bananas: A Global Assessment of Impact (Final Report)*. Sussex: Institute of Development Studies, University of Sussex.

Soluri, J. 2003. "Banana Cultures: Linking the Production and Consumption of Export Bananas, 1800–1980". In *Banana Wars: Power, Production and History in the Americas*, edited by S. Striffler and M. Moberg, 48–79. Durham, NC: Duke University Press.

Spenceley, A. 2008. "Introduction: Responsible Tourism in Southern Africa". In *Responsible Tourism: Critical Issues for Conservation and Development*, edited by A. Spenceley, 1–24. London: Earthscan.

Stanfield, D. 1987. "Land Registration, Tenure Security and Agricultural Development". In *Proceedings of a Symposium on Land Registration, Tenure Reform and Land Information Systems in the Caribbean* (6–8 October 1986, Castries, Saint Lucia), 23–34. Castries: Government of Saint Lucia, and Washington, DC Organization of American States.

Stark, J., P. Lajoie and A.G. Green. 1966. *Soil and Land Use Surveys No. 20: St Lucia*. St Augustine, Trinidad and Tobago: Soil Research and Survey Section, Imperial College of Tropical Agriculture, University of the West Indies.

Strachan, A. 1983. "Return Migration to Guyana". *Social and Economic Studies* 32 (3): 121–42.

Stronza, A. 2001. "Anthropology of Tourism: Forging New Ground for Ecotourism and Other Alternatives". *Annual Review of Anthropology* 30:261–83.

Strunz, S. 2012. "Is Conceptual Vagueness an Asset? Arguments from Philosophy of Science to the Concept of Resilience". *Ecological Economics* 76:112–18.

Sunderlin, W., and I. Resosudarmo. 1999. "The Effect of Population and Migration on Forest Cover in Indonesia". *Journal of Development Studies* 8 (2): 152–69.

Tanner, A. 2007. "On Understanding Too Quickly: Colonial and Postcolonial Misrepresentation of Indigenous Fijian Land Tenure". *Human Organization* 66 (1): 69–77.

Thirgood, J.V. 1989. "Man's Impact on the Forests of Europe". *Journal of World Forest Resources Management* 4:127–67.

Thomas, B. 1954. *Migration and Economic Growth*. London: Cambridge University Press.

Thomas, G. 2010. "Doing Case Study: Abduction not Induction, Phronesis not Theory". *Qualitative Inquiry* 16:575–82.

Thomas, M. 2006. *From Slavery to Freedom: Some Aspects of the Impact of Slavery on Saint Lucia*. Castries: Saint Lucia National Commission for UNESCO, Ministry of Education, Human Resource Development, Youth and Sports, Government of Saint Lucia.

Thomas-Hope, E. 1992. *Explanation in Caribbean Migration: Perception and the Image – Jamaica, Barbados, St Vincent*. London: Warwick University Caribbean Studies, Macmillan Caribbean.

——. 1993. "Population Mobility and Land Assets in Hill Farming Areas of Jamaica". *Caribbean Geography* 4 (1): 49–63.

Timms, B. 2006. "Caribbean Agriculture-Tourism Linkages in a Neoliberal World: Problems and Prospects for St Lucia". *International Development Planning Review* 28 (1): 35–56.

——. 2008. "Development Theory and Domestic Agriculture in the Caribbean: Recurring Crises and Missed Opportunities". *Caribbean Geography* 15 (2): 101–17.

Timms, B., J. Hayes and M. McCracken. 2013. "From Deforestation to Reforestation: Applying the Forest Transition to the Cockpit Country of Jamaica". *Area* 45:77–87.

Tobias, P. 1980. "The Social Context of Grenadian Emigration". *Social and Economic Studies* 29 (1): 40–59.

Torgerson, A.M. 2010. "Fair Trade Banana Production in the Windward Islands: Local Survival and Global Resistance". *Agriculture and Human Values* 27:475–87.

Torres, R., and J.H. Momsen. 2004. "Challenges and Potential for Linking Tourism and Agriculture to Achieve Pro-Poor Tourism Objectives". *Progress in Development Studies* 4 (4): 294–318.

Trancoso, R., A. Filho, J. Tomasella, J. Schietti, B. Forsberg and R. Miller. 2010. "Deforestation and Conservation in Major Watersheds of the Brazilian Amazon". *Environmental Conservation* 36 (4): 277–88.

Tucker, C.M. 1999. "Private versus Common Property Forests: Forest Conditions and Tenure in a Honduran Community". *Human Ecology* 27 (2): 201–30.

Tucker, C.M., J.C. Randolph and E.J. Castellanos. 2007. "Institutions, Biophysical Factors and History: An Integrative Analysis of Private and Common Property Forests in Guatemala and Honduras". *Human Ecology* 35:259–74.

Turner, B.L., II and P. Robbins. 2008. "Land-Change Science and Political Ecology: Similarities, Differences, and Implications for Sustainability Science". *Annual Review of Environment and Resources* 33:6.1–6.22.

Turner, B.L., II, R. Kasperson, P. Matson, J. McCarthy, R. Corell, L. Chistensen, N.

Eckley, J. Kasperson, A. Luers, M. Martello, C. Polsky, A. Pulsipher and A. Schiller. 2003a. "A Framework for Vulnerability Analysis in Sustainability Science". *Proceedings of the National Academy of Sciences* 100 (14): 8074–79.

Turner, B.L. II, E.F. Lambin and A. Reenberg. 2007. "The Emergence of Land Change Science for Global Environmental Change and Sustainability". *Proceedings of the National Academy of Sciences* 104:20666–71.

Turner, B.L., II, J. Geoghegan, D. Lawrence, C. Radel, B. Schmook, C. Vance, S. Manson, E. Keys, D. Foster, P. Klepeis, H. Vester, J. Rogan, R.R. Chowdhury, L. Schneider, R. Dickson and Y. Ogenva-Himmelberger. 2016. "Land System Science and the Social-Environmental System: The Case of Southern Yucatan Peninsular Region (SYPR) Project". *Current Opinion on Environment and Sustainability* 19:18–29.

UNESCO (United Nations Educational, Scientific and Cultural Organization). 2014. "State of Conservation of the Pitons Management Area (Saint Lucia)". Paris: UNESCO. http://whc.unesco.org/en/soc/2889, accessed 25 November 2015.

UNSD (United Nations Statistics Division). 1992. *Agenda 21*. United Nations Conference on Environment and Development, Rio de Janeiro, 3–14 June. https://sustainabledevelopment.un.org/content/documents/Agenda21.pdf.

van Andel, T., B. van der Hoorn, M. Stech, S.B. Arostegui and J. Miller. 2016. "A Quantitative Assessment of the Vegetation Types on the Island of St Eustatius, Dutch Caribbean". *Global Ecology and Conservation* 7:59–69.

Vargas, A., and D. Stanfield. 2003a. *St Lucia Country Study of Land Administration and Management Issues*. Wisconsin: University of Wisconsin Land Tenure Center and Terra Institute.

——, 2003b. "St Lucia Country Study of Land Administration and Management Issues". In *Land in the Caribbean. Proceedings of a Workshop on Land Policy, Administration and Management in the English-Speaking Caribbean*, edited by A.N. Williams, 281–307. Madison: University of Wisconsin Land Tenure Center and Caribbean Land Policy Network.

Vayda, A.P. 2006. "Causal Explanation of Indonesian Forest Fires: Concepts, Applications, and Research Priorities". *Human Ecology* 34:615–35.

——. 2009. *Explaining Human Actions and Environmental Changes*. Lanham, MD: AltaMira Press.

——. 2013. "Causal Explanation for Environmental Anthropologists". In *Environmental Anthropology: Future Trends*, edited by H. Kopnina and E. Ouimet. London: Routledge.

Vayda, A.P., and B.B. Walters. 1999. "Against Political Ecology". *Human Ecology* 27:167–79.

——. 2011. "Introduction: Pragmatic Methods and Causal-History Explanations". In

Causal Explanation for Social Sciences: A Reader, edited by A.P. Vayda and B.B. Walters, 1–21. Lanham, MD: AltaMira Press.

Vayda, A.P., and B.B. Walters, eds. 2011. *Causal Explanation for Social Sciences: A Reader.* Lanham, MD: AltaMira Press.

Veburg, P.H., K. Kok, R.G. Pontius and A. Veldkamp. 2006. "Modeling Land-Use and Land-Cover Change". In *Land-Use and Land-Cover Change: Local Processes and Global Impacts,* edited by E.F. Lambin and H. Geist, 117–35. Berlin: Springer-Verlag.

Vidal, J. 2007. "Saving Saint Lucia: UK Supermarket Sweeps Up to 100m Bananas". *Guardian,* 26 February.

Wahlberg, T.H. 2013. "Elder-Vass on the Causal Power of Social Structures". *Philosophy of the Social Sciences* 20 (10): 1–18.

Walker, B., L. Gunderson, A. Kinzig, C. Folke, S. Carpenter, and L. Schultz. 2006. "A Handful of Heuristics and Some Propositions for Understanding Resilience in Social-Ecological Systems". *Ecology and Society* 11 (1): 13p.

Walker, P.A. 2005. "Political Ecology: Where Is the Ecology?" *Progress in Human Geography* 29:73–82.

Walters, B.B. 2004. "Local Management of Mangrove Forests in the Philippines: Successful Conservation or Efficient Resource Exploitation?" *Human Ecology* 32:177–95.

——. 2005. "Ecological Effects of Small-Scale Cutting on Philippine Mangrove Forests". *Forest Ecology and Management* 206:331–48.

——. 2007. "Competing Use of Marine Space in a Modernizing Fishery: Salmon Farming Meets Lobster Fishing on the Bay of Fundy". *Canadian Geographer* 51 (2): 139–59.

——. 2012a. "An Event-Based Methodology for Climate Change and Human-Environment Research". *Danish Journal of Geography* 112 (2): 135–43.

——. 2012b. "Do Property Rights Matter for Conservation? Family Land, Forests and Trees in St Lucia, West Indies". *Human Ecology* 40:863–78.

——. 2016a. "Migration, Land Use and Forest Change in St Lucia, West Indies". *Land Use Policy* 51:290–300.

——. 2016b. "Saint Lucia's Tourism Landscapes: Economic Development and Environmental Change in the West Indies". *Caribbean Geography* 21:5–23.

——. 2017. "Explaining Rural Land Use Change and Reforestation: A Causal-Historical Approach". *Land Use Policy* 67:608–24.

Walters, B.B., A.M. Cadelina, A. Cardano and E. Visitacion. 1999. "Community History and Rural Development: Why Some Farmers Participate More Readily Than Others". *Agricultural Systems* 59:193–214.

Walters, B.B., and Y. Renard. 1992. "Community Participation in Protected Areas

Planning and Management in St Lucia". In *Science and the Management of Protected Areas*, edited by J. Martin-Willison, S. Bondrup-Neilson, C. Drysdale, T. Herman, N. Munro and T. Pollock, 217–22. Amsterdam: Elsevier.

Walters, B.B., and A.P. Vayda. 2009. "Event Ecology, Causal Historical Analysis and Human-Environment Research". *Annals of the Association of American Geographers* 99:534–53.

Walters, B.B., and L. Hansen. 2013. "Farmed Landscapes, Trees and Forest Conservation in St Lucia, West Indies". *Environmental Conservation* 40 (3): 211–21.

Wannasai, N., and R.P. Shrestha. 2008. "Role of Land Tenure Security and Farm Household Characteristics on Land Use Change in the Prasae Watershed, Thailand". *Land Use Policy* 25:214–24.

Watson, H. 1982. "Theoretical and Methodological Problems in Commonwealth Caribbean Migration Research: Conditions and Causality". *Social and Economic Studies* 31:165–205.

Watts, D. 1987. *The West Indies: Patterns of Development, Culture and Environmental Change since 1492*. Cambridge: Cambridge University Press.

Watts, M. 2003. "Political Ecology". In *A Companion to Economic Geography*, edited by E. Sheppard and T.J. Barnes, 257–74. London: Blackwell.

——. 2011. "On Confluences and Divergences". *Dialogues in Human Geography* 1:84–89.

Watts, M., and R. Peet. 2004. "Liberating Political Ecology". In *Liberation Ecologies*, 2nd ed., edited by R. Peet and M. Watts, 3–41. London: Routledge.

WCED, 1987. *Our Common Future*. Report of the World Commission on Environment and Development. Oxford: Oxford University Press.

Weaver, D.B. 1988. "The Evolution of a 'Plantation' Tourism Landscape on the Caribbean Island of Antigua". *Tijdschrift voor Economische en Sociale Geografie* 79:319–31.

——. 1993a. "Ecotourism in the Small Island Caribbean". *Geojournal* 31 (4): 457–65.

——. 1993b. "Model of Urban Tourism for Small Caribbean Islands". *Geographical Review* 83 (2): 134–40.

——. 2004. "Manifestations of Ecotourism in the Caribbean". In *Tourism in the Caribbean: Trends, Development, Prospects*, edited by D.T. Duval, 172–86. London: Routledge.

Welch, B. 1968. "Population Density and Emigration in Dominica". *Geographical Journal* 134 (2): 227–35.

——. 1993. "Challenging Economic Irrelevance: The Role of Banana Growers' Associations in St Lucia and Martinique". *Caribbean Geography* 4 (2): 102–15.

——. 1994. "Banana Dependency: Albatross or Life Raft for the Windwards". *Social and Economic Studies* 43 (1): 123–49.

——. 1996a. "The Evolution of Export Banana Cultivation in Dominica and St Lucia: Implications for Sustainability". *Caribbean Geography* 7 (1): 62–74.

——. 1996b. *Survival by Association: Supply Management Landscapes of the Eastern Caribbean*. Kingston: University of the West Indies Press.

Widgren, M. 2012a. "Landscape Research in a World of Domesticated Landscapes: The Role of Values, Theory and Concepts". *Quaternary International* 251:117–24.

——. 2012b. "Resilience Thinking vs Political Ecology: Understanding the Dynamics of Small-Scale, Labour-Intensive Farming Landscapes". In *Resilience and the Cultural Landscape: Understanding and Managing Change in Human-Shaped Environments*, edited by T. Plieninger and C. Bieling, chap. 5. Cambridge: Cambridge University Press.

Wiggins, S., J. Kirsten and L. Llambi. 2010. "The Future of Small Farms". *World Development* 38 (10): 1341–48.

Wiley, J. 2008. *The Banana: Empires, Trade Wars and Globalization*. London: University of Nebraska Press.

Wilkinson, P.F. 2004. "Caribbean Tourism Policy and Planning". In *Tourism in the Caribbean: Trends, Development, Prospects*, edited by D.T. Duval, 81–98. London: Routledge.

Williams, G.E. 2001. "Plantation Systems in Saint Lucia". Paper presented at the Regional Expert Meeting on Plantation Systems in the Caribbean, Paramaribo, Surinam, 17–19 July.

Williams, M. 2003. *Deforesting the Earth: From Prehistory to Global Crisis*. Chicago: University of Chicago Press.

Wilson, K.B. 1989. "Trees in Fields in Southern Zimbabwe". *Journal of Southern African Studies* 15 (2): 369–83.

Winkel, T., P. Bommel, M. Chevarria-Lazo, G. Cortes, C. Del Castillo, P. Gasselin, F. Leger, J. Nona-Laura, S. Rambal, M. Tichit, J. Tourrand, J. Vacher, A. Vassas-Toral, M. Viera-Pak and R. Joffre. 2016. "Panarchy of an Indigenous Agroecosystem in the Globalized Market: The Quinoa Production in the Bolivian Altiplano". *Global Environmental Change* 39:195–204.

WIRC (West Indian Royal Commission). 1897. *Norman Commission on the Sugar Industry of St Lucia*. London: West Indian Royal Commission.

Wood, C., and T. McCoy. 1985. "Migration, Remittances and Development: A Study of Caribbean Cane Cutters in Florida". *International Migration Review* 19 (2): 251–77.

Wood, R.E. 2004. "Global Currents: Cruise Ships in the Caribbean Sea". In *Tourism in the Caribbean: Trends, Development, Prospects*, edited by D.T. Duval, 152–71. London: Routledge.

Woodfield, N. 1998. "The Role of Ecotourism in Grenada: A Marketing Ploy or Step towards Sustainable Development". In *Resource Sustainability and Caribbean Development*, edited by D.F.M. McGregor, D. Barker and S.L. Evans, 148–68. Kingston: University of the West Indies Press.

World Bank. 1975. "Caribbean Regional Study, vol. 3: Agriculture". Report No. 566a, Latin America and the Caribbean Regional Office.

——. 1979. "Current Economic Position and Prospects for St Lucia". Report No. 2440-CRB, Latin America and the Caribbean Regional Office.

——. 1980. "Economic Memorandum on Saint Lucia". Report No. 2936-CRG, Latin America and the Caribbean Regional Office.

——. 1982. "Economic Memorandum on Saint Lucia". Report No. 3828-SLU, Latin America and the Caribbean Regional Office.

——. 1983. "St Lucia Economic Memorandum". Report No. 4704-SLU, Latin America and the Caribbean Regional Office.

——. 1985. "Performance and Prospects of the Saint Lucian Economy". Report No. 5603-SLU, Latin America and the Caribbean Regional Office.

——.1988. "St Lucia Economic Memorandum". Report No. 7117-SLU, Latin America and the Caribbean Regional Office.

——. 1990. "Saint Lucia Updating Economic Note". Report No. 8252-SLU, Latin America and the Caribbean Regional Office.

Wrathall, C. 2017. "Maria Islands: The St Lucia Eco-sanctuary Mired in Construction Controversy". *Telegraph*, 15 May.

Yin, R. 2016. "Empirical Linkages between Devolved Tenure Systems and Forest Conditions: An Introduction to the Literature Review". *Forest Policy and Economics* 73:271–76.

Ylikoski, P., and J. Kuorikoski. 2010. "Dissecting Explanatory Power". *Philosophical Studies* 148:201–19.

Young, E. 2001. "State Intervention and Abuse of the Commons: Fisheries Development in Baja California Sur, Mexico". *Annals of the Association of American Geographers* 91 (2): 283–306.

Young, O.R., F. Berkhout, G.C. Gallopin, M.A. Janssen, E. Ostrom and S. van der Leeuw. 2006. "The Globalization of Socio-Ecological Systems: An Agenda for Scientific Research". *Global Environmental Change* 16:304–16.

Young, R., T. Baptiste, A. Donnelly, H. Temple, H. Whitehead, H. Young and M. Morton. 2010. "Potential Impacts of Tourist Developments in St Lucia and the Endangered White-Breasted Thrasher *Ramphocinclus brachyurus*". *Birdlife International* 20:354–64.

Zar, J.H. 1984. *Biostatistical Analysis*, 2nd ed. Englewood Cliffs, NJ: Prentice-Hall.

Zimmerer, K., and T. Bassett, eds. 2003. *Political Ecology: An Integrated Approach to Geography and Environment-Development Studies*. New York: Guildford Press.

Zuvekas, C. 1979. "Land Tenure in Haiti and Its Policy Implications: A Survey of the Literature". *Social and Economic Studies* 28 (4): 1–30.

INDEX

Page numbers in italics refer to figures and tables.